Praise for

POW
CON
NOTH

"A rallying cry for social justice leaps off the pages of this fierce memoir from Connie Rice, a crusading attorney for America's disenfranchised. . . . What's most remarkable about Rice is her dry-eyed idealism." —*More*

"This powerful memoir offers vivid accounts of the fight for social justice from the streets to the courtroom. An excellent read." —*Booklist*

"Rice is the most brilliant legal mind I've ever encountered in my twenty-year broadcast history. I hang on her every word. She concedes nothing without a demand—never has and never will." —Tavis Smiley

"Writing with conviction, Rice's narrative vividly portrays her life's work and her unyielding commitment to our shared family values— the power of education, a dedication to improving the lives of others, and a belief that it does not matter where you came from; it matters where you are going." —Condoleezza Rice

"A powerful new book . . . [Rice] tells the story of how she and her colleagues have worked to free poor neighborhoods of the evils of gang killings, police brutality, poorly run schools, and bad health." —Bill Boyarsky

"Riveting . . . A must-read for anyone interested in innovative approaches to vexing social problems and the civil rights issues they pose." —*California Lawyer*

POWER CONCEDES NOTHING

The Unfinished Fight for
Social Justice in America

CONNIE RICE

SCRIBNER

New York London Toronto Sydney New Delhi

Scribner
A Division of Simon & Schuster, Inc.
1230 Avenue of the Americas
New York, NY 10020

First Scribner trade paperback edition February 2014

SCRIBNER and design are registered trademarks of The Gale Group, Inc.,
used under license by Simon & Schuster, Inc., the publisher of this work.

For information about special discounts for bulk purchases, please contact
Simon & Schuster Special Sales at 1-866-506-1949 or
business@simonandschuster.com.

The Simon & Schuster Speakers Bureau can bring authors to your
live event. For more information or to book an event contact the
Simon & Schuster Speakers Bureau at 1-866-248-3049 or
visit our website at www.simonspeakers.com.

Manufactured in the United States of America

2

Library of Congress Control Number: 2011044089

ISBN 978-1-4165-4473-9 (pbk)
ISBN 978-1-4516-2592-9 (ebook)

For my amazing parents, Anna and Phillip

Power concedes nothing without a demand.
It never did, and it never will.

—Frederick Douglass, Address on West India
    Emancipation, 1857

Contents

POWER
CONCEDES
NOTHING

Prologue

WAKE-UP CALL

The sound of a ringing telephone early in the morning never means good news. In twenty years as a civil rights attorney in Los Angeles, I've had my share of shattering midnight calls from police and gang intervention workers, clients and social workers, all with urgent summons to crime scenes, confrontations, and emergency rooms. But few calls rattled my world like the one that came on a quiet Jacaranda June morning in 2008.

The day had started peacefully enough. The neighborhood rooster had just begun his sun-raising reveille as my blue Prius rolled silently into the predawn darkness that hid the lilac splendor of the Jacaranda trees. Other than spending the night at work, this was my only way to avoid Los Angeles's homicide-inducing rush hour, and to steal some time to think before the chaos of the day kicked in. With the red-light gods asleep, I blazed the nineteen-mile drive from my mountainside home to downtown L.A. in record time, arriving at work just as the sun sliced between the glass-and-chrome towers.

With no other soul in sight, I sailed up the elevator to my office at the Advancement Project, the "action tank" that my law partners, Molly Munger, Steve English, Penda Hair, and I founded to finish what Martin Luther King Jr. started. Once upstairs, I scooped up the newspapers, cut through the kitchen, brewed some tea, and slipped across the hall into the cool darkness of my windowless den. I'd tossed the papers onto the desk and picked up my steaming cup when the phone rang.

"Hello?" I barked at the interruption. There was no good reason for anyone being on my office phone that early. Emergency calls would have rung on my cell or home phone.

The jarred caller caught his breath. "Hello, ma'am, I'm looking for Miss Connie Rice."

I frowned; part of me resisted being called "ma'am," and all of me hated "miss." But he meant no harm, just respect.

"This is she. Who is this?"

"Yes, ma'am," he quavered, "I'm Captain Mendel[1] calling from DOD—the Defense Department in Washington—"

Not again.

"Then you need my cousin," I interrupted. "She's around the corner from you, at the State Department—" I was about to add the obligatory "I'm ConNIE, she's ConDI," but it was his turn to cut me off.

"No, no, ma'am, I'm looking for the Connie Rice in Los Angeles," he said. "My C.O. just heard that you have a gang training academy, and we need to come out and see it."

Who had told his commanding officer that our fledgling gang-intervention training courses were a full-blown "academy"? Barely eighteen months had passed since we'd unleashed our blockbuster report, *A Call to Action: A Case for a Comprehensive Solution to Los Angeles' Gang Epidemic.* In it we'd rebuked L.A. County's thirty-year "war on gangs" and demanded a bold switch from mindless "war" to holistic prevention and family/neighborhood building. Some politicians had cursed it, but the *Los Angeles Daily News* had hailed the report as "a Marshall plan for L.A. gangs." Eighteen months had not been enough time to adjust to the strong support it had won from the police agencies we used to sue. Los Angeles Police Department Chief William Bratton and L.A. County Sheriff Lee Baca, L.A.'s top cops, had even backed our call for an academy to professionalize gang intervention workers, former gang leaders who worked the streets to cut gang violence.

Ending up allied with the police agencies I had repeatedly sued from 1990 to 2006 was a strange place for a civil rights lawyer to be. But it was the right place if the traumatized first-graders of the gang zones were ever to learn reading before they learned to duck bullets in a bathtub. In their neighborhoods, guns and gangs ruled, not civil rights.

Before that June morning in 2008, my most alarming call had involved an ex-gangster and a good cop, both saying I had to foil a curbside execution of a fugitive homicide suspect—by police. But after years of fighting for and winning police reform, we had closed ranks with the good cops and, with a battalion of gang interventionists, had turned to fight L.A.'s widening epidemic of gang power and violence. This DOD call made me worry once again that we were doing way too little, far too late. But we had no choice. To win the civil rights battle of the twenty-first century for safety and viable education—or ever get more than the delusion of homeland security—the "savage inequalities" of L.A.'s gang zones had to end.

It was clear why our report had captured L.A.'s attention. But DOD's?

"Would you mind telling me why DOD is interested in our gang work?" I asked, setting down my tea and trying to sound casual.

"Ma'am, your gangs are like the insurgents in Iraq and Afghanistan," he replied with forthright military stoicism. "And you are using strategies that win cooperation from some gangs to reduce violence. We need your help."

My first thought was: *If DOD thinks our work can help in Baghdad, things outside the Green Zone must be truly desperate.* Then his words sank in: Our gangs were like insurgents? Under the whirlwind of thoughts beginning to spin in my head, my gut told me the man on the phone represented something important. But before going down any road with the military, I'd have to think deeply about the likely blowback.

The last thing L.A.'s gang epidemic needed was more militariza-
tion. After a thirty-year $25 billion war on gangs, L.A. had racked
up an impressive scorecard of a million arrests—but also six times as
many gangs and enough gang violence to alarm the World Health
Organization. "War" had boosted the number of gangs and done
nothing to stop the spread of gang ideology, influence, and power.
The country had made a similar shock-and-awe mistake in the "war
on terrorism," and now this hapless captain had to seek help for
Operation Iraqi Freedom from us. I was deeply disturbed by the
war in Iraq, but I knew that as the secretary of state, Condoleezza
had been pushing hard for diplomacy and community building. The
captain's request signaled a similar change in at least a corner of the
Pentagon. But what did it signal for L.A.?

My mind ran through the parallels between L.A. and Baghdad that
the captain must have seen. Both had hot zones engulfed by violence
that too few had the political will to stop. In L.A., we had no will to
end the conditions and culture that had spawned a thousand gangs. In
Baghdad, there had been no will to halt vicious ethnic and religious
clashes. A failed war on gangs finally had driven L.A. to go beyond
search-and-destroy policing. And a faltering war of choice in Iraq had
driven the military to go beyond search-and-destroy terrorist hunting.
Both places had expended tons of blood and treasure on strategies
that fueled the spread of violent ideology. Both were hobbled by rigid
bureaucracies that were incapable of streamlined cooperation. Both
had enforcers who finally understood they had to win the hearts and
trust of the people by protecting them instead of hostilely occupying
their neighborhoods. And both places had to make tactical alliances
with selected insurgents.

The good news was that in 2008 Americans were spending billions of dollars to remedy the conditions that fueled street violence.
The bad news was that we were doing it in Baghdad and Khandahar,
not in L.A.

The gang violence epidemic in Los Angeles, however, was not a
military or police failure. It was a socioeconomic, policy, and cultural
failure. With eighty thousand gang members county-wide, we would

never arrest or litigate our way out of the problem. L.A. needed to stabilize gang violence, invest in prevention, help neighborhoods and families counter the pull of gang ideology, and push alternatives to *la vida loca* with jobs, good schools, and a cultural movement that rejects violence.

Clear. Hold. Build. Educate. Employ.

Maybe Captain Mendel had called the right place after all. I reassured him that we'd find a way to help, signed off, and then sat in wondrous consternation over his request to observe our work.

At the time, I had no idea that this unsettling call would lead to far more alarming military assessments that would catapult all of our gang and police reform work to the transnational level—and send me down an even more dangerous road. Yet in many ways, this road resembled others I'd been forced to take. It was the road of risk, counterintuitive tactics, unlikely alliances, and unorthodox actions that anyone on a mission to win basic civil rights in America's kill zones had to take.

It was the mission to make sure our poorest kids also reached the mountaintop that Martin Luther King Jr. glimpsed right before he died—and to sound the alarm that the final cost of their chronic destitution would be our own destruction. It was a mission for which I had trained my entire life, one that would take everything I'd ever accomplished in order to fulfill the dreams of my ancestors.

Chapter 1

"WHAT *IS* YOU?"

H e was tiny, black as coal, and in my face. Out of nowhere, he had marched right up, thrust his ashy frown into my chin, and blurted out in exasperation: "What *is* you?"

He scrunched his brow tighter as he scoured my face for clues. I got the impression that he had wrestled with this conundrum for some time. Determined to get an answer, he now confronted the source of his consternation. I stared at him in stunned silence, and he pushed even closer, oblivious that his question had winded me like a good left hook. Before I could sputter out a response, he hit me with his suspicion. "Is you *Japanese?*"

Right hook. He was so close I could feel his breath on my throat, a reminder that my own breathing had stopped. *Japanese?* Still reeling from his first blow, I had wild ideas flitting through my mind. Was he blind? From his query and those searing dark eyes, clearly not. Was it a stunt? It would be just like my mischievous brother Phil to sic this kid on me . . .

It was not a stunt. And Phil had nothing to do with this dustup. It was much simpler than that. My inquisitor, a migrant farmworker's son, had barely adjusted to sharing the only junior high school on the western edge of Phoenix with the mostly white children of soldiers stationed at nearby Luke Air Force Base. Then he saw me, a puzzle piece that did not fit.

It was late fall 1968. I was twelve and, after the eighth military move of my short life, almost acclimated to Arizona. My father, Phillip Leon Rice, Sr., was then a major in the United States Air Force, and my mother, Anna Barnes Rice, was a high school biology teacher who had put her career on hold to raise us full-time. Mom, my younger brothers, Phillip and Norman, and I had just spent a wrenching year at Olmstead Air Force Base, not too far from Three Mile Island, Pennsylvania, praying for Dad to return from Vietnam. I had distracted myself with schoolwork, oil painting, and escaping every Friday night to where no one had gone before via a new TV show called *Star Trek* that Mom let us watch because it had a multiracial cast. On the eve of my twelfth birthday, Walter Cronkite had delivered more terrible news, and I had run into the kitchen to tell Mom that "they've killed our friend." Busy putting a pan of fish under the broiler, she had asked, "Which friend?," then gasped in horror when she realized that Martin Luther King Jr. was gone. But Mom never let outside calamity upend our focus, especially when our tight military family had to survive the anguish of separation during war. By summer's end, our shock over King had been eclipsed by elation over Dad's return. The Air Force could have sent us to Bangladesh, for all I cared, as long as we were together. For whatever reason, the assignment wheel had stopped on Luke AFB outside of Phoenix, Arizona.

Phoenix's staggering heat had taken a little getting used to, and we'd learned to hold our breath while passing the huge pig farms, but otherwise I had not missed a beat. That is, until tiny, determined Mr. What *Is* You thrust his chin into my face and declared me Japanese.

Looking back, I suppose he had connected obvious dots and deduced a reasonable, if wrong, conclusion. He had observed my yellow skin and straightened, almost black hair that was often tied in a topknot, pulling my almond-shaped eyes upward. My thick glasses did magnify their slant. He had watched this ambiguous creature ride the bus, walk, eat, and go to class with the same unthinking entitlement as her white counterparts, but she was not white. And the black people he knew looked, well, blacker. He knew I wasn't Mexican, like his fellow migrant families. He must have figured: not black, not Mexican, and definitely not white, and guessed at what was left: Japanese.

Little could he have known that my family actually had lived in Misawa, Japan, and that my youngest brother, Norman, who was born there, enjoyed dual Japanese and American citizenship. During our two years at Misawa, Phil and I had greeted our Japanese nanny, Keiko, with our four- and three-year-old mastery of Japanese—"*O-hi-o Ka-zyma, Keiko-san!*"—and had watched our mom make Japanese dolls. Had my Arizona accuser even glimpsed our Japanese screens, pottery, kimonos, ceremonial tea sets, hibachi grill, geisha dolls, and obi chairs, he would have convicted me beyond any doubt.

No, there was nothing unreasonable about his speculation, nor wrong with his eleven-year-old's deductive skills. But to me, an African-American preteen living in the overwhelmingly white world of the United States Air Force, his conclusion seemed absurd. What couldn't he see? I was the ultimate transracial token, the pro-verbial raisin—okay, *golden* raisin—in the grits. What little Japanese girl did he think held her breath and prayed for "tiger" every time her white friends sang "Eenie, Meenie, Miney, Mo, Catch a ——— by His Toe"? What Japanese girls endured the ordeal of getting their hair straightened with hot combs to avoid the dreaded fate of appearing in public with nappy hair? What little Japanese girl counted the seconds it took white adults to marvel at how "articu-late" and "well mannered" she was? Surely he knew that only a black girl like me had cringed inside as she picked the African-looking face on an IQ test that asked for the definition of "ugly" and the white face for "pretty," knowing they would be the only "right" answers? And that no little Japanese girl felt compelled to deny that her favorite fruit was watermelon? Who else but a black girl did he think felt obligated to be twice as smart in order to counter stereotypes about her suspect race?

Japanese? What could he be thinking?

These trinkets of tokenism were annoying but had not hindered me in any meaningful way. I was a largely welcome token in my mostly white world of Air Force bases and foreign countries, but surely he could see that even for me, the silent subtext of difference ran like a ticker tape beneath my life. In my mostly white world, race screamed out loud, but the mute button was on.

Mustering as much hyped indignation as was possible during my winded silence, I finally blustered back: "No! I am *not* Japanese. I'm—I'm *black*—just like you!"

His eyes, like bullets, shot back point-blank disbelief. "No you *ain't!*" he fired.

He stepped back, disgustedly shaking his head as he stomped across the dusty gulch back to his side of the campus. As I stared at his receding back, my heart raced, my tongue dried, and my head pounded. "No you *ain't!*" rang in my ears, drowning out all thought and sound. As much as I tried to blot it out, I couldn't. And I knew why.

He was right. I was not black like him.

He was an undernourished, dark-skinned, ebonics-speaking son of migrant farmworkers. I, a light-skinned Black American Princess, spoke the King's English to the Queen's taste and was the only daughter of a highly educated biology teacher and a decorated Air Force officer. I was a tolerated token. He was the discarded "other," consigned to the margins of society. I was the safer preference to him. His undiluted blackness rendered him invisible yet dangerous, pricking the most primordial of European fears.

His blood threatened white existence.

Mine did not.

When my white friends looked into my face, they could still see themselves, and with good reason. I look like a blend of this country's eighteenth-century tribes. My features result from an interracial scramble that, after two hundred years, roughly tallies one fifth Native American (Cherokee, Seminole, and Cree), two fifths African (likely including Gullah, from whence we suspect comes the Rice gap between the front teeth), and two fifths Scotch-Irish/Welsh/Anglo Saxon. In sum, I am an Indo-African Celt, the kind of forbidden blend that sends Ku Klux Klansmen lunging for their hoods and ironists for their pens.

With this mix, I can sign my own reparations check.

This heritage separated me from my dark-skinned challenger not only by blood but also by color caste and belonging. North America is the only place where my cocktail lineage could have been concocted. And while I will always be anguished by the soul-vanquishing torment that slavery wreaked on my African ancestors, I cannot imagine myself had they escaped the slaver's net. This perverse reconciliation leaves me freer to claim all of America, from her soaring best to her craven worst, without having to deny the truth of our history or myself. And I can do so with the schizophrenic ease unique to folks who accept their tribal jambalaya.

It's why, when I was a teen, my stack of forty-fives had Aretha Franklin's "Since You've Been Gone" and James Brown's "Say It Loud (I'm Black and I'm Proud)" on top of Tony Joe White's "Polk Salad Annie" and John Fogerty's "Have You Ever Seen the Rain?" It's why the posters on my walls spanned the Monkees to Jimi Hendrix, and maybe why Irish step dancing moves me almost as much as Mr. Bojangles's tap.

The irony was that my tangled bloodlines bound me to our nation at an organic level, yet loosened the racial shackles. My Native American ancestors give me a ten-thousand-year-old birthright to this land and ancient wisdom. My African lines, while less traceable, reach back to the beginning of human time and endow me with the defining pathos of this nation, slavery and genocide amid the quest for freedom. And my European ancestors gave me a fast pass to privilege and ties to the continent richest in Western culture. It is easier for the great-great-granddaughter of Native Americans, and the great-granddaughter of African slaves and European slave owners, to reconcile our nation's cruel beginnings with love of America's promise, and to embody her greatest credo, *E Pluribus Unum:* out of many, one.

My musings about bloodlines would have meant nothing to my Arizona accuser. He saw only light skin and knew instinctively that it conferred favor. He might have understood that I enjoyed nothing close to the built-in advantages for white members of the club, but I at least had a day pass to enter the side door of the clubhouse. He was right about the bottom line: The privileges of color caste gave me social passports that lightened the heavy gravity of race. I rarely faced debilitating discrimination, and when I did, it was far more often for being a girl or a nerd than for being black.

But the codes of color caste were the least of our differences. The chasm between my world and his stretched all the way back through our shared heritage of slavery, where our clans had endured different kinds of servitude and emerged on very different rungs of the post-slavery ladder. At slavery's end, Mr. What *Is* You's ancestors had little beyond the rags on their backs. My ancestors had emerged literate, owning property or equipped with a trade that gave them an antebellum head start in post–Civil War America.

I doubt he knew much about his family history. And until my dad wrote his autobiography, *Mixed Bag,* in 2008, I knew only snippets of my own from snatches of conversations overheard on porch swings and in Granddad Barnes's fishing boat, from kitchen kibitzing, notes in the margins of family Bibles, scribbling on the backs of old photos, and rare talks with my grandparents, great-aunts, and uncle Bill. But those memories and a few antebellum letters unearthed by my law partner confirm the consequences of our different paths out of slavery.

From the jumbled partial story of my family's odyssey, I know that four of my great-grandparents on the Rice side were no older than my young Arizona accuser and me when they were freed from slavery. In the Alabama wing of the family, John Wesley Rice, my paternal great-grandfather, was eleven when President Lincoln signed the Emancipation Proclamation and ended slavery. It's unclear whether Wesley, as he was called—believed to be the son of Creek Indian and African parents—ever learned to read. But his wife, my paternal great-grandmother, Julia Head, was literate. The Heads, her white owner kin, placed unusual value on learning, as evidenced in family notations that they prized the size of their libraries, and memorizing Shakespeare's plays.[2] By family lore, Julia Head was the offspring of a neighboring plantation owner, also a Head, and his Native American love. Early in her life, the story goes, Julia had declined her owner's offer to send her to school in France. Mr. What *Is* You's ancestors almost certainly received no such offer and likely would have been whipped for touching a book.

As Dad recounts, his father, William Stantley Rice, was a graduate of Gammon Theological Seminary who spoke Greek and Hebrew, and his mom, Erma Phillips, was the literate daughter of Anna Rainey Phillips, a literate former slave of African and Cherokee descent who attended Clark College in Atlanta, and her literate husband, Robert Phillips, founder of Mount Moriah Methodist United Church in Birmingham, Alabama. They followed a family culture that was devoted to God, driven to achieve, and suspicious of anything resembling fun. My dad grew up in Birmingham with his siblings Vernice, William, Robert, and Wilma, but they left in 1947 after his father, a businessman, landlord, printing-press owner, and professional chef, tired of segregation's setbacks and moved the family to Cleveland, Ohio, where they opened Rice's Restaurant.

Any roadblocks my clan overcame, however, were challenges that my young Arizona accuser's family never had the opportunity to conquer.

The odyssey of my mom's ancestors also landed her family near the top of the post-slavery food chain. Indeed, her grandmother Sarah Catherine Brown Wigenton, my Indian, African, Irish great-grandmother, seems to have won her freedom very early and may even have been emancipated at birth. Her husband, my great-grandfather George Wigenton, was born into slavery in central Virginia.

When his father, my great-great-grandfather Paige Wigenton, was still a boy, his white owner-father "loaned out" Paige to a small farm in nearby Rappahannock County to eliminate the humiliating evidence of extramarital slave children. The slave shack that he lived in with his son still stands four miles south of tiny Amissville, Virginia. When I saw it in the 1990s, its forty-foot-square brick frame featured an old fireplace, wood floors, beamed ceilings, and separate rooms, amenities unknown to most slaves. Farm owners reserved quality housing like this for Virginia's many white indentured servants and for white owners' slave children, such as Paige Wigenton. No one white would have been allowed to live in the slave shacks reserved for the ancestors of Mr. What *Is* You.

Like the Rices, George and Sarah Catherine Wigenton emerged from slavery with resources. They owned their land and farmhouse and operated sugar and flour mills in Amissville. Together they raised thirteen literate children, including my mom's mother, Grace Wigenton. They created an indomitable, can-do family culture of creative risk and dogged work ethic, qualities my grandmother Grace had and also found in her husband, Jesse Barnes. He worked the dangerous factory floors of Bethlehem Steel, pouring molten metal and breathing steel shards for forty years. Grandmom, an industrious, church-loving homemaker, raised my mom and her nine siblings and stretched every nickel brought home until the buffalo screamed. She slaughtered her own chickens and got up at five every morning to bake bread that she shared with her Polish and Italian neighbors, who sent back Italian pasta and Polish casseroles. Like my grandmother Rice, she was creative and thrifty, making over old shoes with cardboard, sewing new clothes from remnants, and creating her own cleaning supplies. When food became scarce, Granddad armed his oldest daughters with hunting rifles and took them into the woods, where they shot dinner and brought it home. With salaries and benefits won by the steelworkers' union, boosts from the GI Bill, and a Sears & Roebuck credit card, my mom's parents lifted their household into the relative comfort of the home-owning, hardscrabble working class.

For both of my parents' clans, accelerated upward mobility got jump-started by the pre-emancipation perks that Paige Wigenton, Julia Head, and other ancestors turned to advantage through gumption, hard work, and grit. They owned land, education, and skills, and from their photographs, you can see they also owned the social entitlement that comes from self-belief and caste privilege.

Pictures of my great-grandparents, taken in the late 1800s and early 1900s, exude that relative social advantage.* Sarah Catherine Brown Wigenton sat for her portrait in a crisp white blouse and topcoat adorned with fancy covered buttons and velvet inlaid collar. Her Indian hair is piled on her head in a braided crown, her posture is ramrod-straight, and her gaze is regal, direct, and challenging. Built stout and sturdy, she looks formidable, like a black Queen Victoria. George Wigenton, in his picture, is standing, his direct and defiant gaze that of a confident, internally powerful man whose six-six height amplified his stature. And in a haunting gray-brown daguerreotype of my father's paternal grandparents, Julia Head and John Wesley Rice sit shoulder to shoulder, looking like a somber black Ma and Pa Kettle, their solemn eyes piercing with their trademark sternness. Other photographs of my great-relatives in their Civil War uniforms, Victorian hats, and carriages show the same gravitas and high expectations. They are photos of people who believe they are in the driver's seats of their destiny.

While my ancestors sat for portraits, Mr. What Is You's ancestors probably did not know cameras existed.

Both of our families suffered enormously through the charnel of slavery and Jim Crow America. But my folks had landed on a much higher rung of the post-slavery ladder. Within three generations of slavery, the Rice and Barnes clans laid claim to at least thirty college graduates, two nursing school graduates, seven holders of master's degrees, and five Ph.D.'s. By the fourth generation, we had seven Ivy League graduates and too many degrees to count. We not only owned our homes and land straight out of slavery, but in four

---

*To view the photographs, please visit www.powerconcedesnothing.com.

generations, we had become landlords, print-shop owners, ministers, school superintendents, principals, nurses, college professors, high school teachers, restaurant owner-operators, chefs, computer technicians, truck drivers, a mayor, a career officer in the U.S. Air Force, five medical doctors—one of whom landed on the faculty of Harvard Medical School—an NBA coach, a librarian, amazing full-time parents, a mathematician, three lawyers, three authors, and a United States secretary of state.

We had emerged from slavery with a firm grasp on the ladder up and had never stopped climbing. Over a hundred years after slavery, Mr. What *Is* You's family still toiled in the fields, and his people held title to nothing. They could not even imagine the deference I assumed every time military officers of all races jumped to attention to salute my father.

Until my encounter with Mr. What *Is* You, I had confronted neither my relative privilege nor the inequality in front of me. Even on the same parched Arizona junior high campus, we were separate, unequal, and estranged. He sat with the other black and Mexican farmworkers' kids in hot trailers, only nominally a part of the same school. I sat with the other military brats in the air-conditioned comfort of cinder-block buildings. Symbolically, I was still in the big house with the owners. He actually was still in the fields. History had charted very different paths for us. And with one exasperated "What *is* you?," he had touched the three hundred years of American convulsions that had forged the paradox of our joined journeys.

But history was not what had rattled my world. He had. I needed to find him again. He had to answer for blitzkrieging my world and then dismissing me! And I needed something else, something that I couldn't quite articulate. Every day after our confrontation, I looked across the gulch, searching for his little round head and cranky frown.

I finally spotted him at the outdoor lunch tables with other farmworker students. I stepped down from the shaded concrete platform that hosted our classrooms and crossed the Mason-Dixon gully separating their trailers from our buildings. I stopped at their lunch area. The long, rusted tin tables stood less than a yard apart, with the black kids at one, the Mexican children at the other. Everyone was staring, whispering, or stifling their giggles at my awkward intrusion. He sat three down in the middle of the black table, eating. I became self-conscious; I was so much bigger than they were. Their clothes, like his, were worn and ill fitting, and their little faces, clenched like his, did not soften into welcome. Shifting my eyes to my quarry, I squinted at him through the glare beading off the metal. And waited. He did not look up. I glowered harder at him, his round face frowning, but not at me—at his wilted bologna sandwich. He was inordinately preoccupied with that sandwich, examining it as if it held some secret to life. I cleared my throat loudly. More snickers.

At last he leveled scoffing eyes. "What choo want?"

Good question. What did I want? Absolution? It wasn't his to give. Closure? There was no closing the yawning gap between us. Truth? This kid had a nose for it—and had rubbed mine in it. Maybe I wanted more. All I knew at that moment was that "No you *ain't!*" could not be the end of what he had started. Our exchange was not finished.

"Where do you live?" I asked with hollow authority.

"Edge o' that field," he said, pointing outside the school gate. "Where you live?" he asked back.

"On Luke—the Air Force base."

"I *knows* what Luke is."

"Can I come see your house?"

"Why?"

"I want to see where you live."

"You kin see my house if I kin see yours."

"Fine."

"When you comin'?"

"Today?"

He couldn't quite suppress a smirk. He seemed to enjoy my clumsy intrusion for what it was, a lame attempt to finish our match. But that was not the whole story. He had wanted a straight answer to a pointed question; I needed from him something more. I wanted the one visa only he could issue. I wanted a passport to his world.

"Okay." He sighed in feigned resignation. "When your last class is? Two-thirty?"

I nodded.

"Meet ya at the gate afta' that."

I nodded again. His dining companions had remained riveted on our volley. I rolled my eyes at the audience and set off for my side of the gully.

At two-thirty, I waited at the front gate, sneakers on. Kids filed by me, climbing into the thrumming school buses waiting to take them back to the base. The buses rumbled out onto the road, heaving a cloud of heated dust. Ten minutes passed. No sign of him. I slipped into the slivered shade of the nearest building, worried that he had meant someplace else and that we'd miss each other. But there weren't any other open gates. Finally, he emerged from behind the front trailer, alone and heading my way. He had no books. Again we skipped any greetings. He trudged past me. I followed.

"Where are your books?" I demanded.

"Ain't got none."

"How do you do your homework?"

"Ain't got none. C'mon, dis way."

It was Arizona hot.

"How far do you walk?"

"Not far."

Half a mile later, we reached the edge of the field, where several shacks stood under a lone grove of trees.

"I got to work soon," he warned.

I glanced over my shoulder at the field where he would pick crops until dark. We closed in on one of the shacks and stopped in his home's doorway. The flat corrugated tin roof was covered in tarp, as if it ever rained. The door had a hole where a lock should have been. He pushed it open. Inside, it was cooler, but not by much. We stepped into a low-ceilinged room that sported a worn wood counter and a dented dinette set on one end and a tattered sofa on the other. The space was maybe thirty feet wide and forty feet long, with floors of wood planks set into dirt. An old iron wood-burning

stove stood in the corner behind the door. It must have done double
duty as a heater in the winter. I stepped far enough inside to spy two
tiny rooms branching off a short hall. They were big enough to line
up twin beds end to end. The beds were made, sheets only, with one
blanket folded neatly over the ends. No bedspreads. No room for
dressers or end tables.

Pointing to a jagged hole in the wall with a dangerous-looking
dangling plug, he noted, "We just got 'lectric. The Mex'cans don't
have 'lectric yet." His flat tone didn't quite mask the pride of tribal
advantage. I nodded at the wires and socket and saw an old lamp
unplugged on the floor but nowhere to read or study. There was a
radio but no television. And no refrigerator. I glanced around for
the bathroom. He pointed out the window to a rusted shed in the
backyard.

"Need ta use it?" he offered. I did. But after peering out at my
first outhouse, I decided I didn't know how and declined. Next to
it sat the shower—a hose slung over a curtained plastic bin. Clothes
hung on a line.

Back inside, he was scooping out a glass of water from a bucket
near the counter. He finished and dipped out some for me. I sipped.
It tasted metallic. The windows had curtains made from old sheets,
the table a cloth of remnants. There were no pictures of his family or
him, only a yellowed portrait of a haloed Jesus Christ above the sofa.
I nodded thanks for my unfinished glass before setting it down on
the counter and turned to meet his steady eyes. I took in his round,
creased face. His scowl no longer seemed angry, only watchful. His
eyes were no longer burning but searching. After a long minute, I
worried that he might be able to see what stirred behind my eyes.

Shame burned up the sides of my face. Not for him, for me. He
owned nothing, but he had something I wanted. He may not have
been able to puzzle through the "what" of my identity, but he knew
the "who" of his. He seemed to have grit and tenacity enough to
create rungs and a ladder where none existed. Unbowed by priva-
tion, he had taken the only prize he needed: the right to define
himself and to claim a place the world had never intended for him

to have. He had learned in eleven tough years what would take me twenty-one.

As we stood on those bare floorboards, the gulf between us felt different, the advantage unclear. We stood almost as close as the day he confronted me. Hoping my ears weren't as red as they felt, I tried to work up the courage to say what needed to be said: that I was not black like him but was nonetheless of and with him. But I saw the small upturn at the corners of his mouth that was as close to a smile as he would come, and I knew there was no need. Our eyes held in quiet recognition, each of the other. He pursed his lips in taut acknowledgment and nodded curtly at the unspoken respect he saw in my eyes. I pursed mine and nodded back.

"Now when can you come by my place?" I asked, breaking the moment before it got mushy.

He strode to the door, work gloves and cap in hand, and swung it open for both of us to leave. "Soon 'nuf."

We stepped back out into the sweltering sun. For a hundred yards or so, we walked together. At field's edge, he forked left, and I continued the way we'd come in from the school.

"Take the shortcut 'cross the field," he called over his shoulder. He tipped his hat and then disappeared down the rows.

My books bouncing on my back, I raced back to the school in time to catch the last bus back to the base. Covered in the same dust that had encrusted his face, I wheezed into my seat for the ride back to my world. Twenty minutes later, the bus chugged past the military guards at the base gate and stopped near my house. I stepped down onto the sidewalk and gasped as it hit me that I did not know his name.

For the rest of the year, I looked across the dirt gulley, scanning for his frowning round face, but I never saw him again. Perhaps, as for so many migrant kids, I had lost him to the next harvest. It didn't matter. I did not need to know his name to keep his gift. The journey to answer his challenge had begun. What was I?

Chapter 2

TRIBE OF FIVE

M r. What *Is* You never knew his impact on my life. Shortly after visiting his home, I confronted my homeroom teacher over the lack of lockers, covered lunch areas, and air-conditioning for migrant workers' kids. When she cooed, "Those children are happy," I knew then I was expected to join the conspiracy of inequity that had paved their dirt path into the fields. Angry, I snapped back that I did not believe her. In that defiant instant, I had resolved to end the conspiracy, not join it. For the first time, I had directly stared down power. I was twelve. This budding bent for challenging injustice, however, did not begin in that dusty Arizona schoolyard. It began with Mom and Dad.

Phillip Rice, Sr., and Anna Barnes Rice are the central forces that shaped my life. Growing up under their energetic direction and rich intelligence, I had no choice but to thrive, to strive and succeed. By age four, I knew that my destination was someplace called college.

My core identity has always been as my parents' daughter and, by extension, my own woman. Our nomadic military life intensified this paradox of self-sufficiency and family attachment. Our tight little band moved from place to place as we absorbed our parents' stolid values and mission mind-set. Over twenty-two years, we moved seventeen times. I attended three different grade schools, two junior highs, and three high schools. But in my parents' skillful hands, my brothers and I never dwelled for long on the constant disruption or the lost friendships. My mother seemed to move our household around the world with the ease of throwing a birthday party, transforming the dislocation into adventure as she showed us how to master each new place. My father also modeled confidence and success, whether as a pilot breaking sound barriers at Edwards Air Force Base or as a diplomat breaching Cold War walls. The feeling my parents gave us was one of always pushing forward, upward, and with purpose. As Dad climbed the ranks, Mom, Phil, Norm, and I followed him like the contrails of a comet. We had one another and the open road of life, always beckoning us to make something great out of whatever awaited. As long as I was with the four of them and under the wings of our parents, all was right with the world.

When I look back, I see that this was, of course, just one of the illusions they created to ensure our success. They shielded us from off-base protests against blacks attending the local elementary school outside of Johnson Air Force Base in Goldsboro, North Carolina. They never let us know that in 1957, death threats against the white woman who rented us an apartment in Enid, Oklahoma, forced Mom and me to go live with Dad's parents in Cleveland. On the road, they always made sure restaurants and gas stations would let us use the bathrooms so we kids never suffered the humiliation of the racial rejection they knew firsthand.

My intelligence comes from both parents, but my yen for solitude comes from my father. He is the lone wolf, and I am his cub. When my brothers and I were young, his stoic reserve masked his complexity: the rigid soldier who prizes freedom; the dean of discipline who cherishes the creative chaos of jazz; the introvert who can be the most gracious of hosts; the cautious protector who flies dangerous missions; the military maven who detests war. Despite his reserve, we learned the soldier's way by reading between his actions: Life is serious business. Selfless dedication is its own reward. Do the right thing. Failure is not an option. Integrity is all. Stand and deliver. These were not slogans he ever uttered. Just principles he lives.

To the outside world, Dad is sober and accomplished. But at home, my brothers and I could see beneath the armor and medals. Too duty-bound and disciplined to ever be accused of passion, he did not need to talk much for us to see that we were an important part of his life's mission. That mission seemed to fuel a relentless work ethic and need to set—and keep raising—the bar. He was always on a quest of mastery, as if becoming a serial achiever would pave our way to a summit he wanted for us but not for himself. A college degree, advanced military training, and fluency in Russian were not enough, so after I left college, he rose before dawn for two years to study for and earn his executive MBA degree. After his kids earned graduate degrees, he entered Columbia University's education doctoral program and, at age sixty, earned his own Ivy League Ph.D.

Soldier's bearing and courage notwithstanding, my dad is not without faults. In addition to a chronic infatuation with new cars, he adores his daughter and can never tell me no. This is no flaw but his best gift, one that my mother stopped trying to moderate after what she laments as our point of no return when I was six. After hearing my sobbing disappointment over her sensible decision to buy everyone but me new bedroom furniture, he promptly went shopping to fill my bedroom with princess-white bedroom furniture. Forty-five years later, it sits in my house, a memento of Dad's love and my life lesson in why no is never the end of a negotiation.

That was one of very few battles my wondrous mom lost. Anna Rice is the temperamental opposite of my dad. She is an extrovert, a whirling dervish of joyful fussing, empathy, and bristling energy. She radiates happiness and no-nonsense purpose. Her warmth and bubbly exterior mask her intense intelligence, sharp wit, and staunch will. Even her superior IQ is second to her uncanny EQ—emotional intelligence. My mom reads people better than a Geiger counter reads radiation. There's no one's company I love more.

Born in 1931 in Reading, Pennsylvania, she grew up with her nine brothers and sisters. The five girls—Agnes, Rita, Betty, Anna, and Jessie arrived first, followed by the boys—Carl, Allen, Kelly, Curtis, and Malcolm. Mom, the fourth of the five girls, was a shy, geeky, straight-A student with super-thick braids and thicker glasses. She devoured books and everything her teachers taught. Her dad couldn't read, so he kept on his dresser a piece of cardboard with the symbol of an A, and if his kids' report cards didn't match that symbol, they got spanked—until a teacher explained to him that a B was okay, too. Mom never got that spanking. My grit, confidence, and terminal optimism come in large part from her and her parents, people who clawed success out of constant hardship and generated grace in the face of hostility.

Mom attended really good integrated public schools and decided to follow her oldest sisters to college. She ignored her dad's belief that his daughters' paychecks, like those of the Italian and Polish girls, should pay for their brothers' college educations. She kept her money from her job at the local mental hospital and followed Rita and Agnes to Howard College, where she majored in biology and met Dad. She remembers they slow-danced to "Laura" and met later to exchange German textbooks, and she decided he was the one. They dated for four years, and when Dad joined the Air Force after graduation, she followed him to his first training assignment in San Antonio, Texas. They married there in 1952.

Four years later, at Bolling Air Force Base just outside of Washington, D.C., Mom gave birth to me, a tiny five-pound thing, half of which was my full head of jet-black hair. I can't imagine the luck of the gods that landed me in Anna Rice's baby bassinette, and for a wondrous spell of eighteen months, I had her all to myself while Dad completed his flight training. She poured herself into her first child, and as the center of her world, I flourished, until the shocking arrival of my huge-headed, high-octane brother Phillip. After failing to get rid of the voracious little intruder (I buried him in toy dishes and rolled him off the couch), I slowly adjusted to his arrival. By age three, I had rechristened him Buster, he called me Dabby, and we were thick as thieves, even as I tried to limit his rambunctious impact on my world. Phil, it soon became clear, was far smarter than I would ever be, with twice the will.

Norman, our baby brother, arrived in 1961 when I was five and Phil was three and a half. On the snow-packed January morning of his birth, we were stationed at Misawa Air Force Base, Japan, living in another forgettable bungalow. Upon meeting him, Buster and I agreed that he could stay. As a kid, he had to duck my smothering and Phil's determination to make him his personal human toy. Norm was just as smart as his geekier older sibs, though he had the added advantage of a much higher social IQ. At his wedding, Norman had friends from third grade. Phil and I couldn't even name a third-grade friend. Norm emerged on his own terms, accomplished, athletic, socially gifted, and business-savvy, like our granddad Barnes.

The three of us thrived because of our parents. Growing up with Mom as a full-time parent was an extraordinary gift. Over fifteen years of full-time parenting, she poured her love, wisdom, and zest for life into us. She was a joyous commandant who would wake us up every morning like a spinning Mary Poppins, full of sunshine and purpose. With verve and laughter, she presented life as a banquet of adventure for which we should eagerly prepare. And prepare us she did. On top of her relentless academic tasks, she dunked us in whatever the new local culture offered—ballet, piano lessons, new food, painting, crafts, ceramics, horseback riding, archery, bowling, swim teams, drama, skiing, county fairs, high tea, or square dancing. My first standing ovation, at age four, followed my first dance recital. En tutu, I curtsied to my adoring public for a performance that consisted of exactly ten steps and one plié, but given the vigor of her clapping—in white gloves and pearls—you'd have thought I had just danced the entire *Nutcracker* suite.

Her most ardent passion was ensuring that we read well by age four. She was a certified teacher, but that didn't explain her monopolar obsession with reading. It wasn't until I saw her read the entire A section of *The New York Times* out loud to her twenty-week-old granddaughter ("Ashley! Let's see what trouble President Clinton has gotten himself into today!") that I fully understood how manic her reading mission with us had been. While we were in the cradle, she talked incessantly to us, marinating us in a sea of words. As soon as we could burp and sit upright, out came the international zoo of storybooks that either she or Dad read over and over to us, at all hours of the day and every night before bed. Once we hit late toddlerdom, like a boot-camp sergeant, she whipped out the flash cards, drilling us in vowels, consonants, vocabulary, and spelling. By age five, I thought phonics was a holy catechism. There was no task too mundane to escape a reading moment. Grocery shopping, she'd help us read labels on cans. Cooking, she'd make us read the recipes. Driving, we'd read her directions and the names of the street signs. She pushed books as if they were crack cocaine. And it worked. Addicted, my brothers and I were never far from the fix that only a good book could provide.

By focusing on the serious traits and events that set my later direction, I don't mean to paint a misleading picture of joyless little robots who never attended a birthday party or watched a cartoon (we were allowed to watch three on Saturday mornings). In most ways we were normal kids who jostled and bickered all day and did regular kid stuff like skateboarding, sleepovers, and going to the movies. I loved riding horses and walking on stilts and felt certain that in a former life I'd been a cat. There's also no denying that our itinerant upbringing was different and that, while I liked being around other kids, joining their cliques never appealed. I just don't do groups. Luckily, my peers always waived the rules and seemed to accept me, though it wouldn't have mattered much if they hadn't. Besides, whatever social gaps ailed me, they didn't outweigh my one advantage: I could dance, the one indispensable skill needed for black circles and a prized rarity in my European-American world.

My brothers and I weren't perfect, far from it. We got into occasional trouble. But we never let anything get between us and our parents or our path to college. In every new place, we fought guidance counselors to get into the toughest courses, worked for the highest grades, practiced our music, strived in sports, and as teens, worked in jobs that required the highest trust and responsibility—as lifeguards, babysitters, and cashiers. We had taken the best from each new place, given our best back, and moved on to the next adventure. We had known since sentience that we were going to college, and we had paved our way accomplishment by accomplishment, school by school, into the country's best colleges. With or without affirmative action, we'd have attended the top schools because we had worked hard, scored well, and had the unique outlook of world travelers.

Without robbing us of our childhood or individuality, our parents had managed to equip us with humane values, purpose, and a Trojan work ethic. Their gift—the love and devotion that molded us into secure, creative, giving human beings—was the greatest legacy that a parent can leave a child.

The traits of being secure, driven, and independent that let me choose my path came from my parents and upbringing but also from five key formative experiences, in addition to my confrontation with young Mr. What *Is* You.

In Goldsboro, North Carolina, I remember a playground incident involving Mona, my blond, blue-eyed best friend in first grade. Some local kids had barred her from joining a jump-rope contest because she had "a nigger friend." I told her to go ahead without me. She refused and felt so bad after our clash with the budding Aryans that she sobbed inconsolably. She could not understand why I wasn't crushed, but I did. She had not lived my life. In my almost all-white Air Force world, I knew too many genuinely good people, including my parents' white friends who looked after us, and every Jewish person I had ever encountered. For every racist, there were always a thousand benign and fifty overtly good people, like Mona. She also did not have my mother's secret weapon against racism: pity. I had taken to heart Mom's breezy explanation of racism as a mental affliction that warranted medical intervention. "There are some really pitiful people who are so sick"—she laughed—"they feel they're better than we are because we're black and they're white! Can you imagine anyone being that silly?" They couldn't help themselves, she added, and it was sad that they had to go through life with that kind of mental illness. "We just have to help them get over it, " she ended. With that, racism had rolled off me like water off a duck.

By the time I was seven, another incident showed that I had Mom's empathy, Dad's loner courage, and both parents' dislike of bullies. Halfway through my first-grade year in North Carolina, we returned to my birthplace, Washington, D.C., to prepare for an overseas tour in London, England. We moved into a small ground-floor apartment in the Anacostia district, and I finished first grade in a beaten-down city school named Moton Elementary. It was my first all-black environment. I walked daily up a steep hill to a high-walled, forbidding stone building that looked more like a fortress or mausoleum than a school. Its dark halls, dirty bathrooms, and broken asphalt were depressing, the teachers were unwelcoming, and the kids seemed mean.

On my first day, a fellow first-grader who also had transferred to this school after Christmas break grabbed my arm for help as I passed by him to get through the gate. I knew immediately that he was sick, and not just because he wheezed up the stairs behind me. He reeked of urine. His kidneys did not work properly. He had an unforgivably cruel last name: Peabody. His first name was Robert. I led him to our classroom, and he followed me in.

The classrooms had old wood double desks with inkwells. When the teacher assigned the seat next to Robert, the first kid refused, theatrically holding his nose while the room laughed. My heart broke as Robert's face cratered under the humiliation. As tears streamed down his cheeks, I strode to his desk, sat down next to him, and smiled. Robert took the tissues I quietly passed under the desk and seemed to take comfort from my note that said everything would be okay. He nodded and, for the first time, showed me a glimpse of his smile, a shy, crooked, chipped-toothed grin that sealed our bond. Our first day done, I waited with him at the gate until his mother arrived.

My guardianship would become a permanent job. Every day he waited anxiously for me at the gate. I escorted him through the halls, stared down his taunters, helped him complete his work, defended him on the playground, and ate the afternoon snack with him. I loathed the odor and resented the inability of adults to stop his tormentors or help him get better. But I don't remember him as a burden, and no thought of abandoning him entered my mind. The duty had been instinctive; the commitment, total.

One day later that spring, Robert wasn't waiting at the gate. When he didn't show by the warning bell, I left for class. His side of the desk sat empty that day. The next day, empty again, and the day after, the same. After a week, I gave up.

He never returned. It was as if he had never existed. My shields kicked in, and I shifted into the safety of hyper-focus on getting all A's, as only a child with mild obsessive-compulsive disorder can. Robert Peabody no longer entered my mind.

Thirty years later, while I was racewalking around the Hollywood Reservoir in Los Angeles, a baffling wave of grief welled up and hobbled me midstride. I dragged myself to the fence and racked my brain for what could have hit me. Out of nowhere, Robert Peabody's long-forgotten face loomed to the front of my mind, and his shy, crooked grin broke my heart all over again. Thirty years later, as a thirtysomething attorney, I finally grieved for my first-grade friend and my inability to save him.

In some ways, Robert Peabody had been my first client.

Shortly after this sad stint in Anacostia, we left for London, England. It was June 1964, and this time we were following Dad to a three-year posting at the American embassy. I enrolled in Town & Country, an academically demanding private British school that required uniforms with gray skirts that Mrs. Paul, our despotic headmistress, measured to ensure strict compliance with her three-inches-above-the-knee limit. She was not having the rage over miniskirts contaminate *her* students. We rode a "coach" to the school's four old redbrick buildings on Eaton Avenue. After that pathetic school in Anacostia, it took a while to adjust to British rigor. I truly felt like I had stepped through the looking glass. But our parents' drilling had paid off. Within two years I had mastered pounds, shillings, and pence; was studying Tudor history; and taking four languages—English, French, Latin, and German—at the same time.

After living in a huge house on the Anson Road edge of Gladstone Park for our first year in England, we moved to an apartment building on Maida Lane, a graceful London street that meandered alongside the Little Venice canal.

My mother's passion for reading was by then my own. At age ten, I was an animal nut who had read every Dr. Dolittle adventure and the *Born Free* novels about freed lions that Mom hoped would heal my traumatized reaction of wanting to free the caged lion at the Cleveland zoo. For the most part, Mom didn't much care what we read as long as we read. Only once did she "request" that I read a particular book.

I was in my tiny garland-rose bedroom, reading my latest Dr. Dolittle adventure, when she waltzed through my door, thrust a small white paperback with a shiny cover into my hands, and announced, "Here, I need you to read this. It's important." I looked at the picture on the cover of the dark-eyed girl with the thick brown hair and winsome smile, wondering what had prompted this unusual command.

I left the world of talking cows and entered the garret realm of the girl with the sparkling dark eyes. The book engulfed me. I shuddered as her hunters neared, grabbed on to her fierce will to live, and fell in love with how she spited darkness with her dreams. She was Anneliese Marie Frank. The book, of course, was *The Diary of a Young Girl.*

The Shoah was beyond my ten-year-old grasp, but Anne Frank's spirit was not. She so captured my imagination that on first reading, I blocked out the diary's end. In suppressed anguish, I raced through it a second time, clinging to the hope in my denial. But there would be no escape, no second shelter, no reprieve.

I was stunned. Who could hunt down a little girl and ship her out to death? Without so much as a smothered protest, a demonic industry had snuffed her beauty from the world. Determined to impose order on the unfathomable, I pulled down *Encyclopaedia Britannica* volumes from our living room shelves—Nazi, Hitler, Third Reich, genocide. I read more, understood less, and felt worse. Why did so many abet and so few defy a continent-wide carnage? Vigorously taught to reject hate, I had no ability to grasp the virulent anti-Semitism that had extinguished her life.

But after *The Diary of a Young Girl,* I understood one thing for sure: If Anne could perish, so could I. It began to dawn on me that few tests in life mattered, but one of them had to be: "Would you have sheltered Anne Frank?" I knew with ice-cold clarity that 90 percent of humanity would fail this test. This was the real reason for the devastation I felt.

By handing me that book, my mother had begun an important quest. She never missed a chance to note the significance of the European genocide of six million Jews. Years later, back in the States, in her casual way of lobbing the profound into the mundane, she said, "What they did to the Jews was monstrous, just unforgivable. They tried to wipe them out with the same hatred they have for us." She wanted me to transcend racism through understanding the trauma of Jewish history. We, too, were uprooted, enslaved, scattered in a diaspora, persecuted, and hunted. Our millions perished, not in millennia of pogroms nor six years of industrialized killing camps, but over centuries of cruel crossings and deadly servitude. The same dehumanization that branded us had indeed fueled the slaughter of Europe's Jews, Gypsies, disabled, and intellectuals. Determined not to sink me with the anvils of American slavery, Mom preferred to fortify me with the lessons of a similar people's trauma and to make their strength my own. By handing me Anne Frank's diary, she had planted her seeds of compassion, passed on the gift of her immense empathy, and permanently oriented me to seek justice.

After a year of studying the reign of the Tudors at my British school, I had discovered my next heroine after Mom and Anne Frank: Queen Elizabeth I. QE1 was my Number One Girl. Her Majesty fascinated me. As the disfavored daughter of a fallen queen, she fought by her wits to stay alive, took the throne and held it, refused to marry at a time women were barely above chattel, and then proceeded to best the world's empires. With brains, guile, and ruthless advisers, she transformed herself from a traitor's bastard into England's greatest monarch, the revered Virgin Queen. When she could, she ruled through inspiration, with uncommon vision and restraint for her time (compared to the murderous reigns of her sister and father, her own murderous reign was mild). She ruled alone, thwarting patriarchy and averting the marriage she was sure would end her freedom and possibly her life. But most important, she backed her privateers and set her island nation on the trail to the New World. It seemed to me that without Good Queen Bess, there would have been no United States.

Enthralled with all things Elizabethan, I played to the hilt every Queen Elizabeth role in our British history and literature classes, which were full of dramatic reenactments. Never mind slavery, the question of whether I, the only black female in my British school, could play the role of Elizabeth I never entered my mind. Of course I could. Mom abetted my infatuation, sewing the jewels on the Elizabethan gowns and, while affixing my crown, clucking approvingly that Elizabeth was, as her mother predicted, an infinitely better monarch than any son of any king.

The only other historic figure who succeeded in captivating my imagination to this extreme was the anti-autocratic redistributionist, Robin Hood. My opportunity to play him would come later.

We returned from England in late 1967. In San Francisco the hippies were celebrating the Summer of Love, while across the bay, in Oakland, the Black Panther Party was gaining traction. Riots were erupting in black communities from Milwaukee to Washington, D.C., but up to that point I had been only vaguely aware of the politics exploding back home. Right before we left for London, the horrific murders of four little girls in the Sixteenth Street church bombing in Birmingham had made my dad angrily ask, "What kind of country kills little girls?" In that instant, the war for Negro civil rights briefly jolted my reality but soon faded into a faint echo an ocean away. When the turmoil of the sixties began surging, I was in London struggling with Latin and playing Beatles forty-fives. But by the close of our tour in Great Britain, Dad's next assignment shattered this sheltered state.

He was going to Vietnam. We could follow him to every assignment except this one. We would wait for his return, one way or another, near Middletown, Pennsylvania, at Olmstead Air Force Base. When he hugged us goodbye at the Greyhound Bus depot in Reading, it was the saddest day of my life. I was in sixth grade, old enough to sense the dread beneath my parents' stoicism. Old enough to understand that he could die. And old enough for a new epiphany of anger, this time at the state's breath-gutting power to upend our lives and endanger my dad. It was an anger that would grow deeper as it slowly became clear the war had started over a trumped-up lie. Yet the only protest among the black-light posters of tigers and butterflies on my bedroom walls was my handmade sign protesting turtle soup on behalf of my Spanish terrapin, Mikie, whom I had rescued from a farmers' market in London. At the Unitarian Universalist church my mother dragged us to that year, there were a lot of anti-war protests. I concluded that the war was wrong, but my focus was on Dad. And on Mom, who bravely carried us through that year and quietly prepared herself to finish raising us alone.

From our Olmstead bungalow in Pennsylvania, he was eight thousand miles overseas, but we were never far from my father while he was in Vietnam. We sent him taped messages every two weeks, our banter dutifully masking the fear that this time our message might return with his effects, unheard. His tapes back to us were equally banal, covering the weather, his lodgings, his food, and other travelogue fare, anything that shielded us from his reality. I don't remember anything specific, just his voice mercifully confirming that he had been alive two weeks before and that he loved us. It felt like I spent that whole year holding my breath.

Then one warm, sunny June day came the greatest gift of my life. He returned. Alive.

My brothers and I waited at the screen door. Dad emerged from the military car in full uniform and strode up the front yard to the door. He stopped and declared, "No one else in this family will ever fight in another war. I've paid that debt for all of you." He opened the door and we collapsed in his arms.

He never burdened us with the toll that debt must have taken. But I found out how miraculously lucky we'd been. We didn't know until after his return that he had rejected the much safer job of dropping bombs and had chosen instead to fly combat rescue missions. His helicopter dangled in a veil of bullets, doors wide open for the grunts who flung themselves and their downed buddies into the hovering hold. After the frontline troops, rescue pilots had the second highest chance of returning in a flag-draped coffin. One picture I saw of a Mekong Delta rescue helicopter reminded me of a Chinese checkers board, spackled with the pocked star-point bullet holes from tail to cockpit. How he returned without a scratch is a mystery for which I'll always be grateful.

A few months later, we were on our way to Luke Air Force Base, the post where Mr. What *Is* You jolted my consciousness about color caste, class, and inequity. I was still too young to adopt the bellowing political rage of the late sixties. After Arizona, I spent eighth grade at Edwards AFB in Southern California, running cross-country races in the desert and winning election to class president within two months of arriving. We next moved to Scott AFB in southern Illinois, where I attended ninth and tenth grade at Mascoutah High School and experienced hayrides, met the strenuous demands of my biology teacher, John Harris, and again was elected class president.

By now I was more than comfortable being an intense, self-assured, interracially fluent teen who neither sought nor needed her peers' approval. With an unusual summer of not moving, I got to stay with the same swim team, friends, and piano teacher for the exorbitant stretch of two years in a row. But for my junior year of high school, we moved again, this time to Dad's home turf, Cleveland, Ohio. We lived near Grandmother Rice, and Phil and I got to experience Shaker Heights High School, one of the few American schools that matched the rigor of our British alma mater. Mom forced the guidance counselors to put us into the highest of Shaker's five college tracks, and I carried a load of five Advanced Placement courses. Seven hours of homework a night was not unusual, which meant often not getting to bed before two A.M. I was entering the last leg of the marathon to college.

The most important formative experience happened right after my junior year at Shaker ended. That was the summer when my bent for challenging injustice merged with my interest in political power. As a budding political junkie, I wanted to do only one thing the summer of 1973: watch the televised Watergate impeachment hearings. This historic fight promised a constitutional donnybrook over abused power—the 1973 summer smackdown of a high-handed and paranoid president. And I wanted a ringside seat so badly that I had promised to do all of the family ironing if, for just one summer, Mom would exempt me from her mandatory pre-moving regimen of swim meets, lifeguarding, and studying and let me watch the hearings. She knew I must be desperate; I equated the ironing board with the rack. Since we weren't moving from our Ohio home to our next post in Texas until later in the summer, she relented.

Gavel-to-gavel coverage! Alone in the basement! No laps in freezing water at six in the morning! No supervising spoiled brats in the pool! I was in heaven. Every day, after scouring the newspapers for behind-the-scenes analysis, I stood at the ironing board, glued to the television. At first the Judiciary Committee's hearings, a cross between a constitutional show trial and a suspense-filled soap opera, were riveting enough. "As the Tape Turns"—about power, lies, and audiotapes—bristled with more lawyers, betrayal, and plot twists than the Grisham novels that would come along a decade later.

During the second week of congressional sparring with White House aides, the hearings leaped from satisfying to transporting. From the committee chairman's left, a stentorian voice boomed superbly enunciated, dramatically drawn-out syllables in an authoritarian clap that silenced everyone: "Mistah Speaker, may the gentlewoman from the great state of Texas be recognized?" The chair graciously yielded, and she continued, "Thank you, Mistah Speaker . . . The Constitution of these United States, that most august and prescient of documents, demands a response from the executive . . ."

I froze at the ironing board, transfixed as this formidable woman proceeded to thunder in dignity her perfected objections to Nixon's denigration of this nation's sacred texts. I had never heard anyone like her. Her every utterance thrilled me. I looked for her every day of the hearings. When she cross-examined a witness, challenged her colleagues on the committee, or parried with lawyers, I felt I was watching Elizabeth I incarnated as a black congresswoman from Texas. On the eve of the historic vote to impeach the president of the United States, the Great Lady from the Great State of Texas rose to address the committee and the nation with an epic final performance. Her basso alto brought the hearings to a standstill. With a gravitas to match the voice of God, she marshaled a tornado of reasoning that harkened back to the founding fathers and powered through history to the tragic but inexorable conclusion that President Nixon had abrogated our great Constitution, broken his covenant and bond with the American people, and must step down. I was staggered. She had just shown how to move the will of giants and stand down the most powerful of men with nothing more than eloquence and the majesty of the United States Constitution.

She had just bent the wind.

When I finally regained my wits, I looked down and saw that I had burned a hole right through my father's shirt and into the ironing board cover. They were ruined. I did not care. Barbara Jordan had taken command of the microphone and of history. I had just seen a Praetorian Guard of freedom in action. And my life's direction was set.

The answer to "What *is* you?" crystallized. I was a champion in training to run the relay race for justice. My job was to see that every kid had the same chance to thrive and forge her talent's destiny that I'd had. To end the inequality conspiracy, not join it. Like a peregrine falcon prepped and honed for the hunt, I had spent fourteen years of relentless testing, endless study, constant exams, dance and music recitals, track meets, swim meets, chess, lifeguarding, oil painting, debate tournaments, student council elections, and learning the human tapestry from every place and person on my nomadic odyssey, honing myself to fight for that vision. Like the falcon, hooded and sheathed, I had completed the first level of training and awaited the next, in further preparation for my day of release, when I would soar and attack.

If Dad had been a special operations commander for the Air Force, I was going to be a Delta Force for equality. If Mom had been a master teacher, I would become a master fixer—not for oligarchs who culled riches and power for themselves but for Barbara Jordan's and Martin Luther King's vision of freedom and justice.

At age seventeen, I knew I was driven to achieve, but until that moment, I had not known to what end. I knew only that money did not move me. Fame was silly. Status felt empty. Romance was optional. My aspiration was for something more, and Barbara Jordan had named it. It was the same thing that had propelled a little girl to free a lion, shield Robert Peabody, repel first-grade racists, and challenge an Arizona teacher for the rights of a new friend.

The call I heard was King's trumpet of conscience. The quest for justice beckoned.

To answer it, I would have to learn to bend the wind.

Chapter 3

THE POWER FACTORY

As much as I might have indulged the idea of being a falcon awaiting advanced training, I assiduously avoided all thoughts of leaving the nest. My parents actually had to push me out. I was the only high school kid I knew who dreaded leaving her family after graduation. That summer of Watergate, we moved back to Texas, where I would finish high school at Randolph Air Force Base, just outside San Antonio. After the rigor of Shaker Heights High School, my Texas school was a joke.

Unable to pursue serious academic work, I spent my senior year in a riptide of college entrance rituals and drama club contests. I joined the Thespians under the direction of Signey Scoggins, my cool just-out-of-college speech and language arts teacher who insisted we call her by her first name. To the provincial Texans running our high school, Signey was a Communist, and we, her students, a Red Cell. We did subversive activities like debate, read poetry, speak extemporaneously, and perform plays. Signey disdained high school musicals, so we replaced *A Christmas Carol* with an esoteric David Mamet play that no one understood. Our teams swept city competitions.

Filling in at the last minute for a sick teammate, I won first place in a citywide poetry reading by quickly memorizing a Joan Baez song, removing my Coke-bottle glasses so I couldn't see the audience, and getting onstage ten minutes later to deliver the prizewinning recitation. I also was a wickedly fast and sassy extemporaneous speaker. But thanks to the urging of my classmate Renee Haines, debate was where I ruled.

Renee, a tall, sharp girl with wild curly brown hair and a renegade's spirit, had convinced me to team up with her to lay siege to the genteel world of Texas debate. Renee's only way of paying for college after her parents' divorce was to win the state debate championship and its full scholarship to the University of Texas. The state competition topic that year was about full employment. According to Renee, since we were in Texas, where contestants were used to repeating a fixed set of arguments and facts, it would not be hard to wipe out our opponents with updated arguments based on recent data from weekly newsmagazines and the financial news. She was right. With relentless updates and a ruthless style, our salt-and-pepper duo took the Texas debating circuit by storm, scandalizing the Bible Belt judges with our pantsuits (one wrote on her comment card that "Young ladies should *never* appear in public in trousers!") and our disdain for every ladylike norm known to man. In the most exhilarating moment of my life, we won the state championship that spring, and Renee got her scholarship to UT Austin. But I had other plans, with only one requirement—not to attend college in football-crazy Texas.

I did not have to. My SAT scores had been in the eighty-sixth percentile, good enough for applications from around the country to pour into my mailbox. Sorting through them, I realized I didn't want to leave behind the world of debate, speaking, and drama. I thought that an undergraduate degree in investigative journalism and communications might work. Hadn't journalists Bob Woodward and Carl Bernstein unraveled Watergate and held power to account? Besides, my reasoning went, journalism would be good training for law school or other graduate paths, since almost any mission that leveled playing fields would require marshaling facts and telling truth to power. There was another reason for this thinking. I had grown up admiring newscasters. My mother hadn't let us watch more than one prime-time TV show a week—she was afraid it would rot our brains—except the news and *60 Minutes.*

I had followed great newscasters like Eric Sevareid, Huntley and Brinkley, Charles Kuralt, Dan Rather, Ed Bradley, and Jessica Savitch, but only one stood head and shoulders above the rest: the incomparable Walter Cronkite. The CBS anchorman had mesmerized me with his sensible, authoritative voice. At age six, I would change into a clean T-shirt each night before his broadcast, because that's what we were trained to do when guests came to the house. In sixth grade, I sent him a letter of admiration that notified him I would be ready to take his chair at the anchor desk when he retired. I must have missed his reply.

Broadcast journalism seemed as good a conduit as any to the arenas of power and policy. And the best communications/broadcast journalism program was at Northwestern University in Chicago, so it became my top pick. However, Dad had other ideas. After returning from a winter trip to Boston, he handed me one additional application—to Radcliffe College for Women. Paying no attention to the footnote on the cover that said it was part of Harvard University, I filled it out and sent it in as my last application. By April I had acceptance letters from every school, including Northwestern. But there was no arguing with my dad. Radcliffe, the women's portal to Harvard, was the most prestigious choice and a symbolic leap for the Rice family. Since my parents were paying the bills, Radcliffe College in Cambridge, Massachusetts, was where I would go. I consoled myself with the thought that as one of the Ivy League Seven Sisters, it was a women's school, at least, and my parents promised that if I didn't like it, I could transfer to Northwestern.

My future was charted. I had two months to go in my senior year. I relaxed enough to play hooky twice and ride inner tubes down the San Antonio River with friends. I played tennis, discovered Chaka Khan, and in my pathetic version of sowing wild oats, stayed out all night after my senior prom. Neither the pending thrill of going to college nor these senior-year antics could quell my anxiety about leaving home.

By the time graduation day came, Dad's next military assignment had already arrived. We were headed back to Illinois, this time to Chanute AFB in the northern end of the state, from where I would travel east to college at summer's end. Our band of five packed up and set out across the land we had traversed together all my life. It was too hard to accept that this trek would be my last.

We arrived at Chanute before our housing was ready and checked in to a trailer park just outside the base. Two weeks later, the morning finally came when Mom was to drive me five states away to Cambridge. Norman and Phil were unnaturally quiet as we loaded the Chrysler Newport with steamer trunks of supplies for my dorm room. When it was time to hug them goodbye, I couldn't do it. After so many years, alone together against the world, we were like part of the same organism. Separating from them felt like cutting off my limbs. I sobbed to my dad that I didn't want to leave. He, my eternal rescuer, told me I didn't have to go if I didn't want to. Mom, who had been in the car impatiently gunning the engine, saw what was happening and came back into the trailer to yell at my father, "Don't tell her that! She's going to college—NOW!" Mom was frantic at the thought that her first fledgling might fail to exit the nest on schedule. She was right. I wasn't going to become a champion for anything, staying there in a trailer park. So I took one last forlorn look at my father and brothers and slumped into the car.

My whimpering ceased after the first ten miles. Mom and I drove familiar turnpikes and interstates across the Midwest and through a sequence of Poconos Mountain tunnels I knew by heart. Two days later, we arrived in cobblestoned Cambridge. Mom dropped me off at my dorm in the Radcliffe Quad on the north end of the campus. When she saw me in my tiny, dark room on the second floor of North House, she offered to take me to her hotel, but I sucked up my quivering courage and said no. The time had come to be on my own. She hung around for a few more days, ostensibly to outfit my dorm room with rugs, curtains, and pillows. Then she hugged me goodbye and hit the road back to Chanute to settle her depleted flock into yet another base house.

The beehive of college activity soon reduced my homesickness to a dull ache. I had never shared a bedroom. But nothing, not even living with two brothers, could have prepared me for the experiment of coed bathrooms or the shock of finding someone's pet ocelot sitting on the ironing board in the laundry room. Ever the adapter, I got along with my roommate, Judy Gaddie, found a new gaggle of companions, and mastered the wobbled gait required to walk over cobblestones with a backpack full of books. Then the wonder of being at Harvard and in Cambridge began to take over. I roamed the magnificent Widener Library in Harvard Yard, explored the observatory, tried out for the crew team, signed up for a Chinese-language course, and figured out where to shop for clothes and shoes—already an emerging addiction.

Until I got there, I hadn't realized that Radcliffe did not exist as a separate college, independent of Harvard College (they would officially merge the next year). I must have been the only kid there who had inadvertently gotten in to Harvard. I proved equally clueless on other subjects. Within two months I had learned that tone-deaf people like me not only can't sing, they also cannot take Chinese. That economics was a confusing pseudoscience that believed in invisible hands. That in the stretch between Harvard-Radcliffe and MIT lay an entire mile where I didn't stand out as a nerd. That what I called writing, Harvard called drivel. And that what I considered reading, Harvard considered unfocused browsing. That success in honors high school math notwithstanding, I had the mathematical aptitude of an earthworm. And that while I was intelligent enough, at Harvard, I was a hundred-watt bulb on a campus of halogen torches. I also understood that this was how everyone felt and that it didn't matter.

I had entered the Thunderdome of competitive power education from a pitiful little high school. But I had arrived at the premier power factory equipped with the right stuff. Except for the math and the Chinese, my gaps were easily filled. As I watched some of my more neurotic classmates, I silently thanked my parents for my inner serenity, for my generous outlook, and for my not wanting to be anyone else. I was comfortable with the fact that I lacked the intellectual's yen for total immersion into a single academic subject. My goal was not to be the smartest one in a Harvard room but to sharpen my thinking and to graduate with an understanding of how people, the world, and power worked.

These weren't bad goals. But I was eighteen and, for the first time, free from my parents' formidable constraints. It was almost inevitable that I would crash into some hurdles and run off course a few times before making it across the finish line of college graduation. I made my biggest mistakes early. I wasted way too much of my freshman year cobbling together an unworkable special major in communications and plotting a transfer to Northwestern. Ever the late bloomer socially, I had not really dated in high school and so had arrived at Harvard with the heterosexual social acumen of a turtle. And while my college girlfriends and I ignored the male freshmen (they dubbed us the "NBI" crew for "no booty involved"), the attentions of the upper classmen proved too exciting to ignore.

To my European-American and Jewish friends, I added a dizzying mix of folks with a dazzling range of talents from Holland, India, Nigeria, Japan, and Singapore. For daily living, my primary companions were a group of African-American women, two of whom, Jennifer Davis and Kim Roberts, I met our freshman year at North House. We ate together, studied together, went to dances together, and commiserated about men together. Kim, Jen, and I decided to be sophomore roommates and moved down to Harvard's Quincy House, where we later roomed with Alison Arnold, Kathy Miles, Leslie Walker, and Linda Hodges.

My closest friend by far was Jennifer. Jen had grown up in Brooklyn with her mother and brother and had attended a Catholic girls' school, Saint Angela Hall. She was graceful, friendly, and calming amid Harvard's high-strung atmosphere. We shared a natural skepticism and humor about our presence in the strange world at Harvard-Radcliffe. We had a great time laughing at ourselves, at our interracially clueless classmates, and at scandalizing discoveries like the eighteenth-century exhibits in the bowels of the old bio labs depicting African tribes and apes together, as if they were the same species. Jen was deeply intelligent, with the same uncanny ability to read people that my mom had, and she was my refuge during those cold and sometimes dispiriting years in Cambridge. Many of my best experiences, much of my laughter, and all of my feeling that I had found family were due to her. Thirty-eight years later, she is still my closest friend, and her husband, Bob Carrie, who had the misfortune of living below us in Quincy House, is, too.

During this same time, my feminist bent took flight. In my last year of high school, I loved the way that Renee and I had detonated our way through the Texas debate circuit with blunt, hard-edged talk and behavior that offered none of the deference and finesse expected from girls. We had dismissed the corseted confines of traditional femininity, and I had never felt so powerful, in control, or mentally free. I never wanted to lose that outlook. Radcliffe was the perfect place to make sure that didn't happen. I hit the feminist road with copies of *The Feminine Mystique, Our Bodies Ourselves,* and *For Colored Girls Who Have Considered Suicide When the Rainbow Is Enuf,* and I never looked back.

My best college experience would happen in a dojo. Following a physical assault by a male junior in my dorm kitchen, I decided that my next attacker would end up in the ICU. I trekked down to the old Intercollegiate Athletic Building and signed up for a Korean martial arts class. My life in Tae Kwon Do began in an old second-floor wrestling room, full of grunting students punching and kicking their way up and down the thick bloodred wrestling mat. I took to it like a dolphin to water. What started as recovery quickly became revelation. I was built for Tae Kwon Do. My long torso, strong legs, low center of gravity, and fast hands were perfect for the sport. My double-jointed ankles landed the balls of my feet into my opponents with stunning penetration. But it was my instructor, Suk Young Chung, who figured out the oddity of my fighting edge: Psychologically, I saw my five-five self as being over six feet tall, and this delusion caused my blows to land in completely unexpected places.

It didn't take long before I was obsessively practicing, working out every day, endlessly punching, kicking, blocking, sparring with pros, and perfecting the *kata,* the beautiful stylized sequences of moves that form almost a dance of set techniques. I soon joined Mr. Chung's off-campus Tae Kwon Do studio, where I found a family of truck haulers, taxi drivers, cooks, and carpet cleaners to balance my power-elite realm. By the time I'd earned my brown belt, pushing beyond physical limits had become routine. I could fly and kill with my hands. The best gift from Tae Kwon Do, however, was not physical mastery. It was cerebral transcendence. Through extreme exertion, I hurled myself into soaring, boundless mental planes beyond all constraint. It was not the flying side kicks but the mental leaps of flight that liberated. All fear and any sense of limits vanished. And for the first time, I owned my space on this earth. I had found my first portal to spiritual freedom, a priceless gift that no academic class could ever match.

There were other good reasons to learn self-defense at Harvard. During the mid-1970s, Boston and its suburbs were among the most dangerous places to be black. Almost twenty years after *Mendez v. Westminster*[3] and *Brown v. Board of Education* outlawed segregated schools, the working-class white suburbs of Boston had erupted over Judge W. Arthur Garrity's order to integrate with black schools. Angry Irish-American holdouts in South Boston rioted, burned buses, and, as documented in an iconic photo, beat up black bystanders with the American flag.* Gangs of white males from Southie roamed the trains and back streets of Cambridge, looking for black students. One night a carload of white males chased Kathy Miles and me down Garden Street, yelling racial epithets. We escaped. On another day, riding the Red Line train back to Cambridge, Jen, Kim, and I barely pulled our classmate Lisa Poyer away from an attack by the angry white father of a kid who had been stabbed during a busing brawl.

The first real racial danger of my life was occurring in the same northern city where Crispus Attucks, a freed slave, had fought in

---

*To view the photo, please visit www.powerconcedesnothing.com.

the American Revolution. Once the adrenaline subsided, I could understand the rage of our attackers. All they had to hold on to was that insular patch of turf and their white identity, and now a court was taking that away. The tribal outlashing was predictable. They didn't have to know *me*, only that I was a black woman attending an Ivy League school that they never would. As I thought about it, it made no sense to bus poor white kids to an academically failed black school and poor black kids to an equally failed white school. They should have merged the two populations into a new top-of-the-line school that advanced both disadvantaged populations at the same time. But that would have cost the kind of money rarely spent on poor kids of any race.

My social relationships with other students may have been important, but they should not have taken up as much oxygen as they did that first college year. Distracted and insufficiently focused, I had trouble connecting to my freshman courses with the energy they demanded. After a less-than-stellar freshman year, I returned home for the summer to work as a lifeguard while I cleared my head. I was overjoyed to see my family again, but Phil was busy getting ready to enter Stanford (he had declined Harvard because I was there), and Norm was a big man on campus, busy studying, working, and playing high school football.

I returned sophomore year with a slightly better attitude, kicking myself into high gear after an early come-to-Jesus meeting with myself on the rocky shores of Maine. *For the love of Mary,* I silently yelled at myself as the surf pounded, *you are at HARVARD, the world's greatest power factory, and you are wasting the opportunity! Are you insane?* In what better place would I learn how to use power, or bend the wind, like Barbara Jordan? My parents had knocked themselves out to get me here, and I was wasting time lamenting Northwestern. It was time to grow up and get serious. It was time to learn.

Though the stature of my professors became clearer to me after I left Harvard, at the time, I did not fully appreciate the constellation of scholars who delivered our lectures. I had the privilege of hearing lectures by John Kenneth Galbraith, Robert Samuelson, Orlando

Patterson, James Q. Wilson, Matina Horner, Stephen Jay Gould, Theta Scotchborough, Samuel Huntington, Harvey Mansfield, and at a course I sat in on at MIT, Noam Chomsky. We listened to their lectures and asked our questions of the teaching assistants who led our smaller sections, where we debated the issues and dug into the material.

In my government courses, we explored Socrates's truth-seeking challenges to power, parsed the Peloponnesian War, deconstructed The Federalist Papers, plumbed the dangers posed by Hobbes's *Leviathan,* and examined the rules of power and war from masters ranging from Machiavelli and Sun Tzu to Gandhi. From the founding fathers to Mao Tse-tung, I learned how different systems invested power, managed factions, finessed inequality, provided opportunity, controlled access to land, suppressed dissent, protected freedoms and rights, distributed wealth, and enforced privilege. I studied how leaders had mismanaged power and created debacles, hoarded it for venal plunder, or exercised extraordinary wisdom in declining power in order to advance democracy. I concluded that among the many imperfect systems, democracy offered a fairer distribution of wealth and opportunity and better checks on power. But even democracies could be gamed and looted—which was why I disdained ideology in favor of practical controls that curbed the inevitable greed, bias, and corruption that power bred. As far as I could tell, because democratically installed leaders were forced to be closer to the conditions suffered by the governed, no one in a liberal democracy had ever died in a famine.

As should happen in a liberal arts experience, a few non-government classes almost seduced me to switch majors. In Special States of Consciousness, the fascinating neurobiology of the human brain mesmerized me for a semester. Stephen Jay Gould, my favorite professor, was so good at making natural selection come alive that he made me forget my loathing of being in the sun long enough to briefly consider paleontology. I took Orlando Patterson's masterful and soul-wrenching courses in African slavery that made our progress seem all the more surreal. How, in four generations, my family had ever gotten from slav-

ery to me sitting at Harvard became more, not less, amazing. I also
indulged a brief flight of fancy over feminist studies but settled for
lectures on women's roles in patriarchal society, the colonization of
women's bodies, and the sociological dynamics of the Salem witch
trials. By far my most mind-expanding course was in a field for which
I had zero aptitude but which extended my frame of reference more
radically than any other. Introduction to Astronomy gave me a way to
imagine infinity before and after the universe. It made me weep for
the wondrous vista it had opened and for my inability to think in the
advanced math needed to do it. Each time these and other areas beckoned, I returned to my senses and to the prosaic major about power:
government.

Rocky start notwithstanding, my experience at Harvard-Radcliffe
turned out well. I had studied governance and formal power and
glimpsed its money and how its social webs in the strange Harvard
clubs wove the family of the ruling elite. Harvard molded an oli-
garchy of strivers and scions from around the world and dispatched
them into a global network of gatekeepers. For better or worse, I was
about to become one of its products.

I had learned enough. Harvard's second most important lesson
was summed up in its motto: VERITAS. Truth, however, was often the
last thing institutions like Harvard really wanted known. My thinking
was now rigorous enough to winnow through even the chaff cloud-
ing the truth about Harvard and its secrets. The reality was, even in
the face of hard facts that proved the need to change, power rarely
bent to truth. Even in the face of manifest injustice that betrayed
cherished values, power did not yield to moral mandates. Veritas was
mutable. And power conceded nothing. Which was why Harvard's
most important lesson was best summed up by Frederick Douglass:
"Power concedes nothing without a demand. It never has, and it
never will."

I had emerged from Harvard-Radcliffe equipped to face anything.
I was ready for the next step.

Finally, on a glorious morning, June 18, 1978, I sat in sweet exhaustion on the slate stone berm below the Quincy House cafeteria, sipping a cup of tea. This was graduation day, and before my hungover classmates recovered sufficiently to greet their proud parents, I wanted to savor the moment. The still beauty of my dorm's courtyard warmed my deep satisfaction. Quincy's soaring trees, heavy with new leaves, shimmered in the light. The lavender rhododendrons had ruptured everywhere like fireworks. The trilling of songbirds filled the air, a prelude to celebration. Under the crush of college life, I had never been able to enjoy the Quincy courtyard at this time of year. June always meant morphing into a sleep-deprived zombie during final exams, then quickly vacating the dorm to make way for graduates and their families. But not this June; others would be making way for us.

I was leaving college with a better understanding of the universe, the world, and myself, but more important, of how little I knew. Still, I had managed to acquire some basic wisdom: *Find out enough to ask the right questions. Study every problem through different lenses and angles. Listen closely to your adversaries, especially if you dislike them, then walk in their shoes. Nothing is what it seems, so stay nimble. Brilliant theory is often just a bad start. Outside of science, facts rarely determine anything. Context determines everything, and it changes. Strive for a reasonable balance of risks, then act. Markets and human beings are irrational. Question all givens. Environment matters. Value the many kinds of intelligence, and don't underestimate the kind you don't have. The universe is relative, strange, and amoral. Absolutes and their rigid human counterparts, ideologues, are dangerous. Figure out what is important. Listen to your heart, but act with your brain. Compete against your best self and then push her a little harder. Keep the faults you like and purge the rest. Enjoy others' success as your own. Be ruthlessly honest with yourself and honest enough with everyone else. Claim what you want and go get it. Define yourself and your destiny. If you want flowers, send them. Protect your gift, like Katharine Hepburn did. Physical exercise heals everything, but when that fails, put on some Earth Wind & Fire and read* For Colored Girls Who Have Considered Suicide When the Rainbow Is Enuf.

College, my second training ground, had clarified my vision. Journalism, the world of words and ideas, would not provide enough direct impact. If talking didn't work, I would need to force action without ending up in prison. That would require a law degree. But after sixteen years, I needed a break from racking up academic credentials and wanted to earn another kind of diploma: my black belt from Mr. Chung. At age twenty-two, I was a senior citizen in the world of martial artists. It was then or never for Tae Kwon Do.

My parents didn't mind my decision not to go straight to law school. They were just relieved that I was graduating. That summer I would live with Mrs. Arnold, the mother of my roommate Alison, in Roxbury, my first all-black community, where I'd exchange my armor of otherness for the armor that color caste requires. I would work in the Harvard-Radcliffe undergraduate admissions office as an admissions officer, a position I would love for its fun and the irony of joining the moat-masters to the king's castle. Since Phil was already applying to medical school, and Norman was starting his senior year in high school, having one kid out in the world and supporting herself wasn't so bad.

With the morning sun gaining strength and edging me off my perch, I downed the last of my tea and headed back upstairs to get ready. I met Jen in the living room and gave her a long hug. Before long we were all attired for "Pomp and Circumstance" in black robes and tasseled mortar boards. We sailed down the elevator and walked together through the courtyard to greet our families at the Quincy House gate. I quickly spotted my parents, Norman, and Grandmother Rice in the throng. Only Phil, who was still finishing his finals at Stanford, was missing. Before I could complete the hugs, Grandmom had struggled up out of her wheelchair, planted her orthopedic shoes firmly on the cobblestones, lifted her regal chin, and proclaimed, "I have stepped on the hallowed grounds of Harvard, and I can now die in peace." I thought to myself that "harrowing" was more the word but said nothing to deflate her moment of triumph. Three hours later, Norman, my parents, and she watched me walk across the stage to receive the diploma that my ancestors had worked for all of their lives.

Chapter 4

THE CRUCIBLE

In 1979 I earned my black belt from Mr. Chung after a terrifying exam of breaking thick wood boards, multiple-opponent combat, and other death-defying feats. I went on to win several medals in national Tae Kwon Do championships and even fought in Madison Square Garden. But after three idyllic years of Tae Kwon Do and working as a Harvard admissions officer, I was ready to resume a life of deeper purpose. In the fall of 1981, I entered New York University School of Law on a Root-Tilden-Snow Scholarship.

Gladiator school had begun. I was ready. My vision and agenda were clear. At NYU, I would get the skills needed to bend the powerful. I would learn to take power and wield it responsibly. Not the venal power of glory or greed but the transformative power of public good, the power that levels inclines and extends ladders to folks without it. Or as Martin Luther King Jr. put it:

> The problem of transforming the ghetto ... is ... a problem
> of power—confrontation of the forces ... demanding change
> and the forces ... dedicated to ... preserving ... the status quo.

[P]ower . . . is nothing but . . . the strength required to bring about social and economic change.[4]

It was also, he added, quoting labor leader Walter Reuther, the ability to make the richest corporation in the world say yes when it wants to say no.[5]

My version of his vision was much simpler: I wanted enough power to extend a fair shot in life to Mr. What *Is* You, and to ensure that we didn't leave folks so bereft that they died without hope in hidden hollers and coal mines or drowned on rooftops. Until Mr. What *Is* You had a free and clear path to realize his gifts, it would be my job to open one. Law school had a lot of tools to contribute to my toolbox. The civil rights revolution had ended King's life, but the opportunity revolution he sparked was a long way from finished.

I had been twelve when King's death ended the first phase of the civil rights movement, which had been the fight to end legal inequality and the unimaginable brutality of the old Jim Crow South. We'd reduced the brutality, but in the forty years since his assassination, we had aborted the second phase of that movement, which he called "realizing equality." He'd called on our courage to "radically restructure" our economic and political systems—by which he meant create a humane capitalism that fairly distributed opportunity and the public wealth that, in vast disproportion, we automatically funneled to the powerful. King warned that if we failed to rebuild our three-hundred-year-old house of inequality from its struts to its retaining walls, we would reap "social catastrophe."

He warned us.

Standing at the starting line of law school, I had no way of knowing how hard it would be to heed that warning. How hard it would be to get the beneficiaries of King's revolution to reach down for those left at the bottom of the well. How blind we'd be to the swelling tide of the new Jim Crow as a thirty-year juggernaut of jail-and-fail mass criminalization and hundredfold sentencing differentials mindlessly disenfranchised two thirds of poor black men for largely nonviolent offenses and pretextual stops. Or how thirty years of unhinged enrichment and casino capitalism at the top would devastate the middle class and make the need for King's "radical restructuring" a "fierce imperative" for everyone living outside of Bel Air. I had no idea that these and many more lessons would begin, for me, on Death Row. But before any of these lessons could happen, first I had to get through the notorious paper chase of One L.

During my first year of law school, luck landed me in a single room in the new Mercer Street dorm, four blocks from the law school. I lugged back heavy casebooks from the bookstore, dusted off my typewriter, and got to work. It took me two classes to figure out that the book list left out the books we really needed—the treatises and hornbooks that explained the cases and told you how to answer the Socratic questioning in class. It took me five classes to figure out that law school required a complete inversion of the learning pattern I had used in the first sixteen years of my education. In grades K through college, you go from the macro to the micro, as in learning broad background before specializing on a subtopic, usually in a paper. In law school, you start with the micro—a single case—and deduce up to the macro—the general principles, frameworks, and systems of law.

My scholarship required me to work twenty hours a week in a public service job, so that first year my routine included riding the E train down to Tower 2 of the World Trade Center to do legal research for the New York State Attorney General's Office. By the fifth week, I actually liked law school. My bent for arguing had finally found a welcome mat. It was competitive but not hostile. I wrote well and answered confidently in class. And I liked the people. With notable sharklike exceptions, most of my classmates were the same high-caliber players with whom I'd attended college—geeky, driven, smart, and multitalented, with many unable to hide their wide streaks of decency. The professors, also with a few exceptions, were dedicated and skilled. I had found many colleagues; a few buddies; one close friend, Lynn Dummett; and even my obsessive focus couldn't block out the magic of living in the world's greatest city.

After a good first year, I returned home the summer of 1982 to save money and worked at the Connecticut Women's Education and Legal Fund researching sex discrimination law. Following my parents' retirement from the Air Force in 1977, they had settled in Hartford, where Dad put his MBA to use at United Technologies and Mom resumed her career as a masterful high school biology and chemistry teacher at Bloomfield High School. Phil was challenging the accuracy of his professors' lectures at Howard Medical School, and Norman was forging his own path through Harvard and taking up Tae Kwon Do with Mr. Chung. Everyone was crazy-busy, but it was good to be home again.

By my second year, the paper chase really suited me. I felt in control because I had a clear vision of what a legal education should do *for* me, not to me. I had taught myself to flip even the driest courses into tools for my systems-change arsenal. Civil Procedure and Property Law were nail strips and cages to slow attacks and box in opponents. Contracts struck me as brackets that imposed order, protected expectations, and tied down remedies much tighter than civil rights law did. State and Local Government's guide to delegated power was like the building blueprints that told you where all the pipes, joints, and wires lay. Bankruptcy's framework for fresh starts was like a pressure release valve, and Corporate Law was a Dalkon Shield that deflected responsibility for harm committed while making money as a group. Since we locked in property rights much more stringently than human rights, and protected business deals better than children, I would have to transfer tools from the stronger areas to my areas.

By the end of second year, I had earned high enough grades to interview for summer jobs with the biggest and best white-shoe law firms. However, I wasn't gunning for Wall Street. I was headed to Hood Alley. I had to make rules designed to protect the elite work for those without voice or clout. Like a Jujitsu artist, I had to convert what *is* into what *should be*. To learn that, I needed an internship with Jujitsu lawyers. Thurgood Marshall's law firm, the NAACP Legal Defense and Education Fund, had pioneered and perfected that model.

Before he became the first black Justice of the United States Supreme Court, Marshall carved out his place in history as the director of the NAACP Legal Defense and Educational Fund, Inc., the nation's premier civil rights law firm. Known as the "Inc. Fund" or just "LDF," the group of lawyers had championed almost every landmark lawsuit that had advanced the cause of equal rights and social justice in the mid- and late twentieth century. During his tenure at LDF, Marshall won twenty-nine of the thirty-four cases he brought before the Supreme Court. In 1954 he argued the historic *Brown v. Board of Education,* the unanimous Supreme Court case that ended legal racial segregation in public education and kicked the civil rights revolution into high gear. In that war, the dual crusades of King in the streets and Marshall in the courts had dealt the death blows to the old Jim Crow system that my great-grandparents had hated. Marshall left LDF when President John F. Kennedy appointed him to a federal judgeship, and in 1967 he ascended to his seat on the Supreme Court. LDF had carried on the fight. And I wanted in.

Thrilled to have won an internship there for my second summer of law school, I arrived early for the orientation. LDF's flagship headquarters overlooked Columbus Circle in Manhattan, five stops north of NYU on the D train. Headed by Jack Greenberg, LDF was in the hands of the legal legends who had won *Brown* and boasted an all-star lineup of the country's top civil rights lawyers. Steve Ralston, Gail Collins, Judith Reed, and Janet Levine headed up major employment rights cases. Lani Guinier, a Supreme Court superstar, led voting rights. Ted Shaw, Clyde Murphy, and the legendary James Nabrit III covered multiple areas and spearheaded the housing discrimination docket. And LDF's vaunted Capital Punishment Project was directed by a soft-spoken ordained pastor and lawyer from North Carolina named John Charles Boger or, as we would come to know him, Jack Boger.

After the orientation in LDF's small law library, the dozen or so interns scrambled to stake out a carrel in the library or a vacant desk in the hallways. A blond woman from Yale Law who was rumored to have sailed through her first year with uncommon brilliance took the workstation next to mine. She introduced herself as Julia Boaz. She radiated intelligence but was also funny, irreverent, and ballerina-beautiful. We hit it off and soon became viewed as the precocious JAP/BAP (Jewish American Princess, Black American Princess) duo. We later formed a troika with another summer law student, Iyeaa Orokuma, who was an *actual* princess from Nigeria. Thankfully, when Iyeaa's brains, Alek Wek–like beauty, and defiance had clashed hazardously with her tribe's expectations of royalty, Iyeaa's parents had packed her off to the United States.

Fresh from finishing a paper on compound sex-and-race job discrim-ination, I had set my sights on LDF's cutting-edge employment bias cases. Julia had her heart set on working voting rights cases with Lani Guinier. That first week, the U.S. Supreme Court's last decisions for its 1982 term landed like live grenades in LDF's lobby and blew up both of our plans. The capital punishment team had just lost four key death penalty cases in the nation's court of last resort. LDF's carefully engi-neered national moratorium on state executions had finally collapsed.

LDF's long-standing mission to end capital punishment stemmed from the historic use of the death penalty as a special instrument of state suppression and terror against slaves, ex-slaves, and innocent blacks. In the late 1800s, the Jim Crow South featured a lynching every four days. For the longest time, capital punishment had been little more than state-sanctioned lynching. Death row had always had a decided political tilt, and its modern tilt was still unmistakable: over-whelmingly, and unwarrantedly, poor, male, uneducated, and black.

In 1972 LDF won an actual, if temporary, moratorium from the Supreme Court in a cluster of lawsuits known collectively as *Fur-man v. Georgia*. Crafted under the ingenious leadership of Anthony Amsterdam, the moratorium had taken years of chess moves to achieve. After LDF's Elaine Jones argued and won *Furman,* that vic-tory effectively emptied death rows in forty states and commuted the sentences of 629 condemned inmates. While states conformed their death schemes to the new standards, there had been a few executions, but most of the states had been holding back until they got a clear "go" signal from the Supreme Court.

Now they had four. Death Row, USA, was back in business.

For two days, LDF's death penalty jocks wandered the halls dazed, bemoaning the mangled, underlined opinions in their hands. Intrigued, Julia and I retreated to the library with copies to examine what the fuss was about. The Court's rejection had been sweeping, dismissing core justice issues with cavalier ease. Send a defendant to death based on quacklike speculation about "future dangerousness" that the American Psychiatric Association condemned as unreliable? No harm done, the execution can proceed (*Barefoot v. Estelle*). Kill an inmate based on an admittedly unconstitutional aggravating circumstance? No problem (*Barclay v. Florida*). Scare the jury into irrationally choosing death with the remote possibility that a governor would free a murderer? Irrelevant to jury deliberations (*California v. Ramos*). Remove all jurors who express qualms about death sentences, but keep all pro-death jurors? There couldn't possibly be a skewing or rigging impact from this practice (*Banks v. Texas*). So it went in several more procedural denials of stays of execution.

After an hour of reading legal reasoning that reminded me of the rationalizations in the *Notes of the Spanish Inquisition,* I looked up at Julia, aghast at what this string of defeats meant. Julia was already there. If they went unanswered, there could be a deluge of death. The states would now set execution dates for scores of LDF clients and others on death rows across the country. Even with help from local attorneys and automatic stays, there would be too few lawyers to file all of the appeals and petitions for stays of execution in state courts, and habeas corpus review in federal courts.

The summer belonged to death. We found Jack Boger, the head of the capital punishment team, and volunteered to step into the breach. He gratefully accepted our offer. Back in the library, we decided that none of our death row clients was going to die that summer. Not on our watch. Without an iota of hesitation, we posted ourselves as the last defenders of death row cells across the country. Iyeaa quickly threw in with us.

Our capital punishment bosses gave us a brief overview, a little direction, and some examples of the federal habeas corpus petitions through which lawyers used federal law to attack state convictions and challenge the state's right to hold a prisoner. Jack then handed us a list of inmates with death dates and, as he and the other lawyers left to do hearings for several weeks, wished us luck.

We'd need more than luck. LDF didn't even have a master list of death row clients. We called every death row prison and capital lawyer in the country and created one. Julia, Iyeaa, and I then determined that we could file competent petitions to get our clients past the most imminent execution dates. It didn't occur to us to think otherwise, just as it didn't occur to us not to refer to inmates as our clients. Law students don't have clients. It's illegal. But to us, that was irrelevant. We had vowed to do whatever it took to keep everyone alive. We were too inexperienced to know that it could not be done.

Regularly working from seven in the morning until three the next morning, we churned out petitions for inmates on countdowns to death in eight states. My subway ride home on the D train up to the Bronx, and Julia's on the Number 1 to Harlem, were little more than groggy turnaround trips. In the worst stretch, we didn't see our beds for four days.

For each case, we pored over years of trial and appellate records, looking for grounds to appeal. Whether our client was guilty or not, I first focused on the murder victim so the other moral center of the work did not get displaced by the mission of stopping state murder. This was no contradiction. Protecting the innocent from wrongful conviction required the most zealous defense of the most heinous defendants. I was defending murderers in order to defend the integrity of a criminal justice system whose constitutional protections I deeply believed in at the time.

For me there was no question that murderers should be severely punished or that dangerous people needed to be locked up. Were someone to kill my loved ones, the police had better find him before my Tae Kwon Do–trained hands did. Nonetheless, in our system, the accused has to be vigorously defended, fairly prosecuted, impartially judged, and justly punished, without bias, politics, or corruption. If we chose to kill in order to show that killing was wrong, the machinery of death had to be infallible.

But our death mill was further from infallible than Satan was from salvation.

Jack's death circuit stories, like scenes out of *Brubaker* or an eighteenth-century chain gang, appalled us with how grotesquely fallible and biased it was. We gawked as he told us about the self-described "hangin' judge" in Hondo, Texas, who for two years after *Furman* had handed out illegal death sentences without ever reading the Supreme Court's *Furman* opinions. He explained to Jack that "if it don't make it onto the bookmobile, we probably didn't get a copy of it." Or the Mississippi opinion with no case law that cited a prayer for the victim and brimmed with Old Testament passages about "reaping what ye shall sow" and stoning errant sinners. Evidently, in Mississippi, separation of church and state was just a suggestion. And the judge who, upon being forced to set one of our clients free, proudly mentioned, off the record, his "honorary Klansman" plaque and declared, "Well, if Ah haf to let a nigga' off death row, at least he killed a Jew." Jack didn't even blink. He was beyond being shocked by the judicial brain stems sitting on Southern courts.

Beyond Jack's war stories, everything I learned about the death penalty that summer showed that its application was biased, obscenely uneven, and unjust. Often, death wasn't given to the most culpable killers, as in a case where the getaway driver was executed after the actual killer, or "triggerman," walked out of prison a free man. Many defendants had watched their unqualified or sleeping lawyers deliver them to the row. Even competent court-appointed lawyers had no funds to hire investigators, and others couldn't stay sober long enough to file proper motions. Police lying, frame-ups, and shoddy investigations were a sordid norm. We saw far too many prosecutors who were willing to kill someone innocent rather than admit they had convicted the wrong person. These were the tip of a very dirty iceberg.

Occasionally, we had to leave the stifling safety of LDF's library and travel to death rows to interview our condemned clients. The prisons formed a medieval lineup: Parchman, Angola, Huntsville. Descending behind their suffocating walls was like sinking into a void. Dueling with their sexist guards and wardens was always eye-opening. But nothing was as invigorating or grounding as meeting the human beings whose lives rested in our hands. The clients who were innocent, mentally retarded, or not the triggermen were, emotionally, the hardest to interview. Clients who lived up to their reputations as narcissists and sociopaths proved easier to handle but far more annoying. Julia and I had been only half kidding when we told Iyeaa to abandon one moron client who, six days out from his date in the gas chamber, declined to work on a declaration but wanted Iyeaa to bring him the latest edition of *Black Jugs*.

Death row became my crucible, a realm that forged me into a really good lawyer.

In doing the petitions to halt our clients' dates with death, Julia, Iyeaa, and I scoured trial transcripts for errors by the judge, the prosecutor, the defense lawyers, the jury, the court reporter—anybody. We were good because in every petition, we exercised more penetrating legal analysis, creative argument, and vigorous use of the facts, and we would not consider using the boilerplate a lot of lawyers cut and pasted. We enhanced the standard hooks—the Eighth Amendment requirements to avoid capricious, unusual, or cruel actions; the great Fourteenth Amendment's requirements for fair rebuttal, clean evidence, and unbiased procedures; the Fifth Amendment's bedrock of protection against self-incrimination; the Sixth Amendment's elusive promise of effective counsel.

What impressed our bosses was what we did when the standard hooks *didn't* work. If gaps in the record left out evidence, we retrieved it. If the existing facts didn't offer a platform for effective appeal, we found new facts and grounds for getting them considered. And if traditional grounds for appeal looked doomed, we invented new grounds.

For one particularly heinous murder committed by a uniquely unsympathetic client, I had no choice but to find a novel argument.

This particular client was unusual for LDF. For starters, he was an avowed white supremacist. In the 1980 murder that earned him a seat on North Carolina's death row, he had run over his victim with a truck while she was alive.

When LDF attorney Steve Winter handed me his file, I thought, *Terrific. The National Association for the Advancement of Colored People is fighting to save the life of a swastika-festooned racist.* But given my sanctimonious stance that it was immoral to represent only African-Americans on death row, I could hardly refuse. I accepted with the caveat that Julia and I asserted with other terminally violent clients: Our work extended to reversing only his death sentence, not his conviction. Mr. Serial Killer was right where he needed to be, permanently behind bars.

Not to worry. On this record, there was zero chance of winning life without parole, never mind overturning the conviction. I didn't need to read the record to know that traditional arguments, like our client, were dead on arrival. With gruesome facts and little doubt about his guilt, we'd be lucky if the ultraconservative judges of the North Carolina Supreme Court even bothered to have their law clerks read our petition. Only a riveting argument would get their attention and be heard. It was our job to find it.

To my surprise, it didn't take much digging: North Carolina's own actions had helped create this monster. Our client was the child of a family who so routinely sent its kids to school burned, cut, and bruised that their chronic abuse was county-wide lore. The father thrashed his kids with whatever farm tools or appliances he could lift, and at night locked them in a rat-filled bin where they screamed themselves into delirium. Their mother was so pathologically dysfunctional that feces and pet carcasses regularly covered the floor of the house. The county ignored the pleas of teachers and neighbors for years, in which time the boys blossomed into full-fledged sadists. When the county finally did remove the kids from their house of horrors, they placed them in the state's foster-care system, which *60 Minutes* later reported hired guards who formed a raging pedophile ring.

Steve Winter and I concluded that this extraordinary record supported an unusual claim of equitable estoppel: North Carolina's reckless actions nullified its right to kill him. The argument got the court's attention, landed an unexpected hearing, and sparked a spirited debate on the bench. A majority of the justices agreed that the state indeed had contributed to our client's dangerous condition. In the end, though, it was the best, last all-out effort possible on behalf of a client like him, it would not be enough. It bought him three more years, at the end of which he went to his death in North Carolina's electric chair.

Beyond finding viable claims for impossible cases like his, there were other reasons our student team was viewed as exceptional. As someone with MENSA intellect and poetic eloquence, Julia wrote sublimely. Her briefs and petitions read like stories, not legal mumbo jumbo, and they seduced the reader into our client's experience.

I brought different talents to the team. I knew how to glue my butt to a chair until the material got into my head and into a good document. I marshaled persuasive arguments and was good at framing them for different audiences. And I was fearless, stopping at nothing to get the petitions filed, including, in those days before FedEx, chartering a plane—without permission—to fly state court papers up from Mississippi. Most important, I understood the larger mission. This was war. After we cranked out the petitions to halt individual executions, our job would be to help Jack roll out the next battle plan for stopping the whole country's death industrial complex.

Despite our grueling routine of grim tasks, we were hardly doomsday divas. We regularly lightened our foxhole intensity with humor, which occasionally turned dark. One mid-July morning at five A.M., Julia and I were racing to get a petition copied when LDF's gargantuan and temperamental Xerox machine jammed. We frantically flung the thing open to fix it but stopped dead in our tracks at the thick neon yellow band screaming: WARNING, 25,000 VOLTS WILL ELECTROCUTE—CALL TECHNICIAN. LDF staffers Oscar and Earl arrived at five-thirty A.M. to find us writhing on the floor in meltdown laughter over the hilarity of two death penalty lawyers getting electrocuted by a copy machine. They stepped over us, shaking their heads at our rapidly deteriorating state, and fixed the paper jam.

Despite our own camaraderie, our links with the rest of LDF's legal staff remained complicated. I often heard people talking about us with irritated admiration. The irritation was justified. We barreled through the halls in jeans and work boots, unapologetically commandeering whatever we needed. We were impatient with lawyers and other law students who worked normal hours. And they in turn resented our high-handedness, which only grew worse as our victories mounted. A few of the older male lawyers found us unsettling because we ignored hierarchy, didn't ask permission, and rototilled gender norms. On my first day at work, I got into a lunchtime shouting match with lawyer Ted Shaw over the portrayal of black men in the movie *The Color Purple.* Shaw stormed out of the restaurant, proclaiming that I was barred from coming near his cases—or him. Ted and I eventually became friends, but in those early days, our crop of female law students was a jolt to LDF's patrician culture.

Looking back, I can see that at times we were out of bounds. Most of the men we worked with did not mean any harm; they just didn't know how to deal with women who were beyond responding to the old gender cues. With time, I mellowed and learned to deflect benign gender gaffes with the same tolerant humor my mother had taught me for racial mistakes.

Our bosses in capital punishment, however, did not care about our lagging social skills. Our legal skills had paid off in droves: Every scheduled execution had been stopped. No one had died on our watch. We should have declared victory over this amazing feat and called it a summer, but by the end of July, our bosses needed our help on an even more daunting project. The case was called *McCleskey v. Kemp,* and in it, LDF would unveil a groundbreaking, state-of-the-art statistical study that proved Georgia's death-sentencing scheme was riddled with impermissible racial effects. It was LDF's last hope to throw a permanent wrench in the resurging U.S. death machine.

Chapter 5

TINKERING WITH DEATH

N o one was surprised when eleven white jurors and one black juror sentenced the namesake of the *McCleskey* case to death. Warren McCleskey, a black man, had been convicted in 1978 of felony murder in the death of a white police officer during a robbery in Georgia. His sentence was practically preordained, which made his case an unlikely vehicle for carrying an ambitious statistical study that unmasked the invisible hand of race in Georgia's capital sentencing. Nonetheless, several years earlier, Jack had chosen *McCleskey* for that mission. Led by three law professors, David Baldus, Charles Pulaski, and George Woodworth, the study showed that if the murder victim was white, the killer had a much higher probability of getting death than if the victim was black. Black murderers of whites could expect to get dealt the death card 4.3 times more often. The findings, released in 1980, finally offered proof that race corrupted capital sentencing, and it had sparked debate in the press and elsewhere.

Early in the appeals, Jack had decided to attack McCleskey's death sentence using the Baldus study. The time had arrived to test that theory before a federal judge in Atlanta in a trial that would turn into the latest showdown over the constitutionality of the death penalty. Jack had a copilot, a hotshot death penalty expert from Washington state named Tim Ford, but he also needed our help. Jack had taught us how to write successful petitions that stopped executions and even reversed some death sentences. But he didn't know what to teach us to get through the *McCleskey* hearing. No one had ever done—never mind presented to a federal judge—a study this immense in size, complexity, and audacity. If the court agreed to hear it, the *McCleskey* study would be a Titan missile aimed at Georgia's death machine.

After July, our Summer of McCleskey shifted into warp speed. Julia commandeered an absent attorney's office and set up our war room. The Baldus study filled twelve superthick three-ring binders. Professor Baldus and his partners, George Woodworth and Charles Pulaski, had analyzed the complete records from more than 2,500 murder cases in Georgia, breaking each case down into thousands of variables that covered every aspect of the killing and the trial proceeding. No detail of the crime was too small to escape coding— from the amount of blood on a weapon to the race of the prosecutors. These variables were loaded into what at that time passed for a powerful computer sorting them to isolate the impact of race—a technique called multivariate regression analysis.

I didn't know a variable from a donut. That did not stop Jack from handing me the twelve binders and telling me to figure out how to get them into evidence. Law was supposed to be a sanctuary from statistics or any other quantitative reasoning. All I knew was that our opponents, the prosecutors from the Georgia Attorney General's Office, would be enraged by our suggestion that the Peachtree State's death machine wasn't racially pristine, and would rabidly attack every line of code, every variable, every data-entry procedure, and every "choice" the computer made in this multivariate regression analysis. In order to master the study better than they would, I would have to sleep, bathe, and eat multivariate regression for weeks. My worst vision of hell was coming true.

Along with regression analysis, I got to traipse through the evidentiary minefield of hearsay evidence. Hearsay is an out-of-court statement offered in court for the truth, and it is not admissible unless it slips in under one of the hearsay exceptions. If I overhear a woman in the supermarket remark that she saw O. J. Simpson running down Bundy Drive with a bloody knife in his hand, unfortunately, I cannot take the stand and offer that hearsay statement for the truth—not unless it fits under an exception, like a statement against interest, an excited utterance, or a deathbed confession. In the McCleskey study, when the computer picked different variables, it arguably was making statements that we would be offering in court as evidence of what the study said was the truth about Georgia's sentencing process. Neither the computer nor the code that directed its actions could be cross-examined about the computer's choices. Consequently, we had to be ready for the prosecutors' howling objections that the study presented inadmissible *double* hearsay. Despite the torture of doing it, I found solid grounds for insisting that the study was not hearsay. If it were deemed such, exceptions applied. Trust me, you don't want to know any more than this. I also prepared a set of index cards printed with the hearsay exceptions to hand to Jack and Tim, who had attended law school before these federal rules of evidence existed.

Jack also was counting on us to prepare a precise copy of the Baldus study for the judge, the Honorable J. Owen Forrester. Jack needed us to arrange the complicated study into an easily understood, orderly presentation that the judge could follow page by carefully checked page during the hearing. If just one page of what was in his meticulously constructed binder differed from the evidence, Judge Forrester's ire was not all that we risked: The integrity of the entire study could be open to attack.

In Atlanta, Jack and Tim would need us as pack mules, Sherpas, proxies, and writers. There were a million things to do before jetting down to Atlanta, but the day Jack gave us our chores, Julia and I were on the verge of collapse, so we took that afternoon off to ponder the new adventure. It would be our only break in the summer of death, and our big outing consisted of walking around Columbus Circle and into Central Park for the extravagance of an ice cream cone. Outside, the dirty heat and rushing crowds felt strangely alive and good. At the sight of ourselves in a picture window, we startled. The faces looking back at us were unrecognizable. What little color I had arrived with had faded away entirely under LDF's fluorescent lights, leaving me with the enticing pallor of a poached chicken. Julia's porcelain skin had no hue whatsoever. We were beyond makeup and well into spackling-paste terrain. Our hair looked like unkempt mops, and we'd both dropped way too much weight. Appalled, Julia announced a new regimen of healthy food, vitamins, and exercise, which I predicted had zero chance of lasting beyond our walk. I savored the ice cream and the momentary freedom of losing myself in the summer bustle of Manhattan. That break was our last, but it would not be the last time that I let work hijack my life to the point where even eating fell to the wayside.

At the airport, our tattered suitcases looked pitiful, but we couldn't spare the attention for our luggage; we had to keep our eyes glued on the eight litigation bags into which we had crammed the binders and critical documents. The flight attendant balked as we squeezed them into six overhead bins, and I had to verbally back her down to stop her from forcing us to check them, where they'd surely end up lost on a baggage-claim carousel in Madagascar.

Tim Ford was waiting for our flight, anxious to see that the binders had made it down to Atlanta intact. When we walked out into the Atlanta heat, it felt like someone had smacked us into a wet, hot wall. We loaded the trunk and climbed into a car that was hotter than a Swiss steam room. As he drove, Tim cheerily tormented us with the news that there was no elevator in the ACLU building where we were squatting, and no air-conditioning after hours.

After a look at our borrowed second-floor offices, we headed out for a quick meal in the chilliest air-conditioned restaurant we could find. Hard to believe, but it was the first time all four members of Team McCleskey had sat down together. One of the first things I had learned about Jack Boger, who was a minister as well as a lawyer, was that his folksy manner and decency were not a show. His gentle demeanor hid a driven, cerebral crusader whose determination was powered by a deep belief in redemption and a spiritual revulsion against revenge murder. Where Jack was humble, Tim Ford exuded a tough, steely-eyed confidence, his slight swagger hinting at the bravado it had taken to halt the majority of executions west of the Mississippi. Tall, with craggy good looks, he spoke in a lean staccato uncluttered by emotion, but beneath his cowboy hide, Tim harbored a fierce and roiling hatred of the death mills. Jack united our team, and it worked because our strengths were complementary. There were none of the high-drama antics, personal rivalries, or hidden agendas that derailed so many high-stakes cases. We were driven by mission, bonded through affection, bound by total trust, and dedicated to getting every detail right because life, and possibly history, depended on it. This was LDF at its best.

That night we headed "home" to a condo in a worn subdivision several miles north and west of the city. Jack's bosses at LDF had fretted about female law clerks sharing living quarters with male lawyers—even wondering if they should ask our fathers' permission. Jack assured them we could handle it, but he had to promise LDF management to sequester Julia and me in a separate suite with a separate bathroom.

The next day was the last before the whirlwind in court began. We sped to the ACLU for final prep with the remaining experts. The next morning Julia and I bolted out of bed before dawn, scrambled into mismatched skirts and jackets, and loaded the car. Tacky outfits on and litigation bags packed, we piled into the rental car and made our way to the Richard B. Russell Federal Building and Courthouse for the Northern District of Georgia.

The features of the courthouse were lost on us as we searched for the right floor, found the right courtroom, struggled past guards with the heavy cases full of sacred binders, searched for our experts, and set up shop on our side, the left side, of the courtroom. Five feet away at the state's table sat the team of prosecutors from the Georgia Attorney General's Office, bristling with indignation at having to defend themselves and the integrity of the great state of Georgia's criminal justice system.

All rose as the Honorable J. Owen Forrester entered the court.

Built like a football player, he was an engineer by training, a gradu-ate of Georgia Tech who prided himself on having the statistical and mathematical background to understand the complexities of this study, if not the case. Credentials notwithstanding, he would be a hard sell.

In a smooth Georgia drawl, Judge Forrester greeted the parties. His hands spanning the black binders in front of him, he acknowl-edged the odd subject and nature of the hearing. He noted that sociological studies about race belonged in universities, not federal courts. But his court had an obligation to confront head-on any credible challenge to the fundamental integrity of the criminal judi-cial system. He intended to do so with a hard eye but an even hand.

As he spoke, my breathing all but shut down, and I became all ears. The edge of his remarks revealed a skeptic, though one who had convinced himself he had an open mind. From what I heard, Judge Forrester was willing to let us present the study, but that was all too likely to be the only victory we and Warren McCleskey would see. Forrester had sternly signaled that at best, he was letting us take a swing at a very long shot. In the business of death, long shots are the only ones you have. It was good enough.

Jack rose to give his opening remarks. As he gently traced the story of the case, Forrester's diffidence faded, and he leaned forward to listen. Jack and Forrester came from the same place. They under-stood the South and loved her, warts and all. I knew from the judge's interest and the state attorney's tense discomfort that Jack was on the right track. The latter's shrill opening statement had all of the court-side manner of a cyborg. As the judge turned to his binder, Julia and I closed our eyes and prayed to the gods of accuracy that every page would hold up.

The historic *McCleskey* hearing was under way. From the lofty and dangerous to the seedy, it sizzled with all of the human, political, and legal drama of a Grisham novel: a son-of-the-South judge who wrestled with Dixie's racial dilemmas, the masterful sparring of our elite credentialed Ph.D.s defending the study from the state's third-string hacks, the gladiators dueling for the judge's favor, and the entire battle playing out against a torrid backdrop of lust for Georgia's first execution in twenty-two years. There was even a bomb scare serious enough to make us evacuate the ACLU. Today the *McCleskey* hearing would have been a high-stakes reality show with expert fights, death row showdowns, and the domestic comedy of feminist law students living with their male bosses. The story of Team McCleskey's war against death is its own book. Someday Julia and I may write it, but there aren't enough pages here.

Our work in Atlanta extended beyond Forrester's courtroom. The second front of the war was to keep our clients with new death dates alive. After our long days doing the McCleskey hearing, we trudged back to the ACLU, where Tim and I prepared the next day's testimony—and Julia and Jack hammered out petitions for stays of upcoming execution dates. We had two clients with fast-approaching death dates. John Eldon Smith, on death row for murder for hire, was reaching his end game in three weeks. And Billy Neal Moore had a date early that fall for shooting Edgar Stapleton in a home robbery. With Jack and Tim tied up in court, Julia and I headed down to Georgia's death house to brief Eldon on his last appeals for a stay of execution and to check in with Moore.

We borrowed the rental car, and in our usual division of labor, Julia navigated while I drove too fast to the Georgia Diagnostic and Classification Center, right off the I-75 freeway south of Atlanta. Scoffing at the prison's Orwellian name, we wheeled onto the compound grounds and sped up to the guard kiosk.

With the molten asphalt sucking at our heels, we marched our pantsuited selves toward the prison's bunker entrance. We proceeded down a long, cool underground tunnel that was equipped with cameras, gun turrets, and armored panels that could drop like guillotines to abort escapes. It made me think of the tunnel in the TV show *Get Smart*. We passed through the gauntlet projecting confidence but feeling dread—not of the searches or the menacing guards we were about to face. Not of the hard looks or the smells of human confinement. We dreaded that we could not bring to Eldon the one thing he needed, which was hope. After three full rounds of appeals, there weren't a lot of good arguments left for his case.

As we crossed a corridor leading to the attorney meeting rooms, my stomach clenched at the sight of prison staff excitedly mowing patches of lawn, edging flower beds, and sweeping the walks. Julia and I knew this sinister rite of housekeeping meant one thing: The electric chair, aka "Ol' Sparkie," was at long last about to get some new business. If we failed, Smith's would be Georgia's first execution in over twenty years, and they were sprucing up for the special occasion.

Neither Eldon Smith nor Billy Moore was the typical LDF client. Eldon was a white middle-aged insurance agent who was convicted, along with his wife, of murdering her ex-husband and his bride for an insurance payout. He wasn't retarded or mentally ill. His crime had been premeditated, not stupid or inadvertent. But like almost everyone on death row, he had been rendered harmless, and then the terrorization of scheduled death had hollowed him. Moore was unique. In his ten years on the row, he had somehow grown into a spiritually compelling figure who, upon meeting us, radiated serenity, not fear. He was the only death row inmate I ever saw counsel guards who sought his company.

The noncondemned can never know, but to survive entombment on the row, you must first die inside. Most cling to some hope in their legal appeals, many find God for the first time, and a few create relationships with outsiders, guards, or lawyers. The lucky have family who stick by them; the unlucky have unhinged groupies or no one. In the last attorney visits during the steeplechase run up to an execution, the weaker inmates can come unglued. But from Eldon there would be no histrionics.

We sat at a table in the counsel meeting room as the guard removed Eldon's handcuffs. He gazed at us from behind his glasses, sizing up the new young members of his team. He asked how we got in without Jack. After small talk about the *McCleskey* hearing, Julia took him through the latest appeal. Eldon quietly asked what the chances looked like. He knew the answer to his question. The recent Supreme Court rulings had lengthened already long odds.

The prison was abuzz with his pending execution. He could hear snippets of excited chatter from the guards and see the averted eyes of his row-mates whenever he left his cell. Self-preservation kept him from talking about his fears. He simply adjusted his glasses, stood, shook our hands, and said thanks. Before surrendering to the waiting guard, he turned and asked if we would be back. We said yes. He nodded, and the guard took him from the room.

Emerging from the cold tunnel into the blast furnace, we strode to the car and, once on the freeway, drove back in drained silence. Eldon had three weeks left. The lightning run of last petitions to stop his execution had begun.

Jack and Julia left the *McCleskey* hearing to present Eldon's latest petition in an emergency evening hearing. They could have saved their angst. The judge summarily denied the appeal. Jack and Julia returned to the condo, their faces ashen. Radio commentators crowed about the denial in breathless "death countdown" coverage. The next morning in Judge Forrester's court, we beat back more state attacks on the study and then raced back to the ACLU, where Jack and Julia plunged into the next appeal.

Four hours and three pizzas later, they had a draft. It would have to do. Jack handed it to me and said I had to get it filed the next day at the courthouse in Macon, seventy miles south of Atlanta. I told him to consider it done.

How much trouble could one filing be? I pulled the map out to figure out how far I'd be driving the next day. While the three of them slogged through day seven of *McCleskey,* I would be sailing down I-75, enjoying a leisurely drive to picturesque Macon. I looked forward to my easy day.

At five-thirty the next morning, I fixed some instant coffee and turned the radio on low. As I began slicing a peach for breakfast, a baritone on the AM news station warned listeners to strap on an icepack for the heat and then announced, "Attorneys for John Eldon Smith will be filing an appeal from the denial of a stay of execution in the county courthouse in Macon today. The appeal is expected to be one of his last before his execution, set for . . ." I almost sliced my finger off. They'd seen the notice of appeal already? I ditched the peach, poured more coffee, and set out for the car. The day was going to be hot in more ways than one. After a quick stop to pick up a document at the ACLU, I headed down to Macon.

My leisurely drive turned into a spectacle. Reporters who had staked out the ACLU followed my car. Twenty miles down I-75, I looked up to find a caravan of six cars and police cruisers trailing behind me, and above, an air armada of helicopters circling. On the radio I couldn't escape the hyperventilating, mile-by-mile radio coverage. I gripped the steering wheel tighter and slowed down. Missing the filing deadline because I'd been hauled to jail by the Georgia highway patrol for speeding was not an option.

As I passed the exit for the prison, I silently cursed all of our clients. Iyeaa had phoned the day before to wish us luck on her way to some Caribbean resort for a hard-earned vacation. But for us, the death marathon held no end in sight. I took a deep breath to focus; this was not about us. Half an hour later, the exit to Macon came into view. I veered onto the ramp and glanced in the mirror. The procession had grown. Macon's town square was a Southern-colonial affair of redbrick buildings with spires, columns, and graceful porticos. I headed toward the building with the U.S. flag that looked more like a courthouse than a post office, and pulled into one of the angled parking spaces. My escorts pulled in on either side of me.

Showtime. I switched out my Coke-bottle wire rims for wicked-cool prescription sunglasses, set my face on stern, and marched to the door. Inside the cool air of the foyer, more reporters joined the throng, which piled into the elevator with me. The questions began. Would I give them my name? Would I confirm that I was Mr. Smith's lawyer? How long did I think the court would take to rule on the appeal? I declined comment and focused on the elevator. I had seen snails climb trees faster. The door finally opened onto the second floor. The office of the clerk was right there.

I set the litigation bag on a chair, pulled out our documents, and moved to the low counter separating the public from the clerks. Of all the absurdities that morning, the worst offender was getting out of her chair from behind one of the desks and heading toward me. She was about five-four, but the teased blond beehive on top of her head added almost another foot. "How kin Ah hep ya, honey?" she drawled through a wall of bright red lipstick. I was momentarily speechless, mesmerized by the helmet on top of her head, wondering if it housed wildlife. She was looking at me, too, and said with a sneer, "Oh, you must be the one that come down to file that appeal."

I snapped out of it and offered my papers to Madam Beehive. "I need this filed right away," I said. "I also need a stamped copy, a receipt, and notification of the presiding judge that the original is here."

She didn't move. "Well, you ain't gittin' none of what all you say you need without paying the seventy-five-dollar filing fee first."

Seventy-five dollars? Jack hadn't said anything about a fee, and he hadn't given me any money. The most I had was ten dollars in cash. I steadied myself and kept my face on stoic. "One moment, please." I walked back over to the litigation case and pulled out my checkbook.

She cackled. "We don't accept checks not from around here; it'll have to be a check from a law firm or a cashier's check." The alarms in my head went off. What did she mean, "not from around here"?

I turned back to her. "Well, ma'am, that can't be right—"

Before I could finish, she cut me off. "Whatever I say is what's right, honey. You kin forget filing any appeal here unless you comply with the rules I say you do."

"May I speak to your supervisor?" I said through gritted teeth.

By now the other clerks were watching.

"You're talkin' to her. And by the way, you ain't gonna be able to get a cashier's check today nohow. The bank is closed."

The time for civil banter had ended. I slammed my fist down to rattle her, lurched my upper body across the counter into as much of her cheap-perfumed space as I could reach, and snarled just loud enough for her, "I don't have to pay you with any damned cashier's check. The due process and equal protection provisions of the constitutions of the United States and the state of Georgia do not permit someone to die for want of a cashier's check. This appeal is getting filed whether your beehived ass wants it to or not! Now, unless you want me to start shouting for those reporters to come in here, you'd better find a waiver or make up some new rule that gets this appeal filed."

A male clerk who could hear my menacing tone started to rise out of his chair. Ms. Beehive dropped her hands from her hips and backed away from the counter. I kept pressing, switching to a loud "black" voice that I saved for special combat. I summoned everyone to "listen up" and announced that I was there to file the Eldon Smith appeal and needed to speak to someone in authority.

A door to an enclosed office opened behind the counter. A balding man with an enormous paunch and sweat-stained armpits stepped out just as one of the reporters poked his head in to see what the commotion was about. Clearing his throat as he passed Ms. Beehive without a word, he took the documents and handed them over to another clerk, came back to the counter, and said the appeal would be filed and that I could go. I thanked him but said I preferred to wait and confirm that the documents got stamped and officially filed; handing him my two copies, I added a request that they also be stamped. He shook his head at what the world was coming to.

Minutes later, with reporters as witnesses, I thrust a stamped copy of the appeal into the trembling hands of the judge's law clerk one floor up. That way I knew for sure that the appeal had been delivered to the judge's chambers and not ditched down the elevator shaft. Taking my last ride down on the world's slowest elevator, I marveled again at how important the nameless minions of any office always proved to be, and at how utterly fearless I'd become of menacing guards and even beehive-haired clerks from hell.

Mission accomplished, I drove back to Atlanta without further incident. Almost twelve hours after the beginning of my easy day, I trudged up the ACLU's back stairs and sank into the chair at my desk. Jack and Tim burst into the office, looking for me. "Well?" Jack impatiently prompted.

I decided to let them dangle. "Jack, you didn't tell me there was a seventy-five-dollar filing fee. I didn't have any money, the bank had closed early, and the clerk from hell refused my personal check." I shrugged haplessly at the day's misfortune.

Jack's face paled. "Oh my God, I didn't think . . ."

I ended his misery and slapped the date-stamped filing receipt into his hand. He sagged in relief and laughed, and Tim high-fived me. Neither man had a clue how much higher their already substantial tab had gone up.

In the nail-biting court runs over the next few days, the state appeals courts turned Eldon down, and the federal U.S. district court also said no to a stay. Finally, a day and a half before the execution, the Eleventh Circuit granted a temporary stay to review the case one last time. The steeplechase of death had ended—for a few more moments.

By the end of August, we were in the home stretch of the *McCleskey* hearing. It was summer's end, and trial's end, and the Georgia state attorneys had failed to stop Judge Forrester from considering the Baldus study as evidence for his decision in *McCleskey v. Kemp*. We had won the evidentiary showdown and gotten the study before a federal judge. But it was a temporary victory. Julia and I knew better than to hope that science and solid legal reasoning would dislodge the deeply rooted racial tilt of American capital punishment. We geared up for closing arguments. Jack gave a rousing summation that the significance of the study was irrefutable: There was a racial ghost in Georgia's capital sentencing machine that rendered it unconstitutional. It guaranteed that killers of black victims faced a 4.3 times higher chance of getting the death card. And it could not stand. Georgia argued that no mumbo-jumbo statistical study, however big or state-of-the-art, could prove systemic discrimination.

As expected, Judge Forrester denied McCleskey's appeal. Jack appealed again to the Eleventh Circuit, and finally, in 1987, to the U.S. Supreme Court, where the study and case had been destined to go from the beginning. The U.S. Supreme Court delivered a devastating blow in its five-to-four decision dismissing the relevance of evidence that racial factors played a significant role in Georgia's death penalty system. Unless those factors amounted to intentional discrimination, they didn't matter.

Tony Amsterdam called the ruling "the *Dred Scott* decision of our time." Much later, when Supreme Court Justice Lewis Powell was asked if he would have changed his vote in any cases, he replied, "Yes, *McCleskey v. Kemp.*" After serving as a Supreme Court justice for thirty years, during which he backed the constitutionality of capital punishment through 1,100 executions, in 2010 a retired Justice John Paul Stevens reversed his support and declared the death penalty to be unconstitutional. In 2010, he would reaffirm his condemnation of the decision in *McCleskey v. Kemp* as effectively permitting "race-based prosecutorial decisions." "That the murder of black victims is treated as less culpable than the murder of white victims," he wrote, "provides a haunting reminder of once-prevalent Southern lynchings."[6]

For Warren McCleskey, these reconsiderations would come thirty years too late. The 1984 Supreme Court decision rejecting the significance of the Baldus study meant the beginning of his end. The courts excluded Jack's late discovery of police-induced lying that negated the testimony establishing Warren as the triggerman. Warren's final date with death got set for September 28, 1991. Jack, who left LDF in 1990 to teach law school in North Carolina, returned to the row one last time, and stayed with him right to the end.

That August 1983, however, the *McCleskey* hearing had ended, but the next phase of the fight had begun. After returning to New York, Jack asked Julia and me to draft the McCleskey post-hearing brief and continue to prepare Billy Moore's appeal for clemency. We took a brief break. Julia, ever wiser than her sidekick, took the year off from Yale to keep working on capital punishment cases. Technically, I returned to NYU for my last year of law school. But my work with Julia and Jack on Billy Moore's appeal for clemency and other cases took so much time that one professor complained he had never seen me before the final exam. I did not care. After my summer of death, the lessons of law school seemed irrelevant.

I had been baptized in the bowels of injustice. No course or prestigious stint on *Law Review* could match that experience. Death row had ripped off law school's Socratic mask and shown me the sordid underbelly of our warped bar of justice. Law school's pristine parsing of constitutional principles, lofty notions of liberty, and abstractions on the sanctity of due process had almost nothing to do with the mess I'd seen on the death circuit. And not one professor could answer the muffled question screaming in the back of my mind: If we determined the most important decision of any legal system—whom to kill—with this bias-riddled, corrupt, error-laden system, then how much integrity could our legal system really have?

Law school had no answer to this question.

During my third year, Justice Thurgood Marshall did. In a defiant address that he delivered at NYU in 1983, the old champion vowed to eternally fight the death penalty as a biased, arbitrary mistake that was destined to murder the innocent. After what I'd seen that summer, his words were balm to my soul. For all of the setbacks he had lived through, he still believed that our system of laws would evolve until we got it right. Like Martin Luther King Jr., he believed that we could bend the moral universe toward justice.

His words were a little too effective, because they inspired me to take leave of my senses and accost the legal demigod right after he finished his address. He was a notorious curmudgeon who would never waste time talking to vapid law students like me. So I left the auditorium early, hid under a stairwell near the front doors, and waited. As Justice Marshall barreled toward the entrance, clearly intent on diving into his Town Car for a quick escape, I jumped out and hurled myself into the path of Mr. Justice, forcing him to careen to an abrupt and tottering halt. Standing under his massive swaying frame, I ridiculously proceeded to introduce myself as an LDF student intern, and to tell him, as if he possibly could have cared, my intent to become a lawyer at LDF. Exasperated, he shook his great jowls in disbelief and snapped, "Well, you'll have to do a hell of a lot better than we did." Then he pushed past me, muttering curses and shaking his great lion's head on the way out the door.

He was right. We would have to do better. A few weeks later, in my dorm room, Julia and I numbed ourselves to get through the night that John Eldon Smith would not. Georgia executed him on December 15, 1983.

After that summer, I knew firsthand why Justices Brennan and Marshall opposed all capital sentences and declined to "tinker with the machinery of death." All summer, that was what we had been doing, tinkering with death—and shoveling quicksand. I had learned that superhuman dedication and superb legal skill would never be able to fix the rigged machinery. We were using legal and statistical weapons in what was fundamentally a political war. Until the public purged bloodlust from politics, prosecutors would continue to ride death into political power, snaring the slowest instead of the most culpable, and elevating symbolic retribution over doing justice. Ending the death mills—transformative change—would take public understanding that human fallibility means executing the innocent, and a consensus that it is too high a price to pay for vengeance.

During this time, 1982–1983, I heard that a lawyer named Barry Scheck had just started what he called "an innocence project" at Yeshiva Law School. The science of DNA would have to catch up to his vision of showing the tragic fallibility of capital sentencing, and it would be decades before DNA proved what we knew—that death row housed dozens of innocent defendants. By 2008 we would see 129 death row inmates exonerated and freed, 17 of them using DNA evidence. Yet routinely, prosecutors would fight reviewing DNA evidence to determine whether innocent defendants had been put to death, and in 2011 the Supreme Court backed prosecutors who hid exonerating eyewitness and blood evidence from an innocent man they sent to death row for fourteen years.[7]

I now knew the depth of inequity that awaited and that I had what it took to fight it. After a lifelong, valiant run in the courts, a disappointed Thurgood Marshall still believed in the promise of this system to someday deliver justice that operated without bias, corruption, or brutality. As the beneficiary of all he and our ancestors had sacrificed, I had to at least try to run the next leg of the relay. During my last year of law school, I returned to LDF, and Julia and I went back down to Georgia and enlisted the support of Sarah Farmer, the sister of the victim, to free Billy Moore from death row. We finished his thousand-page clemency petition that spring of 1984, and I took my last final exams of the paper chase.

I would be leaving law school with good enough grades to land a prestigious clerkship with a federal appellate judge on the U.S. Court of Appeals for the Sixth Circuit. But I could not savor that prospect or enjoy my graduation on May 22, 1984. Billy Moore, the prisoner whose case had consumed my third year of law school, was scheduled to die at the stroke of midnight. I was stricken with guilt for not staying in Georgia with Julia and Jack. By now the guards had shaved his head so his hair would not catch fire, and had patched his leg so the current would run smoothly. I could not block from my brain the horror that all of them would soon face if his appeal was denied.

I poured myself coffee, flipped on the air-conditioning, and stepped into the shower to wash away the pall. Graduation from law school had to be the order of the day. Draped in cap and gown, I greeted Mom, Dad, and Norman at the auditorium, and an hour later, I received my Juris Doctorate diploma and the Vanderbilt Prize for public service. I handed both to my ever loving parents and sat through a family dinner to celebrate this latest milestone. But all the time I was numb. Billy had three hours left. At last I kissed them goodbye and raced back to my dorm and up the stairs to catch the ringing phone. It was Julia. From Jack's trembling hands, she read me the Eleventh Circuit's order for a stay of execution.[8]

It would take years before I understood how extraordinary our work had been during those eighteen months in the crucible of death. I would later joke that my best legal work had been done as a student and that my career had gone downhill from there. As New York and law school receded in my rearview mirror, I knew that I was done with death, but another day with LDF lay ahead, as did on-the-job training. My formal instruction, however, was over. The falcon's hood could come off. I was a lawyer. It was time to fly.

Chapter 6

Chapter 6

THE BLUE GRIP

I n the first four years following law school, I deliberately racked up more elite credentials. That way it would be crystal clear that representing people without money or clout was my first choice and not my last resort. My colleagues would know that the prestige, money, and power they enjoyed had been mine to refuse. After LDF, I also wanted to continue learning the practice of law from its best practitioners.

My first stop on this quest was the United States Court of Appeals for the Sixth Circuit in Detroit. Clerking for a judge is a prized credential given to top law graduates. After one of my law school professors opined that I wasn't quite good enough to clerk at the higher federal courts of appeal, I applied to nothing but federal courts of appeal. With the help of my LDF mentor, Lani Guinier, I landed interviews with several federal appellate judges. After a lively session with the Honorable Damon J. Keith, I argued that he needed to hire me that day, before he had a chance to see other candidates. During the interview, the judge put Lani on a speakerphone and mirthfully demanded, "Who is this Connie Rice woman with the nerve to tell me I have to hire her right now?" Laughing, Lani warned him that I was a livewire and a feminist, but that he would never find a more dedicated law clerk. Judge Keith hired me on the spot as his two-year clerk.

It would be one of the best jobs of my life. With my co-clerks, Randall Johnson, David Simmons, and Ezra Greenberg, I prepared the judge to hear oral arguments, teed up the cases for him with bench memos that summarized the facts and law of each appeal, recommended rulings, conducted research, wrote first drafts of opinions, tended his law library, oversaw publication of the opinions, and made sure his chambers in Detroit and Cincinnati ran like clocks. The work taught me the discipline of impartiality: sticking tightly to the facts and law, suspending bias and purging all political bent. In 99 percent of the cases, I did just that, with only two exceptions. The judge knew that in black-lung disease cases for longtime miners, my recommendation would always be to rule in favor of paying the sick miner. And in the rare cases where the facts and law led to a gross miscarriage of justice, Judge Keith expected my recommendations to correct course.

We lived in Detroit, but the seat of the Sixth Circuit, which covered Michigan, Kentucky, Tennessee, and Ohio, was in Cincinnati, where we flew every two months to hear the cases. Judge Keith demanded a lot, but he gave even more back to his clerks, whom he viewed as part of his family. After he picked up the cases of his late friend Judge Harry Phillips, it was not unusual for me to work fifteen-hour days, which, compared to LDF, felt reasonable. I took time only to swim at the YMCA; talk by phone to Dick Berk, a statistics professor I met during the *McCleskey* hearing with whom I'd struck up a long-distance relationship; watch *Miami Vice;* and visit my aunt Betty. Betty, my mom's closest sister, was a gun-toting operating room nurse at Ford Memorial Hospital who drove her carless niece every week to the grocery store and complained to cashiers that I bought more food for my marmalade tabby cat, Meesh, than for myself. And no matter what the job demanded, I made it home for Thanksgiving.

I had chosen this clerkship because, like Thurgood Marshall, Judge Keith saw his job as ensuring the just rule of law, and he had the courage to reverse injustice and tell truth to power. When Lani was his clerk in 1971, he ruled against Richard Nixon's warrantless wiretapping, and much later, in a 2002 case, he would rule against U.S. Attorney General John Ashcroft's secret deportation hearings, declaring that "democracies die behind closed doors" in *Detroit Free Press v. Ashcroft*.

The judge was also a celebrity, which added to my duties. I knew instinctively that he'd be an attractive target, and I kept a sharp eye out for conflicts of interest arising from his vast network of influential friends and nonjudicial activities. An icon of the civil rights era, he already had schools named after him and enough awards to fill a stadium. The photo gallery on the walls of his Detroit chambers chronicled hundreds of encounters he'd had with everyone from Muhammad Ali, Bishop Tutu, Andrei Sakharov, and Martin Luther King Jr. to U.S. presidents. When he asked me why I kept the Code of Judicial Conduct on my desk, I said so I could stop him from crossing any lines. He cracked up when I solemnly vowed that no judge of mine was getting impeached.

The judge grew fond of me, calling me "C" to avoid confusion with his secretaries' C-beginning names, and introducing me as his "feminist law clerk." I certainly deserved the blame when Judge Keith issued a dissent blasting sexually explicit posters, language, and male misconduct suffered by a woman employee of a Northern Michigan oil refinery who had appealed the dismissal of her sex discrimination suit; the other two judges had ruled that modern women were exposed to sexually explicit materials all the time and should be used to it. His scathing dissent in *Rabidue v. Osceola* helped set the stage for later recognition of the claim of a sexually hostile work environment and was cited by Senator Edward Kennedy during the Anita Hill hearings. The judge was lauded for being ahead of his time on that case, but he drew the line when I suggested he hang in his chambers a portrait of a nude male next to the female nude by Diego Rivera.

Clerking was like watching a ball game from behind home plate.

It gave me an umpire's-eye view of the workings of the federal court system—and more specially, a second father. The judge and I had a mutual adoration society, and it hurt to turn down his request that I stay with him as a permanent clerk. (I did, however, send a copy of the judge's request for my lifetime appointment to the professor who had declared me unqualified for a court of appeals clerking.)

I bade the judge farewell and headed west to winter-free San Francisco to earn my next elite credential. As a litigation associate at Morrison & Foerster, I had won a coveted spot at a top-tier law firm and an opportunity to earn my way into a prestigious partnership. I wanted to explore the viability of doing serious public interest work from within a traditional law firm.

Once at work, I chose the securities litigation team. Not that I even knew what a stock was, but I liked Mel Goldman, the head of the team. He was a wise man who had a smart wife, so I figured he could handle me fairly, and he did. After I pointed out that the partners on our team jogged and sat in the sauna with the male associates but not with the female associates, I gave him a choice of taking me to lunch with clients or doing Tae Kwon Do with me. He chose lunch.

The other reason I moved west was to join Dick Berk, the wonderful man I had been dating long-distance. I loved living in San Francisco, not just because it was my favorite city but also because—although it was taking some getting used to—living there with Dick was fun. We had an apartment on the north face of Potrero Hill, overlooking the city and Oakland Bay. While Dick taught at UC Berkeley, I settled into a generous pro bono workload—half of my cases were public interest freebies—and into carrying out the cannibal capitalism of mergers and acquisitions that our big banking clients wanted. Under this yin-yang umbrella of work, I explored whether a private firm was a big enough vehicle for the social-change work I needed to do.

It was not. When UCLA offered Dick a dual appointment in statistics and sociology, I moved to Los Angeles and began to look for work in the nonprofit world. I, too, got a job at UCLA, where I ended up defending their admissions programs from reverse discrimination charges by the Reagan Justice Department. In 1988 Dick and I married. Life with him offered everything I should have wanted, but I realized way too late why our long-distance relationship had worked so well for so long. Whether it was due to the emotional detachment of my nomadic youth or my resurgent loner gene, I could not make the leap into becoming half of a couple. Despite loving him dearly, I yearned to live alone. Dick had promised that if I found marriage untenable, he would let me go, and he kept his word. The marriage ended, but for me, with no regrets, only gratitude. Very few find mutual love, never mind the chance to try life together. Dick and I remain good friends, and he went on to find the marital happiness that was beyond my grasp.

I became free to once again live alone and for my work.

In May 1990 Ted Shaw, my former boss at LDF, asked to meet with me. Ted had landed in Los Angeles in 1987, somewhat against his will, after the new head of LDF, Julius Chambers, sent him to open the first Western Regional Office of the NAACP Legal Defense and Educational Fund with fellow LDF veterans Patrick Paterson and Bill Lann Lee.

After moving beyond our tiff over *The Color Purple,* Ted and I had developed a friendly rivalry. He had kept in touch over the years by firing off occasional postcards depicting warring Amazons or spike-heeled dominatrixes, with endearing notes like "Reminded me of you." Despite my inner feminist, the cards cracked me up and usually ended up on my refrigerator. I half suspected his call now was a setup for another of his pranks.

Ted met me in my UCLA office. Perched on the corner of my desk, he leveled his mandate in the same soft drawl I remembered from New York. "You have to come back to LDF." He was serious. He didn't like L.A. and wanted to return to LDF's headquarters in New York. "Time to come home, E.T.," he said.

He was right. My job at UCLA was done. Both us of knew that I belonged at LDF.

First Ted had to persuade Julius Chambers to rehire me. The new LDF chief was a sardonic, still-waters-run-deep man who absorbed the world from behind oversized eyeglasses. Raised amid the rich paradoxes of Jim Crow, he was part of the second wave of Southern LDF lawyers whose understanding of Dixie's savage suppression was bone-deep and something I would never know. An accomplished man, he was the first black editor of the University of North Carolina *Law Review* and had been part of Thurgood Marshall's *Brown v. Board of Education* team. He courageously opened a civil rights law firm in Charlotte and even more courageously filed the case that forced Charlotte to integrate its schools. In return, racists firebombed his car and house.

After a bad dinner interview during which I told Mr. Chambers he could not smoke his cigar, my fate was unclear. Julius had accurately concluded that I talked too fast, held too many opinions, and would be hard to restrain. He finally relented after ardent lobbying by Ted and Bill Lann Lee.

In September 1990 I began work at LDF's Western Regional Office on the third floor of an ornate, classic L.A. Art Deco building at Third and Olive in a rusty business area just west of downtown. It distantly bordered L.A.'s skid row, where the nation's largest homeless population foraged on city streets and slept in tent cities not too far from Hollywood's glamour. On my first full day at LDF, a skid row denizen named Cookie slid her wheelchair into my path and asked for money, which I gave her. I wondered if she'd ever become a client.

Upstairs, Ted was still clearing out his office. I sat on what would soon be my couch and listened to him talk while he sorted stuff into boxes. He ran down all of the people in L.A. he thought I should meet and what issues he wanted me to investigate, but in between the lines, his frustration smoldered.

"This place is impossible," Ted complained as he tossed a stack of files. "I'd rather deal with Mississippi . . ." Thump. "At least Biloxi is understandable . . . ." Bang. "Furthermore, I refuse to live anywhere the air is so dirty, it can hide an entire mountain range for months."

As I listened to his objections, it was clear the paradox of L.A. had eluded him, like it did many East Coasters and Southerners. Ted had missed the deeper causes of his consternation. L.A. was not the South, LDF's historic turf; nor was it New York, its headquarters. L.A. was not even a city. It was more like a Greek city-state plunked down in a northern territory of Mexico. Unlike ancient Athens or New York, L.A. had no center or coherent identity and no glue. Its countless ethnic and economic communities sprawled across an endless suburban span, fractured and unconnected. And it was huge. The city was nearly five hundred square miles, and it sat in Los Angeles County, which was a staggering four thousand square miles. Its dangers, like the subterranean web of earthquake faults that could level it in an instant, lurked beneath its sun-splashed splendor. It was a land of a thousand unconnected tribes.

Ted's focus had rested mainly on one tribe. Black L.A. was itself a paradoxical terrain hosting the richest African-American communities in the United States, with elegant hillside enclaves like Baldwin Hills and Ladera Heights ringed by gang zones like the Jungle. Anchored to the southeast by historically black Watts, a creative, vibrant, and gang-ridden neighborhood, African-American strongholds were undergoing a rapid influx of Latinos and Asians. Ted couldn't even count on the black community staying black.

As he tossed his last file into a box, his phone rang. He picked it up and barked hello. "Need a quote about offensive rap lyrics? Here, I have someone for ya." With glee, he threw the receiver to me. On the line was an anxious reporter from *USA Today,* a half hour from her deadline. On the spot, I gave her a quick sound bite: "We may not like it, but it is the talking drum of America's mean streets," and tossed the phone back to Ted.

"Not bad." He grinned. "But you always were good at instant bullshit."

I rolled my eyes and turned my attention to my new partner, Bill Lann Lee, who had entered the room to enjoy the banter. Ted and Patrick soon would be gone, and I knew next to nothing about the man who, it turned out, had bargained the hardest to get me the job. On first impression, Bill Lann Lee struck me as steady, level-headed, and scrupulous. Ever self-effacing, he spoke in soft tones that sometimes swallowed his words into a trademark mumble. Bill was a brilliant litigator who had avoided developing the obnoxious persona that usually accompanies that role. He was selfless and driven by deep-seated decency to help the helpless. I would learn that he always thought first of everyone else and reserved the worst tasks for himself. But to mistake his goodness for weakness was a big mistake. Bill was a nationally recognized expert on employment rights, and his professional voice was one of authority. In combat, the altar boy became a gladiator. The gentle generosity disappeared, and an icy, fiercely disciplined zeal took its place, just as it had with Jack. Bill combined to deadly effect a rare mix of meticulous preparation, strategic genius, iron will, and common sense. It was almost always a bad day for anyone opposing Bill in a federal court.

Bill had grown up in Harlem. His Cantonese-speaking parents had worked round-the-clock in their laundry. The family endured the special humiliations reserved for Asians; he could remember dreading the "No tickee, no laundry" mockery that local ignoramuses had directed at them. His mother did not let him handle the dirty clothes for fear it would lower his sights from the higher goals of college and graduate school. But the Lees bypassed resentment and held on to the American credos of liberty and equal justice under law—the very principles Bill now vindicated in courts across America. If anything, Bill and his brother had thrived in the tough African-American neighborhood and had, curiously, conflated the two cultures. His brother became a Baptist preacher, and Bill became a lawyer for LDF. When he traveled to investigate apartheid in South Africa for LDF, Bill was given a visa that assigned him the racial category "honorary white." He filed an appeal to change his designation to "black."

For his own good, I broke the bad news to him: "Bill, you are not black." He responded with a dismissive laugh.

We devised a plan to split the political work: He would deal with our bosses in New York, and I would work cases and be the face of the office. Given the racial politics, I had to be the mascot. The rest of the office was like Bill: dedicated, talented, and not black.

Kevin Reed, fresh out of Harvard Law School, landed in LDF's L.A. office the same time I did, courtesy of a Skadden Fellowship, the generous internship run by the prestigious law firm Skadden, Arps. Had he lived a century earlier, Kevin would have been a woodsman or a cowboy homesteading the frontier. Secure, easygoing, and disarming, he had a wickedly fast sense of humor that could instantly deflate the pompous. A barely repressed rebel, he rode a devil-red motorcycle way too fast, fly-fished, and hunted. Given my objections to guns and killing living creatures for fun (I ruined my only fishing trip at age twelve by liberating Granddad Barnes's basket of writhing fish back into the Schuylkill River), Kevin should have banned me from his NRA orbit. But he was the rare regular guy who relished being around "difficult" women and who instinctively saw what most white people could not: the automated privileges and penalties of a system designed to reward wealth and whiteness. Like me, he was cross-racially fluent, comfortable being the token, and needed no intertribal translation. All I needed to know was that he was a great lawyer and seemed to view making me laugh as part of his job.

Robert Garcia, my third colleague—who arrived a year later—was a recovering Stanford Law School professor who wanted back into the action. Robert was tactically gifted, brainy, prickly, and complex. On the surface, he was affable enough—a charming contrarian—but his inner tumult was never far from view. A former prosecutor in the Southern District of New York, he practiced with a ferocious zeal. Robert's tactics could border on ruthless, but they were in proportion to the outrageous conditions that our clients suffered. Robert was a lawyer you wanted in your foxhole; opponents promised concessions if only we would keep him at bay.

Once assembled, our office lineup sounded like the opening lines of a bar joke: "So a 'black' Chinese-American altar boy, an Irish-American rebel, a Guatemalan-American prosecutor, and a Black American Princess walk into a bar . . ." But LDF, an organization led by African-American and Jewish lawyers, had always been about diverse people bound by the mission of delivering on America's promise of equal treatment, liberty, and opportunity. Carrying out that mission in L.A. required a more multiracially and socioeconomically complex approach. In the city of gefilte-fish tacos and chitlin burritos, what choice did we have?

The immense talent of my colleagues aside, it was hard to see how such a tiny office could make a ripple in the ocean of established charities and nonprofit agencies in L.A. Most of the groups did admirable direct service—sheltering the homeless, aiding addict recovery, teaching reading, coaching minority businesses, tutoring children, running health clinics, helping women escape domestic abuse. Few service providers, however, had the artillery to take aim at ending the root causes of these problems. Sheltering the homeless is a critical service, but permanently breaking the cycle of homelessness requires reengineering the underlying political, economic, policy, medical, and mental health drivers of the disease. As lawyers, we also were focused not on root causes but on our class action cases.

Our business as civil rights lawyers was to file lawsuits that enforced the U.S. Constitution's promises. LDF practiced "impact litigation," class action lawsuits designed to change policy and fix systems that affect lots of people at once. We aimed to open doors, put our clients at the table, influence policy choices, and vindicate rights. LDF had racked up years of tactical victories, winning scores of cases to enforce the relatively limited reach of the civil rights laws won in the 1960s. Unfortunately, I was soon to learn, our courtroom victories rarely touched the deeper problems beyond the reach of a judge. The cases more often restrained unfairness than delivered systemic fairness. I would have to plunge deep into L.A.'s hidden underclass before I truly understood Martin Luther King's warning that "evils . . . rooted deeply in the . . . structure of our society . . . suggest that radical reconstruction of society itself is the real issue to be faced." Ending extreme poverty and racial exclusion could not be done with lawsuits alone. That also required a revolution in values and the political will to restructure our political and economic systems to open opportunity.

I had heard King's admonition that "Justice ... will not flow into society merely from court decisions," but in 1990, there were still many problems the courts could fix, and I needed to do enough cases to learn the possibilities as well as the limits of the law in effecting social change. In 1990 I had to prove two things: first, that my legal skill merited full membership in Thurgood Marshall's law firm; and second, that our tiny office could help remove the biggest barriers blocking opportunity.

Our sister firms like the American Civil Liberties Union, the Center for Law in the Public Interest, the Mexican American Legal Defense and Education Fund (MALDEF), and the Asian Pacific American Legal Center already had filed plenty of class actions to open up voting systems, employment, education, and immigrants' rights. The ACLU, Johnnie Cochran, and a dynamic umbrella group of lawyers called Police Misconduct had also filed scores of police abuse cases to counter L.A. cops' notorious excessive force. Our cases had to go beyond opening a closed door, redrawing a voting district, or rebuking individual abuses of police power. To earn our place on the L.A. stage, we needed go beyond the tactical victories of cases to the transformation that Martin Luther King Jr. had talked about. In other words, I wanted our little office to redefine traditional civil rights for twenty-first-century Los Angeles.

LDF did a lot of cases representing middle-class clients, and the L.A. office had its share of traditional voting rights and job discrimination cases. My focus, however, was fast turning to the problems of poor areas where there was no job discrimination because there were no jobs. It took no investigation to know that voting was not the hot issue for L.A.'s poorest communities. In African-American L.A., that perennial prize belonged to the Los Angeles Police Department. LAPD abuse was the one issue that cut across all classes.

At first I did not understand the depth of the hatred that black residents felt toward LAPD. Fifty years of incessant and pervasive dragnets, pedestrian stops, prone outs, car stops, home tosses, beatings, and roundups of black men and kids—often done with racist taunting and open lawlessness—had achieved a remarkable feat: universal hatred of the police. In South L.A., LAPD ran a police state. As LAPD historian Joe Domanick noted, LAPD officers were told, "You had to hit the street hard and be aggressive. If people were on the streets, they were suspect . . . Confront and Command. Shake them down. Make that arrest. And never, never admit . . . anything wrong . . . The Grip was in."[9] LAPD was the Blue Grip. Its militaristic suppression had stoked rage, emasculated black men, and throttled all trust in law enforcement. To find a more impressive campaign of malignant containment, you would have had to go back to Bull Connor's Birmingham, apartheid South Africa, or sectarian-racked Northern Ireland.

In the leading black newspaper, *The Sentinel,* the LAPD got covered like it was the Gestapo. Every week, its headlines howled LAPD abuses: LAPD DOGS MAUL CHILD. LAPD MAKES BLACK JUDGE LIE ON GROUND. LAPD SHOOTS UNARMED SUSPECT. LAPD KILLS 7 BLACK SUSPECTS WITH ILLE- GAL NECK CHOKEHOLD. LAPD CHIEF SAYS BLACKS DIE BECAUSE NECKS "ABNORMAL." OPERATION HAMMER: LAPD INVADES BLACK LA WITH TANKS! And that was just the news coverage—editorials bellowed even louder outrage.

At first I was skeptical about the histrionics. LAPD couldn't be that bad. I knew from its coverage of LDF that *The Sentinel* was not exactly a font of factual accuracy. But this *was* the only major city with so many police-abuse lawyers that they constituted an entire bar. And why, after decades of court battles, hadn't L.A.'s lawyers beaten LAPD back into the confines of the Constitution? What could LDF achieve that they had not?

I checked out a stack of books on LAPD, seeking to gain some insight into the department's excessive-force policing. The history was not encouraging. In its earliest incarnations during the early 1920s and '30s, LAPD was widely condemned as "a handmaiden to organized crime." In the 1950s the department found a savior in William H. Parker, who transformed the force with a new credo of crisp professionalism and military-style discipline. But the new militaristic policing came with undercurrents of bunker mentality and arrogance. Parker's obsession with strict order fed his delusion that LAPD stood above the law. And his pious rectitude led him to use preemptive dragnets to "eliminate the lice."[10] He ignored civilian rule, flouted Supreme Court rulings, and denounced the U.S. Constitution as a shield for criminals.

In those days, LAPD's motto, TO PROTECT AND SERVE, extended only to privileged white neighborhoods. Parker viewed himself as racially enlightened for the times but nonetheless believed his police force was a thin blue line protecting the "good" people from the hordes of uncivilized "domestics" and "Negroes with violent natures." His top officer in charge of the black community, a white man, was openly called "The Nigger Inspector."[11] And in a precursor to the Republicans' "Southern Strategy" to capitalize on racially fearful white Democrats, Parker baited white voters into blind backing of his excessive-force policing with warnings of violence from "Mexicans who descended from the wild tribes of Mexico" and "wanton Negroes."[12] As for the black officers on his force, he forbade them from having white partners or issuing orders to white officers or civilians. Meanwhile, white civic groups showered Chief Parker with "civil rights" awards every year.

Terrific. The vaunted father of the modern LAPD was an unreconstructed racial suppressionist. But what did I expect? Was there any big-city police force without remnants of the containment suppression used by plantation police during slavery? It would have been more surprising to find a twentieth-century police department that enforced equal treatment.

Parker died in 1966, but his influence would cast a long shadow over LAPD for decades. LAPD headquarters, Parker Center, bore his name, and Parker had trained the three internal chiefs who followed him, including the current chief of police, Daryl Gates. Unfortunately, the Blue Grip looked locked in for the foreseeable future.

I was reading my books on LAPD one day when Chandra Ellington, our receptionist, buzzed me on the phone. "It's a Mr. Johnnie Cochran for you, Connie," she announced.

The Johnnie Cochran? I grabbed the phone.

"Ms. Rice. This is Johnnie Cochran," he said. "I'm a local lawyer calling to welcome you to L.A."

Right. Johnnie Cochran was a local lawyer like Michael Jordan was a weekend basketball player. Though this was years before the O.J. Simpson trial, which would make him a household name, in the early 1990s, Cochran was one of the best trial lawyers in Los Angeles. He had practically pioneered civil lawsuits as a check against LAPD's abuse of force.

He had called to tell me how happy he was to have an LDF office in L.A. and that without the work of Thurgood Marshall and LDF, the only way he ever would have appeared in a courtroom would have been as a defendant. He gave me four phone numbers, told me to call anytime if I needed anything at all, and asked for my help in freeing his client, Geronimo Pratt, from decades in prison on fabricated evidence of murder.

I told him yes and then mentioned my slog through books on LAPD to understand the city's out-of-control police force. He told me books couldn't help me. In Johnnie's view, LAPD was a force run amok that ran a police state in South L.A. And no one except lawyers like us had the guts to restrain it by filing hundreds of cases every year on behalf of the abused. I asked why politicians had not reined LAPD in.

Cochran answered without hesitation. "LAPD compiles files on every politician, and politicians will shell out millions of dollars to pay for abuse claims forever before a single one of them ever grows the backbone to shut them down." The city was paying $20 million that year to settle LAPD excessive-force lawsuits. It was a line item in the city budget.

LAPD kept Stasi-like files and illegally intimidated politicians, like J. Edgar Hoover did? Where did they think they were, East Germany? Hundreds of cases and tens of millions paid out forever? This strategy of launching one patrol boat at a time to attack LAPD's aircraft carrier was not working. I asked Cochran if anyone had tried to use bigger cases, mounting an armada against LAPD's battleships.

He thought for a moment and then explained that even if they knew how to do the bigger cases, plaintiff's lawyers didn't have the resources for a big federal assault on a powerful police department. They'd lose too much money.

I reminded him that for nonprofit lawyers, losing money was a specialty.

He laughed. But then he warned me to get reinforcements if we went down that road. It was dangerous to aggressively take on LAPD. "Just remember," he cautioned, "there's a reason LAPD's black cops fear their own police department. Money is not the only thing that can be lost in challenging a department this intransigent."

Apparently, there was a dark side of the police I had yet to see.

After the call, Bill came into my office, and I told him, "It's unavoidable."

Bill had already filed employment discrimination claims against LAPD on behalf of black officers and was way ahead of me. He knew the appalling history of LAPD and how its mindless use of force and harassment seemed immune to attack. LAPD brushed off individual lawsuits like dandruff. We needed a bigger battering ram. As he headed for my door, he said we needed clients the public could not ignore. We needed more police officers as clients, which he was already lining up. He promised to get back with me after he made some calls. It was a Friday in early March 1991.

Neither of us had any idea that over the weekend, before we'd ever get a chance to reap the results of his calls, LAPD would cause a nine-point earthquake to strike the city. It would smack a tsunami right upside our work, make the public confront police abuse—and alter the course of Los Angeles history.

Chapter 7

THE TAPE

I got home late from work the following Monday night and trudged up the forty steps to my home in the Hollywood Hills. The spring night air was clean and sweet, redolent with the jasmine rose blooming along the patio walls, but I was too tired to enjoy it. Meesh, the orange marmalade tabby I'd inherited from Julia, chirped an impatient meow and followed me in through the French-cottage doors. I flipped on the kitchen television for background noise before putting on the kettle and then fumbled with the can opener and a can of Nine Lives. I was vaguely aware of the breaking-news urgency in the anchors' voices on the eleven o'clock news but had only enough energy to get out of my suit and into the shower. Refreshed and hungry, I padded back to the kitchen and started fishing in the fridge for something edible. The pointless weather forecast of more sun should have been on by then, but the TV anchors were still broadcasting in their serious-news voices, talking over the same jumpy, grainy, badly lit black-and-gray video they'd been playing when I came in. I tried squinting at it again to figure out what the shadowy

figures were doing. I moved closer to the TV. And then it hit me. I
knew what I was watching and why it was breaking news.

On the screen, a ring of police officers circled a prone man.
Twenty-seven cops—twenty-two from LAPD—stood in that ring,
ten with guns drawn. In the middle lay a man facedown on the
ground. Two LAPD officers stood near him. One of them appeared
to reach down and grab his wrist, but both officers jumped away
from him. A wire shot across the dark and landed on the man, who
jerked and writhed spasmodically. They had just shot him with two
Taser darts of fifty thousand volts each. We would later learn that at
this point, officers had begun a singsong taunt of "What's up, killer?
How you feelin', killer? How you feelin'? How you feelin'?" As
they chanted, the man tried to cough out the blood in his mouth,
but before he could, LAPD officer Laurence Powell strode forward
and power-swung his PR-24 metal baton into the prone man's face.
Powell stepped back and wound his arm up for another blow, while
a second officer joined in to deliver similar strikes to the man's torso.
The man bolted upright toward Powell in a frantic, panicked attempt
to flee. The officers set on him like wolves. Whack, whack, whack!
Ten quick strikes felled him to his knees, and then the two officers
began wild spurts of power strokes, battering the batons into his
body. The man jerked and recoiled from the blows, and every flinch
that jerked his body up prompted another strike. An officer would
later claim that the man's defensive spasms had defied their orders for
him to lie completely still.

In eighty-one seconds, three LAPD cops had pummeled Rodney
King with fifty-six blows, several kicks, and a foot-stomp to his neck.
They had knocked out fillings in his teeth, crushed his right eye
socket, broken his cheekbone, fractured eleven bones at the base of
his skull, inflicted a serious concussion, damaged his facial nerves, and
shattered his ankle.

The video took my breath away. The casual brutality jarred me. I
was looking at something that was ten degrees away from a snuff film,
but for LAPD, it was just another night's work. When it was over, the
officers hog-tied King like a trussed boar and left him bleeding at

the side of the road to await the ambulance. Sergeant Stacey Koons, an on-scene supervisor, would later conclude that the arrest had ended satisfactorily:"[King] had not been seriously injured.We don't get injured. He goes to jail. That's the way the system's supposed to work."

Apparently so, because out of the twenty-seven cops at the scene, not one stopped the frenzied beating and Tasering of an unarmed suspect lying on the ground. Not one tried to hide what was happening in the macabre roadside ring. On the video, it is clear that there are witnesses: Cars and a bus drive by, spectators in nearby apartments stand on balconies from which one videographer films the beating. The officers know there will be no price paid. They're simply doing their jobs.

Audiotapes of police radio chatter and of mobile computer transmissions confirmed that a little later, Koons, Powell, and others laughed about the beating as "a little attitude adjustment" and how they "got to play a little hardball game tonight." Powell bragged, "Tased and beat the suspect . . . big-time! . . . I haven't beaten anyone this bad in a long time."The transcripts also revealed that just before the King beating, Powell had responded to a domestic disturbance in a black neighborhood, which he described as something "right out of *Gorillas in the Mist*."

We would learn about this and much more in the months to come. But as I stood in my kitchen on the night of March 4, 1991, the one thing I knew was that after this tape, nothing was going to be the same. The video had shoved police abuse into the living rooms of the upstanding middle class, and there was nowhere to hide. City hall would not be able to duck this one by covering it with a check.

It was midnight, and the local news anchors still seemed more mesmerized by their own shock than by the brutal spectacle on the video. *Now* they expressed concern? Up to that point, mainstream media had ignored the drumbeat of black protests about police mistreatment. L.A. media might have reported big damage awards but otherwise glossed over police abuse. Most reporters no longer bothered to cover barrio and ghetto homicides—they were too common to be considered news. But let a celebutante check into rehab, and stations dispatched enough media trucks to fill the Rose Parade. Annoyed, I flipped off the volume and called ACLU director Ramona Ripston at home. She, too, was glued in horror to her TV screen.

Ramona had forgotten more battles with LAPD than most lawyers ever waged. I wanted her take on whether this beating would get "bluewashed" by LAPD and ignored by George H. W. Bush's Department of Justice.

"I think they've finally done it," she said, "and done it on tape." I agreed. For once LAPD's mindless brutality had no escape hatch and would have to be prosecuted for what it was: unconstitutional excessive force that violated every known human right. I predicted a shock wave. I underestimated the response. The uproar over the King beating was instantaneous, global, and stupendous. CNN's endless broadcasts of the video around the globe had forced a political response that was swift and sweeping.

With photos of the hospitalized King's swollen and bruised face on every front page of every newspaper, Mayor Tom Bradley demanded immediate action from the Police Commission. Commissioners, actually behaving for once as if they ran the police department, suspended Chief Daryl Gates. The City Council, cowed by LAPD's outrage, quickly reversed the suspension and reinstated the chief, proving once again that LAPD ran the city. This time, however, Chief Gates and LAPD could not completely halt what the tape had sparked. On March 14, 1991, a county grand jury returned multiple-count indictments against four LAPD officers, including Koons and Powell, for assault with a deadly weapon, filing false police reports, and inflicting excessive force against a suspect under color of law. The trial was scheduled to start that fall. On April 1, 1991, less than a month after the video had detonated on the airwaves, Mayor Bradley appointed the prominent L.A. attorney and soon-to-be secretary of state for President Clinton, Warren Christopher, to lead a blue-ribbon panel of the city's heaviest power brokers and charged them with taking no longer than three months to complete a sweeping investigation of every aspect of LAPD operations. I told Bill that the commission was a setup for yet another useless report that would excuse police abuse and demand no fundamental changes.

But on July 9, 1991, Warren Christopher dropped a neutron bomb on Daryl Gates and the LAPD. The Christopher Commission report was culled from eight hundred interviews, two hundred testimonials from LAPD brass and officers, and a million documents that featured explosive transcripts of officer radio and digital transmissions chock-full of the worst racist, sexist, anti-Semitic, homophobic vitriol imaginable. Those MDTs—mobile digital terminals—deep-sixed anyone's ability to defend the department. The report demanded a sweeping change in LAPD's xenophobic culture and a radical reorientation from militaristic intimidation policing to community policing. The commission unanimously called for Chief Daryl Gates to resign—and called for the first constraints on LAPD power in eighty years, including the first term limits for the chief of police and an inspector general to be the Police Commission's independent eyes and ears.

Outraged, defiant officers torched a hundred copies of the report on academy grounds. But it was too late. The endgame had begun. The blue-ribbon elites had struck a deal: If Gates stepped down, the worst of the racist MDT transcripts and other damaging evidence would be buried for sixty years in sealed vaults at USC. Gates delayed but eventually stopped fighting and began preparing to step down as chief of police.

Two months after the Christopher report, another King aftershock rumbled through our office. It was a late-starting September morning after a late night, and as I swooped through the office doors, I glimpsed a man sitting on my couch. *Dad!* I thought, but then stopped in my tracks at Chandra's desk. The man was not my father, in some surprise visit, but someone who at that distance looked like his fraternal twin. I turned to Chandra.

"Oh," she whispered. "There's a police commissioner waiting in your office. I told him you'd be here soon." Bill had urged the commissioner to meet with the new black lawyer at LDF-LA.

The man rose as I entered. Like Dad, he was an inch shy of six feet, his ramrod posture beginning to bend with age. His precise white hairline mirrored my dad's, as did the shape of his face and the color and set of his eyes. My visitor's eyes, however, shimmered with a gentle playfulness. He had a lived-in handsomeness, and he radiated the warm grace and steely dignity that seemed to be the hallmark of elite black men from the Jackie Robinson era. He smiled serenely and rose to graciously usher me into my own office.

"Connie, come in, come in," he greeted me. "It's such a pleasure to meet you. My name is Jesse Brewer." He explained that he was a retired deputy chief of the Los Angeles Police Department and that Mayor Bradley had recently appointed him as president of the Los Angeles Police Commission. Still holding my hand, he paused, bade me to sit down, and then closed his other hand on top of mine. "I am here to help you break the Blue Grip of LAPD."

For the next three hours, Brewer recounted his nearly forty-year career of outmaneuvering the Blue Grip. LAPD had tried to shake him off from the start, illegally blocking his entrance to the Police Academy, then rigging every promotion test to block all black cops' ascension through the ranks. "They battled us as if we were an invading virus and they were the white T cells," he joked. "But they weren't sharp enough to cut us out."

I asked him how he had survived such a hostile culture.

Brewer smiled and explained that in his day, black candidates for the Police Academy had college degrees and twice the gray matter of the average white officer. He joked that, fortunately, that had not been a difficult threshold to reach. We laughed. I knew at least three generations who had received this script: If you're black, you have to be twice as good to be considered half as well. The white officers needed only a relative on the force to get in. For black officers, there were two ways to survive LAPD: like Brewer, as an inside resister who ignored the taunts, outsmarted them, outperformed them, and quietly resisted the racism wherever he could; or as an inside opera-tor, becoming bluer than black and outdoing the Blue Grip's dirtiest games and meanest intimidation.

I suggested a third way—open confrontation.

"You asked how to *survive* LAPD," he retorted. "These cats have guns, and they shoot black people with little to no thought all of the time. And as the world has seen, they beat blacks more easily than they breathe."

He stated this as simple fact. Had the statement come from me, it would have been dismissed out of hand by the dominant culture as paranoid racial hype. But LAPD's own statistics backed him up. Between 1963 and 1965, LAPD shot and killed sixty African-Americans, twenty-seven of them in the back.

Brewer was not finished arming me. He turned to strategy.

He said that if we wanted to break LAPD's impunity, we had to change our strategy. Most lawsuits used victims' complaints to challenge LAPD's external behavior—its mistreatment of the public. But, explained Brewer, you wouldn't lay a glove on the department that way. He said, "You have to break LAPD from the inside—shatter the internal cohesion and embolden the reformers hiding inside the department."

What reformers? He answered my unspoken question and said that the younger black and Latino officers Bill had been talking to were the change agents. After years of mistreatment and thwarted promotions, enough minority officers were ready to take a stand and suffer the retaliation. It had taken Brewer a lot longer to reach the same point, but this was hardly his first turn as a whistle-blower. He and his white counterpart, Deputy Chief David Dotson, had been the star witnesses before the Christopher Commission, giving hours of devastating testimony about LAPD's hair-trigger use of force, warrior mentality, and racism. Now Jesse Brewer had turned to help us. With joint action by black, Latino, and Asian-American cops, and help from seasoned veterans like them, we just might have enough to begin breaking the Blue Grip.

Shortly following my session with Brewer, another unexpected and even more extraordinary whistle-blower would emerge, one who vividly revealed the dark side of LAPD that Johnnie Cochran had flagged.

It was on a midweek morning at six, and I was in the office hoping for uninterrupted time to finish a memo when the lobby bell rang. I peered out into the receptionist area, expecting to see another homeless soul who had spied my predawn arrival and knew from Wheelchair Cookie to follow me upstairs for "help." But it was a dark blue LAPD uniform with a sergeant's insignia that filled the glass partition. Filling the uniform was a black woman who looked almost six feet tall, 180 pounds, and built to hurt. On her hips swung an immense gun in a holster and a belt of less lethal weapons and restraints.

I opened the door. "Good morning, Sergeant. Come in. How can I help you?"

Like most officers, the sergeant knew LDF was fighting LAPD. She strode into the office, revealing the smaller guns strapped to her back and ankle, and offered her stolid hand. "Thank you. I'm Sergeant Pauline Reidel,[13] Southeast CRASH. I've come here directly from my morning watch shift. I need your protection."

CRASH—Community Resources Against Street Hoodlums— was LAPD's gang-suppression unit. It accepted only the most aggressive officers and no women. Reidel had to be a first, not to mention off the charts in ability, to have gotten in. If she had just finished morning watch in Southeast, she was coming off the most dangerous night shift in LAPD's most dangerous division. She had three guns that I could see. Yet she needed my protection.

This was going to be good.

She sank into an armchair and closed her eyes. I fetched water for her and coffee for me and sat quietly as, forehead in hand, she composed herself. She thanked me and drank deeply and then scanned me with hard eyes, sizing up what she had heard against what was sitting before her. Her briefly quizzical expression said that I was not what she had expected. She sat back and began her story.

Reidel's shift had started out normally. Before her separate CRASH roll call, she had checked in with the supervisor, inspected her weapons, the car, and other equipment, and huddled with her partner, the only Latino officer in Southeast CRASH, over where they'd "hunt" that night.

At this point I interrupted her. "What in the hell are you doing in CRASH?"

"They take on the toughest criminals, and that's what I wanted."

Before joining LAPD she had been a crack shot, an accomplished athlete, and had graduated high in her class at the LAPD Police Academy. She must have sent shivers up the Blue spine: a black woman who could outthink, outrun, and outshoot them.

"But how did you get past them into the unit?" I persisted, meaning the all-white, all-male CRASH teams.

"Gave them one choice. I don't take no, I don't back down, and I'm too good for them to sink. Had a little luck, too—my partner pulled for me. He's okay. We went through the academy together, so he doesn't break out in hives when I get in the squad car." She smiled slightly and carried on with the story.

Over the five-hour shift, Reidel and her partner had staked out a gang's headquarters, followed some radio calls on the designated CRASH frequency, and helped interrogate a gang leader being held for murder at 77th Division, at the western end of the bureau. An hour before the end of their shift, they circled back to Southeast station. Reidel was walking out of the station to return a rifle to the squad car's trunk when she heard muffled whimpering and muted talking coming through a closed door. She stopped and slowly cracked the door open.

Another CRASH officer was straddling a black teenager strapped to a chair and shoving a gun barrel into the kid's mouth. The quaking youth had urinated on himself and was whimpering in terror as the officer pulled the trigger one round at a time. The cop was chuckling at the kid's rising panic that the next click would blow his head off. Reidel burst through the door, pounced on the officer, dragged him into the hall, and with one hand, slammed him by the throat up against the wall. With the other, she snatched up her rifle, stabbed its butt into his chin, and spat, "If I ever fucking see you fuck with anyone like that again, I'll fucking kill you."

As she recounted the confrontation, her tone was level but intense. She was tamping down her emotions while I was trying not to look stunned. The question struggling to break through my shock at that point was strange: Had this other cop arrived at LAPD already a sociopath, or had Southeast made him one?

Her patrol area was what I called a kill zone—a tiny, high-crime, gang-dominated spot in the ghetto or barrio, no more than four to ten blocks, in which people, opportunity, and hope died premature deaths. A kill zone was a hot spot with no rules. I also called it a Constitution-free zone, where the First, Fourth, Fifth, Sixth, Eighth, Thirteenth, and Fourteenth amendments were inoperative. Forget free speech, effective counsel, or due process. The only constitutional amendment in full effect was the Second. In Southeast, you could find a Glock 9 a lot easier than fresh vegetables.

In 1991 this three-square-mile area of L.A. six miles south of my office was the reigning champion for most dangerous swath of territory in the country. Home to three violent, gang-dominated housing projects, Southeast had more than five hundred reported gunshots every year and more murders than ten individual states. At that moment, the area was in economic collapse and gripped by a deadly crack cocaine war. It had never been this violent. The risk of death from murder in Southeast Division had escalated to an astronomic one in 250—five hundred times higher than the risk in L.A.'s safer neighborhoods.

In America's war zones, like Southeast, police and residents alike expected violent death by strangers to pose a daily threat. But even Southeast's mayhem did not explain the atrocity Reidel had witnessed. "I jammed a cop torturing a kid with Russian roulette," she said, mildly marveling at what had happened. "I lost it. As soon as I had slammed the bastard, I knew they'd never let me get through another shift alive. I got in my car and drove directly to your office."

"Why?" I tested.

"They ambush, cancel backup, and plant evidence on *white* officers who betray them. What do you think they'll do to me?"

She did not need to explain. I had learned from the ACLU and Police Watch lawyers that when cops plant evidence and pull backup, they mean for the target to die. I knew officers who had suffered gunshot wounds because hostile colleagues had canceled their calls for help. Nor did I need to ask if she had reported any of the prior illegal acts she had witnessed by her brothers in blue. At LAPD your duty was to protect and serve other cops. In CRASH, loyalty was a cult. They expected her to "take it to the box," meaning do whatever it took—including going to prison—to protect CRASH officers' actions. But torture was a line Reidel could not cross. And now she had not only threatened a fellow CRASH officer, she had done so for a "scumbag gangbanger."

Her career at LAPD was over. I struggled with what that said about LAPD corruption. The outlaws who ruled L.A.'s police force would back a sadist torturing a kid over an honest officer. But she was not in my office to save her job; she was there to save her life.

Reidel was a military-trained star, a one-woman demolition machine. She was the perfect officer to lead a class action challenge to LAPD's systemic brutality, discrimination, and retaliation. She loved being a cop—and she was good at it. I couldn't advise her to join the lawsuit if it would destroy her future. She found a safer division and left L.A. soon thereafter for a command-level policing job in another county.

I hated to see anyone with her integrity and talent run out of LAPD, but the xenophobic agency purged many of its best as too honest to be trusted. The Blue Grip went after all cops they suspected would not reliably take it to the box: women, minorities, independent thinkers, intellectuals, homosexuals, Jews, and other "outsiders" who didn't send the right signals of blind loyalty. At that early stage of our campaign to curb police abuse, the best we could do for whistle-blowers like Sergeant Reidel was to help save their lives and, if possible, their careers. If we couldn't help a police officer like her fight LAPD, what chance did a civilian stand? Reidel was one of many brave LAPD challengers, but her story that morning made the enormity of what we had to change clear as Lucite. The battle would require an army of litigators, informants, and challengers, so we set about building it case by class action case. We gradually developed a Serpico squadron of whistle-blowers to spearhead our "infiltration" strategy of class actions by cops. Dozens of fed-up officers eventually risked their careers and endangered themselves in order to challenge the racism, sexism, homophobia, illegal policing, and excessive force that corrupted L.A. policing, enraged blacks, and destroyed public-police trust.

From these dramatic beginnings, I began my fifteen-year fight against police abuse in a pitched crusade that at first we waged in the courts with a small army of the best attorneys in L.A. The twenty-plus police misconduct attorneys included mavens like Hugh Manes, Carol Watson, John Burton, and Sergio Diaz, who had spearheaded the majority of L.A. County cases representing poor and working-class victims of police abuse; Paul Hoffman and Carol Sobel of the ACLU of Southern California; Richard Fajardo of MALDEF; Barry Litt and Mercedes Márquez of Litt & Márquez; Dan Stormer and Barbara Hadsell of Stormer & Hadsell; the great excessive-force expert Sam Paz; the police-dog specialists Donald Cook and Robert Mann; Johnnie Cochran and Associates; Doug Mirell; law professors Erwin Chemerinsky, Gary Williams, and Laurie Levenson. With one phone call, we also could summon help from colleagues in every major U.S. city and from LDF's New York and Washington, D.C., offices.

In the early 1990s, armed with insider guidance, we launched a double-barreled barrage of cases in which teams of lawyers attacked L.A. law enforcement externally and internally. We sued with Cook & Mann, Barry Litt, and Paul Hoffman to end the cruel abuse of LAPD's dogs to illegally maul black and brown teenagers. Bill Lee rallied California's anti-discrimination agency to declare that LAPD operated blatantly racially discriminatory promotions—and then used the finding to ram a class action right up LAPD's center, with its best minority officers banding together. Carol Sobel, Abby Leibman of the California Women's Law Center, Barry Litt, Kathy Spillar of the Feminist Majority, and I masterminded another long-running and painful class action led by Detective Terry Tipton, Sergeant Myrna Lewis, and other LAPD female officers who lost their careers taking on the case that finally ended the systematic mistreatment of women cops who suffered everything from rape at the Police Academy to being ambushed by gang members deployed by male officers to attack them.

We also combined the cases of fifteen Police Misconduct lawyers into a massive federal class action challenging systemic abuses by the county sheriffs who covered the county's other eighty-eight cities outside of L.A. that did not have their own police forces. This juggernaut challenged bad shootings, beatings, and brutal interrogations by a cell of deputies who had donned the tattoos and philosophy of the Vikings, a vigilante cops' group. The Honorable Terry J. Hatter, the federal judge hearing the case, repudiated the deputies' tactics and the absurd claim that they had a First Amendment right to call suspects "niggers." Long before prosecutors used injunctions against gangs, this judge ordered a sweeping injunction against the Los Angeles County Sheriff's Department that made banner headlines and caught the attention of state and federal investigators. Taken together, our docket of cases from 1992 to 1997 became hefty battering rams that inflicted more damage than any single case could. The bottom line was that our strategy had dented police impunity. We had broken the united front. And we were winning. We may not have dented very deeply, but we were definitely no longer dandruff.

Police saw this legal whirlwind as war, and they retaliated with no holds barred. Private information from our officer-clients' personnel files appeared in publications. Our clients were left stranded on the job without requested backup and endangered in other ways, too. Anonymous threats became routine. The Police Protective League, the official rank-and-file police union, attacked our clients in the union magazine. Internal Affairs fomented dozens of unfounded investigations against our clients, and creepy police investigators accosted our clients' children. The sabotage extended to the cases and to us personally. I got thrown bodily out of the Police Protective League headquarters, and in the last years of this long fight, during the 2000 DNC convention, some LAPD riot cops took complete leave of their senses and shot Carol Sobel in the eye with a rubber bullet.

Like a junkie starting a twelve-step program, LAPD had to hit bottom and surrender to a higher power, in this case, the United States Constitution, before it could change its direction 180 degrees and move toward community policing as the Christopher Commission had ordered. The department's day of reckoning would not come until years after the final fallout from the King beating. In the months following that seminal videotape, the first forays had just begun.

In late fall 1991, Kevin Reed barged into my office with a worried look on his face.

"Turn on your television," he ordered. "They're changing venue."

"What?" I snapped on the TV behind my desk.

For months we'd been watching with mounting concern the criminal trial of the officers who had beaten Rodney King. Kevin looked over my shoulder as we heard broadcast journalist Furnell Chapman confirm our fears. "This just in, the Second Court of Appeals has just ordered the King beating trial be moved out of Los Angeles County ..."

This was the second time that defense lawyers for the accused LAPD officers had tried to move the trial out of Los Angeles County. The first judge had said no, but this one had reversed the ruling on the grounds that intense local TV coverage of the beating had tainted the jury pool. There wasn't any place on the planet that hadn't had intense coverage. But that was not the worst part. The judge had picked Ventura County as the new location. Kevin looked at me in disbelief. "What the hell is this moron thinking? Doesn't he know?"

The judge, a former prosecutor, did know. Ventura County's jury pool came from Simi Valley, fifty miles into canyon country north of L.A. The area was predominantly white, conservative, and known as a retirement haven for hundreds of police officers. In Simi Valley, there was no such thing as police misconduct. The odds of conviction had just dropped off a cliff.

Tribal tensions in L.A. had continued to mount. Just that morning, all three black radio stations in the city had rocked with bitter rants over another racially charged case: Soon Ja Du, a Korean shop owner, had just received probation for shooting a black teenage girl she feared might rob her store. Three months earlier, a Pasadena man had received six months in jail for killing a dog. Radio callers had raged: smoke a joint, go to jail; kill a dog, go to jail; but kill a black girl, and you get an award. An ugly backlog of anger was building.

Over the next five months, Kevin and I were never far from a television or radio, catching as much of the King trial as we could. It was not going well. The district attorney's office had hobbled itself by appointing as lead prosecutor a recently transferred lawyer with zero experience in the tough specialty of prosecuting police officers. In contrast, lawyers for the accused officers boasted a combined eighty years of expertise in defending cops accused of brutality and corruption. After weeks of jury selection, the final panel of ten lower-middle-class whites, one Latino, one Filipina, and zero blacks could not have looked less promising for the prosecution. The general public was not yet worried—after all, the videotaped beating was a slam dunk. We knew better.

When testimony began, counsel for the defense doubled down on a counterintuitive and brilliant strategy: Blame King for his own beating. Faced with a devastating videotape and a world-famous victim, the defense aimed to attack and destroy those strengths. With straight faces, they argued that King had caused the extensiveness of his beating by failing to freeze like a corpse when the officers struck and electrocuted him. The defense "demonstrated" how every twitch of King's body in response to the blows looked like an "aggressive-combative" threat that provoked the next blows. By writhing in pain, King had forced the officers to beat him senseless! The defense then proceeded to break the video into harmless, time-coded, soundless pixels repeated so often and so slowly that even I was numbed to the fifty-six strikes of steel batons. By the time they were done, the prone, battered, and unarmed Rodney King had been transformed into a dangerous, hulking black menace, and the twenty-seven armed officers had morphed into paragons of restraint. Why, they'd no choice but to bludgeon and Tase King; indeed, they had saved him from being shot. The video? An optical illusion the jury had to ignore.

I understood enough about Simi Valley to know this absurd defense could work. It played in to every brain-stem fear that white America subconsciously harbored about black men. Meanwhile, the prosecution fumbled away, failing to call any of the horrified white witnesses who had seen the beating and heard officers taunting King. And they never presented the victim, Rodney King. So to the jury, he never became a human being.

On the morning of April 29, 1992, I called in to the office to let Chandra know I'd be drafting a brief at home. Working outside on the peaceful brick patio of my hillside cottage was a luxury I rarely indulged. My "desk," a white wrought-iron patio table, sat under a hot-pink bougainvillea bush and was just big enough to hold the essentials: coffee, gum, phone, legal pads, pens, highlighters, law books, radio—and my cat, Meesh.

The King jury had been deliberating for a nerve-shredding week. What was taking a week? There was nothing good about this. Were they deadlocked or about to deliver a mixed verdict that would satisfy no one? The city was perched on a razor. Every news and radio program buzzed with tense countdowns to the zero hour. This had to be the day the jury came in with its verdict.

It was. At three that afternoon the jury came back, and KNX reporters scrambled to their mikes. I stopped writing, cranked the radio up high, and closed my eyes to listen. The foreman began: "On the first count of assault with a deadly weapon against Officer Stacey Koons, how does the jury find?" "Not guilty." "On the second count of the indictment of assault with a deadly weapon . . . how does the jury find?" "Not guilty." Like baton blows came the rest: *Not guilty. Not guilty. Not guilty. Not guilty. Not guilty. Not guilty. Not guilty. Not guilty.* Ten times with one hung verdict against Laurence Powell for assault.

I thought, *Oh, God, no.* Before the final "not guilty" had come out of the foreman's mouth, I had snatched up my phone. "Chandra, tell everyone to go home now."

She tried to protest, but I cut her off.

"*No!*" I barked. "This is not a discussion. I am *ordering* you and the staff to get out of the office *now.* Get your kids and go straight home, *nowhere else,* fast. Put Bill on. *Now!*" I could tell my tone had shocked her, but she wasn't moving fast enough. Bill also was startled but quickly accepted my verdict: The city was about to burn.

Cop-worshiping Simi Valley had just told black, cop-terrorized South L.A.: "Suck on this for justice." I knew how black L.A. was about to answer back.

Within an hour, helicopter shots of the first fires flashed on the television amid ugly footage of black men dragging a helpless white truck driver named Reginald Denny out of his truck and pummeling him with bricks before black Good Samaritans pulled him to safety. Even more ominous was footage of a screaming crowd ripping up and torching the kiosk in front of LAPD headquarters at Parker Center and of furious rioters bashing in windows of police cruisers to attack cops. I swallowed hard. Rage had erased all fear of armed authority. This was going to be worse than I had feared.

Scanning stations, I watched in bafflement as the looting, beatings, and arson bled wider and wider—west into Culver City, Hollywood, mid-Wilshire, and even Beverly Hills. Where were the damned police? Omnipresent in South L.A. any other time, they were now missing in action. As the fires blazed across the entire L.A. basin from Long Beach to Pacoima, Chief Gates was at a fund-raiser in Beverly Hills, and LAPD commanders were at seminars, attending other fund-raisers, at home in exurbia, or otherwise not responding. The department was ducking the rage of a community it had done its best for decades to torment and provoke.

It took three days for twenty thousand California National Guard soldiers and police to quell the violence, but not before the turmoil had reverberated across the country. Harlem demonstrated en masse. San Francisco rioters shut down the city and its bridges in a state of emergency. In Atlanta, black youth shattered storefronts and attacked bewildered white bystanders. Las Vegas forced Nevada to send in its National Guard. And in Madison, Wisconsin, protesters bashed squad-car windows.

The toll in Los Angeles outmatched all of these cities' combined. Fifty-eight dead, over 2,300 injured, a billion dollars' of property damaged, the Bradley legacy tarnished, and faith in government tattered. It had been the biggest riot in American history. The only silver lining I could see was that LAPD would have to answer for it. And for a minute or two, the politicians would have to pay attention to the poor.

The Rodney King riots and their aftermath were a turning point for me. I was furious with LAPD for its arrogance and cowardice. I was disgusted with white America for its entitled indifference. I was livid at black America for forgetting Martin Luther King Jr., and burning our own communities and attacking non-blacks. I was perturbed at the civil rights establishment's incrementalist failures; in forty years, we had desegregated, affirmative-actioned, and voted our way right back into another police-triggered riot. Last but most of all, I was angry at myself for doing what I knew instead of what was needed. For not heeding the fact that while we did a great job as lawyers, real safety and opportunity in the kill zones could not come from lawsuits alone. It would come from the "radical restructuring" and revolution in everyone's priorities and values that King had warned we'd have to do.

I vowed that the end of my run as a lawyer would not be spent wondering why we had failed to stop the fire next time.

Chapter 8

AMERICAN *FAVELA*

National Guard troops were still patrolling the streets of downtown L.A. when the LDF offices reopened for business on the Monday after the riots. That afternoon Bill Lee, Kevin Reed, Robert Garcia, and I gathered in Bill's office for a conference call with New York. Julius Chambers and LDF's president, Robert Preiskel, were flying out the next day to raise money and to check in with their West Coast lawyers. I sat dumbfounded while our bosses complained that their L.A. office was getting too embroiled in riot-related matters. Bill saw the look on my face and signaled for me to zip it and sit tight while he reasoned with them. I fumed in silence. From Bill's window, I could see a National Guard Humvee rolling slowly down the street. On the phone, Julius was explaining why we needed to focus on our cases and not the riot. I had had enough.

"Julius, with all due respect, that's utter crap," I snapped. I reminded everyone that after the '68 riots in Chicago, Detroit, and L.A., LDF had flown lawyers to every city to bail folks out, file riot-related cases, and help NAACP chapters deal with police commissions. The LDF I knew would never question the relevance of a riot.

My outburst was greeted with dead silence in the room and on the line. I had just accused a civil rights legend of abdicating LDF's vision. Bill looked stricken. Kevin suppressed a grin. Robert nodded in agreement. Glaring at me, Bill took back the phone. "Uh, Julius, nerves out here are still a little raw right now," he said. "Why don't we continue this in person when you get here." He punched us off and swiveled back to me. "Want to tell us what you *really* think, Connie? What the hell was that?"

"The truth," I huffed, getting up and leaving his office. Back at my desk, I pulled out the standing letter of resignation I draft on the first day of every new job.

When our bosses arrived from New York the next day, Julius headed straight for the office of his problem child. He still floundered a little when he talked to me. I was such a strange challenge for him. He had no way of understanding me; women in his world were nothing like me. He had thought carefully about the gauntlet I'd thrown down over the phone and told me he really wanted to know why I felt so strongly. It was sad to see him struggling with something that to me was painfully clear. I gently told him that this was bedrock for me, and that if his view of our role in post-riot recovery held, then this organization was not the LDF I knew or that history celebrated. I would rather resign. Julius raised his eyebrows in surprise, nodded soberly, and left my office for Bill's.

Pained at having to break with a leader he revered and loved, Bill said quietly, "If Connie resigns, I will have to resign as well." Robert agreed, and Kevin, ever the jokester, piped up with "Well, you ain't leavin' me, the only white guy, here alone." Julius lit another cigarette and beckoned the whole staff into the conference room. He looked at us pensively as he smoked and reminisced about harder days long gone. He harkened back to the turmoil of '68 and agreed that LDF had unflinchingly flung itself into post-riot activity then. In his judicious and generous way, he delivered his verdict. He told me to put my resignation letter away.

"You do what you think you need to do out here." In a wistful afterthought, he said, chuckling, "Maybe I've been doing this too long and it's time to hand over the reins to you younger folk." With that, he got up and headed out for a fund-raiser.

In the weeks following the riots, every politician imaginable, from the mayor to President Bush, toured the rubble with bevies of TV cameras in tow. Each vowed things would change. Each pledged investment and renewal. We even had a new city committee to explain how the King riots differed from the Watts riots in 1968. Back then the McCone Commission had warned us to end the "spiral of despair" that fueled inner-city clashes with police. We didn't do it in 1968, and it did not look like we were going to do it in 1992.

In America's hot zones, the spiral of despair had continued. The politicians touring the newest rubble offered no solutions to end the chronic Great Depression–level unemployment of 35 percent, with pockets as high as 60 and 70 percent in the poorest spots. At most, pledges of a Denny's, a Kentucky Fried Chicken, and maybe a supermarket were .5 percent of a solution. We were still trimming the tree, not reaching the roots. The maps of the riot fires that the city's Planning Department prints after each eruption showed that while the Watts fires had burned only in black areas, the King fires had singed Long Beach and the edge of Beverly Hills. My focus had to go beyond the courtroom to end the spiral of despair before another twenty-five years of deprivation ignited the next explosion in our backyards.

A few weeks after our bosses had returned to New York, I pranced into Bill's office to propose that my work should focus on the plight of the underclass. I no longer wanted to spend resources fighting to get a promotion for someone with an Ivy League degree when the poorest of the poor suffered without a job of any kind. It would be an underclass barriers docket. He nodded approval but countered with a bid to blend several goals so that every case addressed underclass inequality and police reform. If we represented middle-class probation officers challenging race discrimination in promotion, the case should also correct the unfair distribution of probation resources

that hurt poor kids in the juvenile prison system. All of our employment discrimination cases should be against police departments and
used to seek police reforms that the community wanted.

I agreed his vision was better. Bill had only one question.

"Now, exactly how are you going to go about developing an
underclass equity docket?" I told him that I would ask the women
in the Watts housing projects what they needed and figure it out
from there. He told me to take Kevin or Robert with me. I pretended to agree but thought that the only thing dumber than my
going to black housing projects alone was to drag a white or Latino
man with me.

I also did not tell him that as the result of a call I'd received from
Mercedes "Mercy" Márquez that morning, I'd be heading for Watts
that afternoon. Mercedes Márquez was the Márquez in the civil
rights law firm Litt & Márquez. She had taken on a tragic wrongful death case for the Zunigas, a Latino family who had lived in the
Jordan Downs housing project in Watts. I knew Mercy from working
with her masterful law partner, Barry Litt. From Barry, I was learning advanced court combat. From Mercy, I was learning new lessons
in audacity and getting into trouble. A feisty spark plug of a woman,
Mercy rolled right over rules, boundaries, and egos. She took no guff
and had no fear. We hit it off instantly. I called her the Mexican Fannie Lou Hamer. She dubbed me the black Frida Kahlo. When she
called that morning, her voice told me it was urgent, and there was
no doubt that I'd be doing what she wanted.

She said we had to go to Jordan Downs and persuade the threatened African-American residents to peacefully coexist with their
new Latino neighbors. *Oh great,* I thought. Mercy, a Chicana, and her
barely black sidekick would be confronting angry black folks over
their alleged mistreatment of Latinos with whom they had absolutely
no intention of sharing their crumbs. She was right. The time to fully
engage L.A.'s housing projects had come.

It was early afternoon when I wheeled my pockmarked Honda
Civic away from the federal court on Spring Street onto the 110
South and zipped down to the East 105, the new freeway that had

cut through working-class and poor black neighborhoods. (Bill Lee had successfully sued the freeway project to score millions of dollars for replacement housing, commercial development, and contracting opportunities for the folks the highway had wiped out.) I found Wilmington Boulevard, and headed down 108th to Grape Street and into the heart of one of the most neglected and violent neighborhoods in Los Angeles.

Jordan Downs is a sprawling thirty-five-acre campus of the same two-story row houses in which my family had lived on at least five different Air Force bases. At first glance, it looked as safe as an air base. Jordan Downs, however, was the epicenter of the Southeast kill zone, the area of Sergeant Reidel's last night in CRASH. It was just emerging from a roiling crack cocaine war that had forced families for months to dodge fusillades of gunshots. I had only newspaper accounts in my head, and no real feel for what it meant to the human beings surviving in that racked complex. I am sure that to the hardworking residents of Watts, who were the vast majority of its denizens, Jordan Downs was a tiny, ugly exception to their historic and beloved neighborhood.

To me, Jordan Downs was an American *favela*. It was not nearly as desperate as the hillside shanty towns of Rio de Janeiro, but it was equally isolated and engulfed in disproportionate poverty and violence. In the early 1990s, James Head, the noted poverty economist, estimated that the area around the project posted an adult male unemployment rate that was double the height of the Great Depression's, and that a whopping 80 percent of the immediately adjacent economy was underground. Of that, 60 percent involved the most accessible "professions" of slinging dope, stealing cars, and peddling guns. Jordan and its nearby sister projects, Nickerson Gardens and Imperial Courts, harbored more guns than a small armory. Over time, I calculated that 60 percent of its male residents had been arrested or incarcerated. The risk of death by homicide in the Jordan Downs area in 1992 was *five hundred* times the risk of homicide in my neighborhood. Seventy-five percent of the older adults in Jordan Downs were functionally illiterate, an illiteracy rate destined for intergenerational eternity given the dismal quality of the local schools. The 1992 Jordan High School graduating class had lost 75 percent of its students after the ninth grade.

Like the *favelas*, it left you flabbergasted that there was no urgency about such extreme conditions. The answer was that we had accepted this litany of catastrophic failure as a reasonable state. We proclaimed universal opportunity, but we left the savage inequalities to become the norm for generation after generation. Despite the recent riots, there would be no rush to change it.

The most baffling fact was that the professional managers of the Jordan Downs complex were not in charge. I had been told that if you wanted to use the Jordan gym, you did not call the managers, you called the head of the local street gang. Jordan, a public housing complex paid for by taxpayers, was controlled by the Grape Street Crips, a black street gang named for the street on the complex's west side. Grape Street was one of the city's then estimated three to four hundred street gangs, with its members a growing part of the county's estimated thirty to forty thousand gang members. Grape Street was among the 1 to 5 percent of hard-core gangs that police considered chronically violent. L.A.'s hard-core gangs were the main reason that Jordan Downs and other gang-controlled hot spots in L.A. suffered high violence and trauma, but the street war to control crack cocaine had turned these poor neighborhoods into shooting galleries and the few gangs in that war into killing machines. But apart from the accelerated violence of the drug war, there was little new about this scene.

Street gangs were as much a part of the American fabric as hot dogs. They were a do-it-yourself vehicle for underclass males who had no access to mainstream jobs, upward mobility, or power. Street gangs differed from prison gangs and organized crime, which in the early nineties were still separate from the streets. Father Greg Boyle, an inspiring Jesuit priest whose mission focused on saving gang-ravaged souls, described street gangs as "disorganized crime," whose hopeless members clung to turf as their identity and yearned for a belonging that their broken families did not provide. At that point, I knew very little about the impact of gangs in what LAPD viewed as a gang zone. That was about to change.

This much I had guessed: The Grape Street Crips must have been the geniuses behind the "no Latinos" policy that Mercy was set on reversing. I also guessed that, just as Latino gangs did not allow black families to move into "their" projects, the black gangs would not allow unknown males of another race to penetrate their territory, never mind take up residence in their fortress. In their world, Latinos may as well have been invading extraterrestrials. The Crips had turned on the new arrivals in a campaign of abuse that approached ethnic cleansing. But it was the horrific attack on the Zuniga family that forced Mercy and Barry into federal court and me into joining her in Jordan Downs. What happened to the Zuniga family would never cease to haunt all three of us.

In 1991 Juan Zuniga had moved his extended family into a gray-and-blue two-story Jordan housing unit on 102nd Street. The sixty-five-year-old patriarch, his seventy-eight-year-old mother, Margarita Hernandez, his wife, Guadalupe, and their children and grandchildren had joined the growing minority of Latino families, which by then made up 20 percent of the tenants in Jordan Downs. Juan Zuniga was apprehensive about moving into a historically black complex, but he was grateful to have won the keys to habitable and affordable housing. He could ignore the racial taunts and hostile stares from a few resentful black residents. But he could not fend off repeated demands from the drug dealers and gang members who had taken over the family's stoop to deal drugs. And over six months he made repeated requests for an emergency transfer for safety reasons.

The Housing Authority denied the requests.

After a heated Friday-afternoon confrontation with the drug dealers that ended with direct death threats, Guadalupe Zuniga begged a HACLA employee for an immediate emergency transfer for her family to move that weekend. At six the next morning, thugs poured gasoline through their mail slot, lit a match, and torched the unit. The accelerant roared into flames that reached 1,200 degrees and trapped the Zunigas in their bedrooms. Several black neighbors rushed into the inferno to pull some of the children out. A panicked Juan Zuniga mistook rescuer Gregory Moore as an attacker and shot him by mistake.

The blaze killed five members of the family: Twenty-two-year-old Martha Zuniga perished with her two children, five-year-old Juan Lopez and four-year-old Claudia Zuniga. Margarita Hernandez had tucked her two-year-old great-grandchild, Veronica Lopez, between her legs to shield the baby from the flames, and died trying to protect her. The baby girl was taken to the hospital but died on the Monday following the fire.

Mercy and I were sick. The eventual convictions and life sentences for the thugs who had murdered the family did nothing to lessen the anguish. The Zunigas had died because HACLA had failed to transfer the family away from imminent danger; failed to provide livable and safe premises for its black, Latino, and other residents; and endangered all racially isolated residents.

Mercedes and Barry Litt had filed on behalf of the Zunigas a wrongful death, emotional distress, and violation of civil rights case. They later won at the appellate level, establishing a new duty for public landlords to reasonably protect tenants from criminals who used the premises and regularly assaulted tenants. The court found that HACLA's callous and systematic disregard for the safety of its residents could amount to a civil rights violation. Mercy and Barry won a $1.3 million settlement for the family, but conditions did not materially improve for racially isolated families in L.A.'s gang-controlled public housing complexes.

A year later, the Hazards, a Latino gang that ran the Latino-dominated Ramona Gardens public housing project, firebombed and severely injured the handful of black families who remained there. Mercedes, Barry, and I filed a class action against HACLA on behalf of all racially isolated minorities who were tormented, threatened, and assaulted by the dominant racial group and gang of that housing complex. After six years, the case would result in a settlement and consent decree but no real change on the ground. Black families struggle to live safely in Ramona Gardens and Latino families struggle to feel safe in Jordan to this day.

There would be no deal or sentence that could purge the crime or our failure to push sooner and harder for safer conditions and more professional HACLA staff who would protect residents instead of endangering them. Helping Mercy that day was not a choice. It was an imperative. Cross-tribe violence in a multiracial city like L.A. had to be stopped one way or another.

I parked my car outside a large structure on the western edge of the Jordan Downs complex. It was the Grape Street gymnasium. Mercedes was standing near the double doors on the side of the building. I locked the car and headed in her direction.

"What kind of getup is that?" She laughed. She was smirking at my outfit, a tailored knit suit, pearls, and sling-back pumps. "You're drowning in more pearls than Barbara Bush."

This was vintage Mercy ribbing. I ignored her. We pushed through the steel double doors. Inside the gym was a large group of women and girls seated in four double rows of folding chairs with an aisle down the middle. Mercy led the way to the front of the group. She stopped to shake the hand of an older African-American woman. The woman nodded and Mercy took the floor. She introduced herself and me and went straight into explaining that we were civil right lawyers who needed their help in defusing Latino-black tensions and getting post-riot recovery for the complex.

"Jordan has been home for many of you and your families for years, and I know that if new folks I didn't know started moving into my home, I would find it unsettling," she said. "But I would try to find out if the strangers are good folk, and I'd welcome them. You are seeing new folks, Latinos—my people—moving in, and we need your help in making them a part of life here in Jordan."

Silence. Their eyes were hard and unreceptive. I moved to stand next to Mercy.

They allowed her to continue uninterrupted as she pleaded for cooperation that could yield benefits for everyone who lived in the complex. When she suggested that all groups experienced tension when a new group moved in and that blacks and Latinos had to share the complex and protect each other's rights, a middle-aged woman jumped up and yelled that they didn't have any tensions with anybody who was supposed to be there and demanded that we explain what the hell we were talking about.

The other women clapped and amened.

Mercy, refusing to back down, respectfully disagreed with the woman, who then jabbed her finger in our faces and hissed that "Mex'cans ain't got no rights here." I tapped Mercy on the elbow and tried my hand at interceding. I got no further than reintroducing myself as an NAACP Legal Defense Fund lawyer, whereupon another heavy-jowled woman sitting in front exploded out of her seat.

"NACCP, ma' ass! You light, bright, damn-near-white BITCH," she yelled, slapping the air for dramatic effect. "Where the *fuck* was you when they gunned down both of ma' sons in a gutter? Where the *fuck* was you when the bullets was flying through our walls so bad we had to put our babies to bed in the damn bathtub? TELL ME, MISS HIGH YELLA—WHERE THE FUCK *WAS* YOU?"

She twirled around, stomped her foot, and thrust her face into mine. Later I would learn her name was Mrs. Tolliver. When she finished and the amen choir quieted down, I looked at my interrogator—and potential client—and calmly said the only thing a light, bright, damn-near-white bitch in a St. John's suit could say.

"Yes, ma'am. You're right. The NAACP has abandoned you. You have a right to be angry at all of us who've left you in a war zone with no help. But I am here now. You can tell me how to help or you can tell me to leave. It's up to you."

Mercy, wisely opting out of this intrafamily color-caste spat, was standing very still at my side. I noted two young men hanging on the lip of the side doors, watching and listening. I counted seconds and kept my eyes peeled for signs of agitation. The women, rumbling among themselves, seemed to be mulling over my offer. After a minute or two, the queen bee in this hive, Mrs. Tolliver signaled for a younger woman to respond. The woman, draped in a lovely African shawl, stood and began rocking side to side.

"The only way for you to help us right now is to help our men," she pleaded, not in anger but in grief and desperation. The shootings had become absolutely unbearable. She begged me to help with the cease-fire negotiations between the warring gangs that were taking place nearby. Anguish contorted her face. Her despair lanced right through me. I was watching a discarded woman who could no longer tolerate the intolerable. The riots had been one expression of that point, and her cry to quell the violence, a second.

The others grumbled their agreement, and Mrs. Tolliver, angry eyes averted, nodded her assent. A hundred stupid questions I could not ask flashed through my mind. Exactly how did I help men with guns stop their mindless shooting sprees? Would they accept my help? Or shoot me on sight? How do gangs fighting over drug turf cease firing at one another? Why should anyone help these paragons of Western civilization?

Instead, I inarticulately asked, "How—where are they?"

"Out back of Markham, in that trailer near the tracks." She was referring to the nearby junior high school.

There it was, the unexpected turn of events. I had come to help the women. But their needs were overrun by the problems of the men. For the moment these women just wanted their men to dial back the violence.

I had my mission of marginal improvement.

Mercy and I left the gym, grateful to find our cars intact. We paused near hers and caught our breath.

"That went well," I snapped.

"Okay, Miss High Yella, where the fuck *were* you . . ." I shot her a warning look, but she could not resist. "Shit, they're pissed. They should be. If you NAACP people hadn't left them behind in a shooting gallery . . ." She saw the daggers in my eyes and ended her fun.

We agreed to come back soon with another strategy to halt the cross-racial attacks. Cross-racial mayhem anywhere in L.A. posed a mega-threat. We had too many tribes to indulge ethnic cleansing.

Only a biracial team could tackle it. Eventually, we'd pair terrorized Latinos in Jordan Downs, headed by leaders such as Arturo Ybarra, with equally terrorized blacks in Ramona Gardens, led by the Watts Health Foundation, and sue the Housing Authority for failing to protect its racially isolated minorities. While the suit proceeded, we would have to find immediate protections. On top of everything, I'd promised to dive into the middle of a gang cease-fire.

"I'll call you later this week," Mercy continued. "And chica," she added, lowering herself into the driver's seat, "stay away from those damned men of theirs. You are *loca* if you put yourself in the middle of that gang-truce shit. Go home."

She gunned her engine and shot down Grape Street. I waved her off. Turning back toward the gym, I stopped a passing kid and asked him to show me the bungalow behind Markham Middle School. He looked at me quizzically and told me to follow him.

He left me in front of a corrugated plastic trailer squatting on the back edge of some tarmac. Male voices filtered through the trailer door. Light seeped between the small slats that passed for windows, along with smoke from cigarettes and blunts. I stepped closer and knocked. Silence. I pounded again, harder. The door cracked open. A tall man in sagging pants, a wife-beater undershirt, and a red bandanna tied around his head poked it through the opening. He fixed heavy-lidded eyes on me and frowned. I must have looked ridiculous, standing there suited in pearls and pumps with a briefcase. That probably paled in comparison to how stupid I must have sounded.

"Hi, my name is Connie Rice. I'm a lawyer with the Legal Defense Fund," I announced, careful to leave off NAACP. "I was told you could use some help."

Without a word, he shut the door in my face. *Strike two,* I thought. First the women and now the men. But I could hear voices rumbling behind the door, so I waited. A minute later, the door swung wide open. The trailer was filled wall to wall with gangsters, their heads, necks, and biceps wrapped in red and blue bandannas, like flags. On the left side of the room, red bandannas, as I would soon learn, adorned Bounty Hunter Bloods, the gang from Nickerson Gardens. On the right, blue bandannas decorated Jordan's Grape Street Crips, and one man on each side sported a combined blue and red scarf tied in a cross-colors band around his biceps. The faces ranged in age from mid-teens to early middle age, in hue from black to lighter brown. No "high yellow" here. The visages were granite-hard, the eyes cold, the vibe leaden. All eyes had turned toward the intruder. Me.

Anyone with an ounce of wits about them would have left. My wits, however, had been overwhelmed by my curiosity. I wasn't afraid—more like excited, with every instinct on edge, somewhat like I felt on death row. The tall man in the white tank who had shut the door in my face nodded for me to repeat what I'd said to him. From the doorway, I broadcast my voice to the room.

"My name is Connie Rice. I'm a civil rights lawyer with the Legal Defense Fund. I was told that you are trying to carry out a truce to reduce the cross-colors shootings. I'm here to see if there's any way I can help."

A few frowned. Others exchanged looks of bemusement or disbelief. Most kept their stone masks intact, showing no reaction. But from the Crips side, a short, stocky man built like a barrel leaned in closer to the door. "You a lawyer, right?"

"Yes."

"Can you get us that agreement between the Arabs and the Jews?"

I pressed the surprise out of my voice and responded obtusely, "Would you be referring to the Israeli-Egyptian Sinai peace accords?"

"Yeah. Them." He had no idea what I was talking about but had replied as he should have to my pinheaded educational correctness. The precise title of the treaty was not important, but the big idea was.

"Yeah," he explained, "if the Jews and Arabs can work it out, then we can, too."

I swallowed my elitist wonder. "Yes . . . I can get you a copy of that accord. Anything else?"

A blue-bandanna man with forearms thicker than my waist piped up, "Yeah. Can you stop LAPD from bustin' up our games?"

"Games?" I repeated cluelessly.

A man in the back explained that they used midnight basketball games to enforce cooperation among the younger toughs and would soon need full tournaments as the truce took effect. "We put rivals on the same team and make 'em play."

I put that one off. "Tell me more about that when I come back with the treaty, and maybe I can figure it out." Never overpromise.

They shut the door. I took that to mean our introductory session was over. I had begun to walk back to my car when the bungalow door reopened. "Miss Rice, Miss Rice!" A tree trunk of a man with a perfect bald head was loping after me. He caught up, extended his muscle-bound arm, and introduced himself.

"I'm Fred Williams," he said, a tiny bit out of breath. "Just wanted to welcome you." He whipped out a business card before continuing. "This is my bungalow." He cocked his head over his shoulder at the school property behind us. "I run the Cross Colours Foundation from here. I'm leading these truce enforcement talks, so when you're ready with the treaty, call me before you head down and I'll meet you." He paused, looking at something behind me. "Now follow me. Let me get you to your car."

Fred moved with a big man's bulky grace, like the linemen who glide their heft across the football field. He was about thirty-five, stood a few inches under six feet, and seemed to pack all two hundred pounds of it into muscle-popping arms, shoulders, and legs. His face was a stunning blend of African and Indian beauty. Flawless red-brown skin, a broad hooked nose, and chiseled Cherokee cheekbones struck so high that their flinty ridges seemed to set right under his angled ebony eyes. Added to his physical prowess was a sublime confidence, making for a show-stopping physical presence. It was his manner, however, that held my interest. He had the same physique and style of the other men, but he spoke standard English and fluently used middle-class mannerisms that most of the others could not mimic if their lives depended on it. I suspected that Fred was a man of canny EQ who operated fluidly across worlds—*un bandido sin fronteras.*

Like much in the ghetto, Fred Williams was not entirely what he said or seemed. In a world where physical strength means power and deception means survival, Williams appeared to be a master of his environment. His introduction seemed riddled with illusion. And his genteel overtures to me bristled with ulterior intent. He claimed school property as "his bungalow." He was "leading" the negotiations but had not been free to welcome me earlier in front of his flint-edged colleagues. And gangsters don't have "foundations" or brandish business cards. Was he a bona fide gangster, a poseur, or one of the few who had truly stopped banging?

No matter. There would be time enough to figure him out. At that moment I was relieved to see someone like him in the mix. This clueless tourist had found a guide. Besides, he must have had even more skeptical questions about me, starting with what in the hell was a BAP doing wandering around Watts in pearls, pumps, and a suit?

Fred led me through a shortcut to the front of the school. When we reached my car, he opened the door for me. When I thanked him, he demurred.

"No, thank *you* . . . for comin' down here," he said. "Things are still on edge from the rebellion. But you know, things are always popping off around here. By the way, we know who you are. You're from Thurgood Marshall's group. You're the lawyers—not the damned NAACP." He looked around, signaled to someone I couldn't see, and shut my door. "My crew will lead you out. Drive safe. Remember to call me before you come back down—whenever you're ready."

I didn't know ten black professionals who could tell the difference between LDF and the NAACP, but this genteel gangster could. Before I could get the car in gear, Fred's convoy surrounded my car, and we snaked out of Jordan Downs in an ostentatious procession. As I drove, the exhilaration of entering another world flowed over me, and my gut tingled with satisfaction that I'd linked to something important. This American *favela* was where I needed to be. I hit the 110 North and headed for the county law library to get a copy of the agreement between the Arabs and the Jews.

Upon my return the next day, Sinai accords in hand, Fred "The Gentleman" Williams met me with a posse of Crips, assigned a detail to guard my car, and flamboyantly instructed that no one was to get near me without his say-so. He ushered me into the bunker to present the treaty. After going over it briefly, I handed them the document and left them to their negotiations.

I learned quickly that Fred was not a fake ex-gangster. He had ardent opponents, but no poseur would have been allowed to operate the bungalow or command the loyalty of the younger men in his "crew."

Fred had explained that the Crips-Bloods truce had been hammered out earlier by OG's in meetings right before the King verdict. The older "original gangsters" were men determined to rein in the wildness of younger gangbangers. They had the clout to commit their sets to an agreement. I was never privy to those meetings but sat in on segments of the ongoing breakout sessions that Fred held. These proved educational enough.

The blue- and red-flagged truce leaders I had glimpsed in the trailer were the hardest of the hard core. I guessed that 85 percent of them had seriously considered committing murder, and a smaller subset had commissioned or done it. I reached that staggering calculation after sitting through two surreal sessions of negotiations in which Fred's breakout team debated bylaws for murder that would be taken to a larger meeting. Had their back-and-forth been captured for a Harvard seminar, it would have had a ponderous title like "Comparative Killing Paradigms of the Sicilian, Samurai, Genghis Khan, Sun Tzu, and Centurion Eras," or "The Rules, Regulations, and Relative Merits of Strategic Homicide." Unfortunately, the debate in that bungalow was no academic exercise. By the end of the afternoon, they had merged a range of constraints into one set of tentative rules that I bet myself would last six days before getting violated. From the notes I jotted down in my car, out of their view, they ran something like this:

No drive-by shootings if children were present. No women should be killed. No cross-color killing for gang initiations. No hits on Latino gangs if they stayed in their territory. No killing for refusal to join. No killings stemming from prison fights without express sanction from top shot-callers. No hits ordered for violating the no-killing rules except by order of top shot-callers. No hits ordered for violating the cross-colors truce without agreement and order of top shot-callers. No targeting cops. And finally, kill only when absolutely necessary and according to an escalating scale that included a system for warnings—unless, of course, it was a snitch, in which case the killing could be instant.

Who knew murder was so intricate? And for the love of Mary, what was I, an officer of the court, doing listening to a roomful of gangsters debate a code for killing one another? At the time it seemed the lesser of many evils, and helping them continue to reduce the killing of innocent bystanders was what the women and children of Jordan Downs needed. The cease-fire was not altruism at work. A few OGs were worried that their children, who had also become gang members, would get shot. Other men wanted stability for their drug dealing and to restrain the wild-ass shootings by sloppy youngsters who seemed to kill everyone but the intended target. Whatever their intent, I had absolutely zero business listening to those discussions or interacting with these gang members in any way that validated their dealings. However, abruptly leaving the room could have posed its own, more dire danger.

I could see why the women of Jordan had asked me to help these guys. Their temporary cease-fire had substantially reduced the crazy level of shootings. It was not safe by any means, but it was better. Strangely, the main menace I felt walking back to my car was from the LAPD cops watching us in their squad cars. I could not tell if they were my LAPD allies or the legions of foes, so I assumed the latter.

Back at the office, Kevin read me the riot act.

"Let me get this straight," he began as he untangled rubber tubing from his aquarium, "you drove down to Watts, *crashed* a gangster confab—"

"It was a truce negotiation," I corrected. We were in his office two days after my third foray into Watts. He was cleaning his fish tank.

"Crashed a *gangster summit*," he persisted, "and waltzed into a trailer of convicted felons. What were you smoking?"

"Well, I'm not going to learn what people need sitting downtown—"

"You're not going to learn dead, either."

There wasn't any way to convince Kevin, Bill, or Robert that with Fred's protection I was probably safer in Watts than in our Olive Street parking lot. There also was no way to explain to my colleagues why plunging headfirst into gangland was the best way of figuring out how to help L.A.'s war-ravaged underclass. But my gut said it was, and in those post-riot days, I was following my gut, not my head. Acting like cerebral lawyers—conducting research or waiting for clients to come in the door—would not reach the trustless, discarded people who had just torched this city. The wounded women of Jordan Downs had told me exactly what they first needed: an end to the violence. Besides, it was too late to talk me out of it. From the ashes of the riots, my journey into L.A.'s underworld, the realm of invisible power not taught at Harvard, had already begun.

Chapter 9

LADY LAWYER

"Yo! Lady Lawyer!"

"Insane," a fifteen-year-old Crip with a lisp, had cornered me on the tarmac as I approached the Markham bungalow. After three months of working with Fred, I had seen the free haircuts, school supplies, bags of groceries, and other basics that his off-the-books Cross Colours Common Ground Foundation distributed to Jordan's families. I had joined in the tutoring, chess games, television watching, and counseling that made up the after-school activities for kids in the bungalow.

Very few of the men and teenage boys who worked with Fred's Cross Colours Foundation, mostly ex- and current Grape Street Crips, would speak to me directly, but they were beginning to accept my presence. Insane, who had no such inhibitions, had appointed himself as my roving ambassador to the younger teens. After I had mangled my own introduction and left a group of kids looking puzzled and uneasy, Insane had jumped in and eased their doubts by quipping, "Yo, Connie white—but she down."

Translation: "Look, I know Connie looks and talks strangely—like a white lady—and in our world she may as well *be* a white lady, but she's here to help us, so accept her." His ebonically efficient praise had saved the day.

"Yes, Insane?" I was still choking on my decision to use their street names—"Killer," "Mad Dog," "T-Bone," "Glock," "AK." But I was truly grateful for the name the younger bangers had chosen for me. In that female-phobic world, "Lady Lawyer" was a rare honorific title.

"You gonna get us our money from Cross Colors Clothing that stoled our work?"

I told Insane to hold tight and reassured him that we were taking care of it—legally.

I had dissuaded some angry members of Grape Street from going after some businessmen Fred believed had ripped off his clothing designs. Whether true or not, the owners of a company called Cross Colors Clothing had foolishly left Fred and his crew feeling that their logos and designs for urban street clothes had been taken and sold for a big sum of money that the company was not sharing with Fred. Since it was my suggestion that Fred settle the score through the legal system instead of their street system, I had to make sure it worked. I called Molly Munger, a partner at the Fried Frank law firm and our co-counsel in a lawsuit we had filed against a big Orange County developer for refusing to rent to mixed-race couples.

Molly, a graduate of Harvard Law School and one of the first women in L.A. to make partner at a big downtown law firm, was one of the few people I thought capable of helping Fred. She was sharp, wise, and uncommonly at ease in racial thickets, though I wondered if current and former gangsters would be a bit much even for her. I needn't have worried. When I explained that Fred, a former shot-caller for the Grape Street Crips, needed his intellectual property protected, she did not hesitate. She cleared the way for her white-shoe firm to do the case for free, and we had set our first meeting with her that day. Not sure they'd find the right skyscraper in downtown's confused tangle, I drove down to pick up Fred, Black, his right-hand man, and a young street kid named Molotov.

When we entered the marble lobby, the security guards took one look at Fred's bald-headed gangster gait, steroid build, and baggy pants and tumbled out from behind their desk to halt our entrance. I assured them we had an appointment. They believed not a word and ordered a rattled guard onto the elevator to "escort" us. Fred and Black stood as close to the terrified little man as they could, towering over him and forcing him to engage in small talk. His hands and right leg trembled all the way up. When the elevator doors mercifully closed him off, they busted up in laughter. I shook my head at both the guards' overreaction and Fred's predatory racial intimidation.

We waited for Molly in the reception area. Fred was unimpressed. Black and Molotov wryly ribbed each other over the artwork but seemed genuinely thrilled with the panoramic view of the city. Like little kids, they darted back and forth across the glass panes, identifying landmarks and neighborhoods.

In my fifteen weeks of being around him, Black—so named for his ink-dark skin—had remained flat and unreadable. From what I could tell, he was the stealth shot-caller who was making the Watts gang truce stick, running a skillful team of influentials who conducted Kissingerian street-shuttle diplomacy. They looped through key streets and houses to quell conflicts, tamp down the trigger-happy, and calm the chaos seekers. Black had the rare status of cross-hood cred, credibility within the Crips and sufficient respect from Bloods for both to heed him. I suspected that this special respect came from his close adherence to gang codes, his steadfastness, and an ability to carry out serious violence when required. It was the kind of thing you did not ask about if you wanted to continue being an observer. Guarded and quiet, Black let Fred do the talking while he absorbed and observed. He clearly had not made up his mind about me but, out of loyalty to Fred, was holding his objections for now. Molotov was a young kid whom Fred and Black had in protective custody from a hit order that they assured me would not follow us to the elegant offices of Fried Frank.

What was I doing?

Before I had time to work through that question, Molly glided into the foyer. She had finished a trial a few days before but looked none the worse for wear. As I hugged her hello, the sun filtered behind her, set her hair aglow, and caused her mother-of-pearl skin to seem to radiate light. Black, genuinely startled, jumped back from her and blurted, "She's so bright!"

My friend, who resembled a cross between Catherine Deneuve and Michelle Pfeiffer, often left people mesmerized, but nothing like Black's reaction. He had never met anyone who looked like Molly, and her incandescence had thrown him. She barely paused at his confusion and laughed warmly. I quickly introduced him using his street name.

"Hello, Black," she said, rolling off his name as if it were John. "I'm Molly Munger. It's so good to meet you. And," turning to Fred, "you must be Mr. Williams—Connie has told me about your work in Watts. It's such a pleasure to finally meet you. And who is this young man?"

I introduced Molotov, who was firmly and sullenly fixated on the floor, obviously wishing he could disappear into it. Molly ushered us down the hall and, in a move that endeared her to me forever, circled the floor, introducing her new clients to her dumbfounded colleagues as if Fred and Black were CEOs of a Fortune 500 corporation. We retired to a conference room and hammered out a plan to reverse the alleged transgressions against Fred's creative team. When the company settled with Fred, he and his crews saw that legal tactics could work for folks from his neighborhood and that at least a few elites at Molly's level were willing to help.

Fred's gang truce work had introduced me to a small corner of Watts's gang realm. The glimpses of that world showed us that the gap between gangland and our world was bigger than Molly or I had imagined. It was more than a gap; it was parallel universes.

We lived the code of patrician privilege in the lap of safety. They lived the code of Darwinian desperadoes in a war zone. Our norms would get us killed in gangland, and theirs *did* get them killed, everywhere. The main link between our worlds was a dangerous delusion: that the safety of ours could be ensured by the containment of violence and deprivation in theirs. This was the deal with the devil that almost destroyed Northern Ireland and apartheid South Africa. In 1992, mainstream Los Angeles had no idea it harbored the same delusion and was incubating an extreme subculture of violence in its backyard.

In the months following the April 1992 Rodney King riots, I glimpsed the best and worst of Watts in the microcosm of Jordan Downs. I saw how discarded families fought for decency amid devastating adversity. How many with little to their own names shared what they had. I saw parents desperately trying to shelter their kids from the overwhelming power of the street. And how a few of the violent tried to redeem themselves by shielding their former victims from the toxic destruction.

I also saw how the violent tyranny of some gangs went way beyond destroying individuals to corrupting the entire human ecosystem. My path through Fred's netherworld had lifted the curtain on the deadly conditions that hid individual misconduct, fueled the cult of gangs, seeded the culture of violence, and reinforced the deadly dynamics of the kill zone.

In six months of accompanying them as they worked, I sat in living rooms, listening to Black and other street ambassadors talk twitchy young men with guns into dropping hits, respecting the truce, and playing the midnight basketball tournaments with rivals. I stood like a scarecrow on the sidelines of the gym at eleven o'clock at night to repel hostile officers from LAPD who would retreat upon seeing my suit and briefcase. In more than one home, I forced myself to sit still as mice ran over my pumps and kept silent as johns filed in and out of bedrooms behind us. None of that bothered me as much as the guns. It seemed like everyone owned one, including children. As I followed Fred on street patrol one night, we stumbled onto two U-Haul trucks full of enough semi-automatic weapons to start a war, leaving me wondering how many huge gun caches escaped detection by ATF and local police. I later discovered Crips burying bins of weapons around the complex so that the incessant police stops would not find them illegally armed. No amount of logic dislodged Fred's belief that "the man" had delivered the weapons and drugs into Watts.

It was from street excursions and encounters that I gleaned a little of what made Fred's world turn. I learned from listening to conversations in the Cross Colours bungalow and from complaints of neighborhood women who didn't trust Fred or his penchant for dating much younger women. I learned from watching Black's skilled street moves. Most of what I learned came from what Fred showed me. I had no way of ever knowing Fred's whole story. But of some things I was sure.

Fred, like many I met, was smart. Had he received a passable secondary education, he could have completed a four-year degree at almost any college. He had been steeped in the values of his grandmother and the black church and could read. But his father had left, and as things at home became difficult, at age nine, Fred began escaping to be with the only men he saw with money, power, status, women, and cars—the Grape Street Crips. After years of gangbanging that included time for a murder allegedly committed during his teens, something snapped, and he broke from the Crips and began striving to recover a measure of his humanity. I never probed but guessed that, like many gang members who reached twenty-five, he simply started to use his upper lobes and outgrew gang life. In a magazine interview in the early 1990s, he revealed, "Something hit me that's still burning in me today. I wanted people to recognize me as someone positive. During my new birth of consciousness, I took a look at some of the little fellows and said, no, not them." At their age, Fred had chosen to join Grape Street and a life of crime. Now he was doing what he could to keep them from making that mistake and to keep himself free from the chemical addictions that bedeviled his self-rehabilitation.

In the five years we worked with each other, Fred and I relied on the bounded formality of professionals. He would not have called me a friend. Friendship required trust that neither of us had. He could not trust himself. And I lowered my inner drawbridges for no one. But in the mission of shielding the kids of Jordan Downs from violence and getting them to stay in school, he could call me a reliable stranger, perhaps even an ally.

Despite the professionalism, there were a few moments of mutual vulnerability that were enough for him to see beyond my armor and for me to see beneath his mask. We had wept over the senseless deaths of kids who had died for stepping on someone's shoes, looking at someone the wrong way, or giving the wrong answer to the dreaded gang question "Where you from?" I could count these moments on one hand, rare glimpses of his heart that let me see the abandoned son yearning for the mastery of manhood that his father never taught, the wisdom that his father never revealed, and the love and protection that his father never bestowed. For want of a good father, Fred had lost his way. Now he shielded not only his kids but also Latino residents, at one point planting his body between a Latino family and their attackers in a vivid confrontation caught by an *L.A. Times* photographer in 1993.* In gangland, any impulse to protect, rescue, or atone had as much chance as a candle flickering in a storm. Fred's dedication to all three was, in that world, extraordinary.

Black, by contrast, had never been near the mainstream. He was even smarter than Fred, though he had none of the grounding. Black came from a gang family with four generations in that public housing project. To his surprise, I guessed correctly that his clan had descended from a Mississippi mega-plantation. In everything from his speech and color to his family's brokenness, the vestiges of that extreme isolation were manifest 140 years later. Fred told me that when Black was seven, LAPD swept every adult out of the house into a wagon and left the terrified youngster alone with his eighteen-month-old brother. After four days, Black, hungry and scared, wandered out with the baby to find food and clean diapers. A store manager caught him changing the baby in the diaper aisle and called County Child Services. By the time he reached junior

---

*To view the photo, please visit www.powerconcedesnothing.com.

high school, Black did not need to join Grape Street; he had been born Grape Street. Making his way through multiple stints in L.A.'s juvenile prisons, he was fulfilling his family's tradition as much as my going to college fulfilled mine. The gang was his family. His family was the gang. Jordan and the neighborhood were his world. These were the things for which he would kill and be killed. But with all of this, from Black, at age twenty, I never saw anything but his selfless dedication to the truce and to keeping the younger kids safe.

In the end, Black would stay connected to me much longer than Fred did. In fifteen years of interaction, however, we had only one genuine conversation. It was years later, during the two-hour drive home from the state prison in San Luis Obispo. I picked him up after a stupid eighteen-month stretch that he got for missing one meeting with his lazy parole officer. The first thing he wanted was a Big Mac. Sitting in McDonald's, I pleaded with him to leave Watts and Grape Street's malignance, which would surely land him back in prison. He said he would not survive if he had to leave the only people and place he knew. He ordered more food to go, and we left. Before I backed the car out of its space, Black touched my arm for a rare direct look into my face. He needed me to understand something. I stopped the car. Other than Jordan Downs, he said, prison was the only place he felt that he belonged. In a quieter voice, he added that he expected, sooner than later, to die near Jordan—or in prison. After six years of hearing it, this abject resignation to early death should have lost its punch. It hadn't. I swallowed the lump in my throat and slipped the rap cassette he'd been waiting to hear into the tape deck. We rode in silence, to a hip-hop beat, back to Grape Street.

In 2004 Black was sentenced to twenty-five years to life in federal prison for getting stopped in someone else's car that had a gun in the glove compartment. His past convictions and gang status had transformed a low-level felony into a life sentence.

Over time, it became clear that a majority of men from the violent hard-core set lived similarly hounded lives. If it had been possible to do so safely, most would have traded their mean lives for a saner existence in a second.

Under their masks of callous indifference, many secretly longed for exit ramps out of gang life. But they feared the price of leaving more than the price of staying. Shown those exit ramps, they needed help in order to take them, the kind of all-encompassing help that only a few like Brenda Shockley of Community Build and Father Greg Boyle gave homeboys and *veteranos* trying to leave *la vida loca*.

More extraordinary than any of gangland's dynamics was how the vast majority of residents in that complex and that neighborhood, longing to live normal lives, strained to avoid gangs, dodged the violence, and stayed clear of the police. Most of the parents in Watts and L.A.'s other barrios, like my mother's parents, got up every day, worked hard, sent their kids to school, and came home without shooting or robbing anyone. They rejected gangs and strived to get the basic job of living done with as much dignity as possible in a place where life's basics were much harder to attain than they should have been. Most in Watts strongly rejected the gang mentality but felt powerless to stop its reign of madness.

It was no exaggeration to call what had happened during the worst of the crack wars madness. It was madness to have to sleep on the floor or in a bathtub to avoid a nightly fusillade of bullets. It was madness for 60 percent of kids at Markham to report witnessing a shooting, beating, or dead body. It was madness the day a group of third-graders pushed me inside a house because they recognized that a zigzagging car searching for a target was about to do a drive-by shooting. It was madness in the late '80s when LAPD tried to put a police kiosk inside Jordan Downs and Grape Street blew it up with a bomb. It was madness to accept 50 percent unemployment—the same as Yemen's—or a 25 percent high school graduation rate as normal. It was madness to accept gang control of public property—parks, schools, and housing projects like Jordan Downs, Nickerson Gardens, and Imperial Courts. But we had. Worst of all was the immoral conclusion that as long as the madness stayed "down there," as long as it was only Black's family dying, we would never summon the political will to end it. We were all insane.

What had created this? Over the years I asked this question and found many answers, none of which explained it all. Gangs are the Blowback Mountain of hopelessness, craven criminality, ruptured fatherhood, isolation, and casual emasculation. There is no question that the adult men and women who chose gang life were responsible for the destruction they inflicted. The kids are a different matter. Most are fleeing from abandonment, abuse, or other trauma. Many have no choice.

The explanations pointed to the solutions, but after years of seeing their victims and watching so many gang members end up in coffins or cages, I know nothing justifies the predatory cult of gangs. Self-defense to survive is one thing; but the malignant masculinity that rules through brutality and operates through group banditry and intimidation—never.

I also understand that poverty does not cause gang violence any more than it does terrorism. But it makes a great petri dish in which violence hides and the violent thrive. Even though the number of hard-core violent gangs was a tiny 3 percent of all gangs, their impact on the larger community of normal people was huge. During the twenty-five years since the late 1970s, in the area around these three housing projects, LAPD's South Bureau racked up over eight thousand *unsolved* murders. Most of them were gang-related. The community so mistrusted the police that they would not cooperate in investigations, and the police either endangered or could not protect the few witnesses who were willing to testify.

Eight thousand unsolved murders mean that *everyone knows you can get away with murder.* If you can get away with murder, there is no law. There is no order. There is no Constitution. And there is no freedom from violence—the first rule of civilization—and no right to safety—the first civil right.

Through Fred and his team, I gained access to a narrow band of gangland in Watts—a small subset of the Grape Street Crips. They let me glimpse enough of their world to get from me what they needed. I returned enough to remain in their orbit and useful to their violence-control efforts. But even with time in Fred's world,

I would learn to read only its outer contours. There would be no touching the soul of his world, not for the likes of me. They showed me just enough to admire the steadfast striving of the average residents. Just enough to sense a tiny bit of the overwhelming tragedy. And just enough to see that those of us thriving on the safe side of the thin blue line were doing nothing to end the madness of the kill zone.

After I'd spent about ten months of regularly going down to help Fred in the bungalow and Jordan, he and others began to call me for help with the street trauma that filled his nights. After a while, my car seemed to find its own way down to the emergency room. I went not just to help intercept shooting victims and avert retaliation shootings but also to check on the truce stats. The Watts truce may have temporarily reduced the cross-colors Bloods-Crips shootings, but every other kind of shooting flourished, and gangsters and cops both had reasons to lie about the effectiveness of the truce. Emergency personnel who categorized each shooting as either intra-gang, rival gang, domestic attack, or accident did not lie. In that first year, the ER numbers confirmed that cross-colors gang shootings were down substantially and staying down. According to the *Los Angeles Times,* there were twenty-four gang-related killings in South L.A. between May and August 1992, and only seven involving Crips-Blood rivalries, down from fifty-two killings, thirty-one of them cross-color, during the same period the previous year.

Reduced shootings in one category did nothing to loosen the toxic traction of the gang mind-set and its relentless bent for self-destruction. When one of the younger Crips got shot for the third time, I stood at the foot of his hospital bed and angrily demanded to know if he was trying to die. He glared at me and then spat out self-hatred so virulent that it hurt my heart.

"Yeah, I'm committin' suicide by homicide," he retorted. "I fuckin' kill anyone who fuckin' reminds me of myself. Like that!" He finished by flashing the sign for death with his bandaged hands.

Again in the hospital, when one youngster I really wanted to save got shot a second time, I begged him to leave the streets. In desperation, I guaranteed him any legitimate job he had ever desired. His eyes brightened at my offer, and for a moment his hardened mask softened into a kid's eager visage, and he replied there *was* one job he had dreamed of having: "I always wanted to work that machine at McDonald's—the one with the pictures on it." My heart sank. His dream was the cash register at McDonald's, which the company had to change from numbers to pictures because employees could neither read nor add well enough. It should not have shaken me. He was almost illiterate. Other than gangbanging, what else did he ever see that seemed within his reach?

When a twenty-year-old shot-caller proudly reported that he had impregnated yet another girl, I lost it in a rant about kids he couldn't support that ended with the rude suggestion that he learn "to put a sock on it." Stung, he looked away. He struggled for a moment, groping for words to respond. Before I could soften the blow, he quietly retorted that in my world, birth control may make sense, but not in his: He probably was going to be dead in a few years, and his five kids would be "all I'll have to prove that I was ever even here." I shut my eyes against the pain. It was my turn to be stung. Two years later, his words would rip through me like a chain saw when Fred called to tell me that he had died in a gun battle. Other than the lives he had destroyed, his offspring were indeed his entire legacy.

These incidents were minor compared to the double play of tragedies that would transform me. And when they did, the course of my life changed once again.

Chapter 10

EPIPHANY

One afternoon in early 1993, Fred, who had begun to rely on my observations, asked me to attend a meeting that would showcase the absolute worst from his world. It took place at the only neighborhood "restaurant" at the time, a second-floor walk-up with a makeshift kitchen of fryer pans, toasters, gingham-covered tables, and white plastic chairs. Fred had reluctantly agreed to the meeting with some gang members who had begun grumbling about his growing clout in the neighborhood and chafing at the confines of the truce. He thought the session might soothe things, but his edgy demeanor told me he was ready for it to become testy. He had never brought me to such a meeting; it was a new sign of trust.

We walked upstairs to the makeshift café. Six Blood Bounty Hunters, the gang that dominated Nickerson Gardens, huddled at a table in the back corner. I did not know many Bloods. For my own well-being, the Bloods I met were solely at the behest of Fred or members of Grape Street. Fred approached his rivals guardedly. He coldly introduced me to each of the men but not to the tiny boy with cropped curlicue hair, golden-brown skin, and huge brown eyes who was hovering behind them. Distracted by the child, I heard none of their names, all of them street monikers. Their suppressed smirks pricked my unease as they pushed the little boy forward.

"Pygmy, step up to the lady," the biggest of the seated men ordered. Fred, not expecting the child, was frowning and edged closer to me.

Pygmy (not his real moniker) squeezed out from between their plastic chairs. I pegged his age at an underdeveloped ten. But his stunted appearance was not what set off my alarms. It was his face. His eyes had no light. He looked straight through me with no affect at all.

The men snickered some more. Their cruelty dripped between every snort. Whatever joke was brewing, I knew it would not be funny.

"Tell the lady what you do for a livin'." The big man pushed him closer toward me. The child looked at him for direction. "Go on."

Pygmy turned back to face me and flatlined, "I kill."

My spine went cold. The six chortled a chorus of approving "yeahs," accompanied by fisted high fives. "He's our l'il assassin, ain't you, Pygmy?" said a lanky Bounty Hunter with a pocked face and scarred neck. The hair on the back of my own neck was, at this point, standing straight up.

"See," the pocked Blood expanded, "Pygmy do the job and go to juvi. Leave us free."

A nine-year-old assassin? These assholes actually thought it was cool to use a baby as a shield? If they had really twisted this child into a killer and then been stupid enough to showcase him to me, they had made a serious mistake. Fred, alarmed by my rising ire, looked sick, but he was in flight-or-fight mode, one eye on me and the other on them. I ignored his flashing eyes warning me to stand down and honed in on the child.

"Pygmy, I am glad to meet you." I smoothly approached, stooping down to his level. "My name is Connie. I need you to help me understand something about what you just told me. What do you mean by 'kill'? You don't mean people, do you?" Pygmy looked to his handler, who nodded permission for him to respond.

"Yeah. I kill people—who they tell me." Indicating the satanic six behind him.

"I see. Thank you for clarifying that. Now, do you mind telling me *how* you kill people?"

This conversation should not even have been possible, never mind necessary. As damaging as it was, I had to determine the extent of the child abuse—or to find out if it was just another hoax being played on Fred's clueless high-yellow lawyer.

Unsure where the exchange was headed, and slightly unnerved by my determined tone, Pygmy's patrons had stopped their bemused banter and were glancing warily at one another. *Good,* I thought. *They're squirming.*

Pygmy, not sure if he should say more, looked up seeking their orders, but I slipped myself between him and them and raised myself up a little higher so I was all he could see. Fred, now openly frowning, slowly moved over to my new position.

"Don't worry, they wanted me to know what you do," I pushed, "and they are proud of how well you do it, aren't they? So, if it's your job, tell me a little of how you do it."

Pygmy swallowed hard and licked his chapped lips. No one else offered him water, and he refused mine.

The tiny boy shook his head and tried again to see his handlers but gave up and looked straight at me. He fixed his leaden eyes somewhere beyond us, took a breath, and in a bloodless monotone, described how they—the older men—pointed out or showed him a picture of the mark, positioned him to lie in wait or walk up on or ride a bike to the target; how, beforehand, he chose a gun and the best ammo, how he handled and concealed the gun, how he aimed and "popped 'em," and if he had time, fired again, looked for witnesses, and then ran or rode away to a place where his patrons waited. They then ditched the weapon and hid him until the "heat" cooled. When he finished speaking, Pygmy stood very still, waiting for his next command. I stayed just as still and held his eyes for a long fifteen seconds before touching his arm in silent acknowledgment.

This was no hoax. He knew too much about setups, too much about guns, too much about where to aim, just too damn much about killing. But it was his soulless eyes that bared the truth. Pygmy the child had died with his targets. I was talking to a child soldier.

My mind reeled. How had we allowed sociopaths to twist a child into a robotic killer? What kind of toxic indifference had spawned this outrage? It should not have been possible—not *anywhere* in the richest country the planet has ever known.

Fred, restraining his own revulsion, kept his eyes steady on the six men and the guns they surely had strapped somewhere on their bodies. Pygmy retreated behind their plastic chairs and stood like a tin cutout. I tried to focus. I needed his real name, his address, his parents' names. But the Bloods had become agitated. My reaction to their obscene display had rattled them. The tension ticked upward. Fred, clear that the intended business was no longer possible, began mumbling excuses and nonsense about needing to get back downtown. As he firmly pulled me back by the elbow, I roiled inside over the cost of demanding that Pygmy leave with us. Fred shot a warning glare at me and yanked my arm, almost dragging me away. We backed our way to the stairs and descended.

On the street, out of range from the building, I whirled around to confront Fred. He was fuming, but the fear in his eyes was over me. I was white-hot with anger and in a dangerous state of mind he had never seen. He tried to bring me back down. "Connie, please calm down, you can't—"

"Shut up," I cut him off, ignoring his stunned look. He was about to find out how rage unleashed my imperial streak. "What's that boy's real name, and where does he live?" I demanded icily. Fred mumbled that he did not think Pygmy had another name. He had a shaky expression, one that said, "Oh, shit, what's she gonna do now?" I did not know whether he was lying. Nor had I decided whether his revulsion had been for what had happened or that I had found out one of the things he so carefully concealed from outsiders like me. Fresh out of trust for Fred, I ordered him to find out the information and stormed off for my car.

My dented Honda screeched to a stop four blocks west in front of the Housing Authority office. I marched into the lobby and made a beeline for the pay phone. The number I dialed was on a mangled piece of paper taped to an inside pocket of my briefcase. LAPD Captain Ben Hannity (not his real name) at Southeast Division answered his direct line, but before I could get out a single sentence of tirade, he interrupted me and demanded, "Where are you calling from?" I told him. He barked that the housing office was infiltrated with dozens of Grape Street family members and ordered me to hang up and head for our meeting place near my office, a tacky little hole in the wall that served bad Chinese food.

The captain was one of five white LAPD officers and the only one of command rank, among my most valuable blue angels. Hannity had come up in LAPD a strapping Irish Catholic, true blue, a good ole boy, but had made the mistake of getting a midlife master's degree in urban sociology. It had completely changed him. I knew none of this when, shortly after the riots, he phoned me and identified himself as a white LAPD command officer. He had called to apologize for the King beating, lament the riot, and offer clandestine help. He had not called from a pay phone. He had not whispered. At the time, I thought his offer was a prank, but I took his number anyway. A few weeks later, I dialed it, and we began a covert conversation that had yet to end. At this early point in our relationship, I had no more reason to trust him than I did Fred, but Hannity was the only one who understood enough about the dangers and to whom I could turn for help and uncork without triggering more repercussions.

He had beaten me to the empty restaurant. He stood and waved me over to his table against the back wall. Two glasses of water, chopsticks, and a teapot with teacups set the table. He had poured himself a cup of oolong.

"What did I tell you?" he scolded as he pulled out a chair for me, his gun holster creaking with the movement. He detested my venture into gangland, had reamed me about it over the phone, but had resigned himself to keeping a close eye on my Watts activities. Too upset to sit, I paced back and forth in front of the table and unloaded everything I'd had to repress while with Fred. I excoriated the mindless machismo, the brain stem violence, the lemming loyalty, the stupid self-destruction, the congenital male deficits in upper-lobe activity—and built to a ballistic, profanity-laden explosion over my exchange with Pygmy. I stomped to a stop in front of Hannity and commanded him to immediately open a top-priority investigation into Pygmy's situation. Glancing at the unnerved waitress edging away from our table, Hannity calmly stood up, physically sat me in the chair, and made me drink some water.

"Now breathe," he ordered. I inhaled and drank some more. "Feel better?" he asked. Unsure he wasn't mocking me, I started to rise up, but he waved me back down. "What the hell did you expect?" he demanded. "Boystown? I know what you're trying to do, but dammit, you're tangling with the worst, Connie, and you don't know what the hell you're doing—"

I slammed my fist to the table. "I don't give a shit what you think of what I'm doing," I hissed at him. "This is America—Americans don't let children die. I want that kid protected, and I want those sons of bitches who twisted him gone for good. That's your fucking job. *Do it.*"

Hannity's back stiffened. He had never seen me bent on doing real damage. But the smile that crept around his mouth said he liked it. That was enough for me: I ordered him to personally conduct the investigation, protect Pygmy, and criminally go after the satanic six.

"Anything else, Your Highness?" he cracked. I shook my head no, but refused to retract anything about the way I had just issued four orders to an LAPD captain. Calmer, I sat back, smiled slightly at him, and conceded a thank-you. Hannity would do most of what I'd asked.

I thought he would get up and leave at that point, but to my surprise, he poured me some tea, called over the bug-eyed waitress, ordered some egg rolls, Kung Pao chicken, and an extra plate. A full meal was a new milestone on our jagged journey.

At the restaurant door, he gripped my shoulders to ensure that I was listening. "Okay, Wonder Woman, it's time to listen to the white guy. For now Grape Street is allowing Fred Williams to operate. So as long as he's on the wagon, he's your best bet to stay safe, but under *no* circumstances do you go when he's not there. And watch out for Graveyard; don't get near them."

"Graveyard" were the late-night cops who, like CRASH, were notorious for vigilante mind-sets and insubordination. Like Sergeant Reidel, Hannity worried as much about Graveyard as he did the gangsters. It was more unwelcome confirmation that the good guys in LAPD were not in charge. Hannity reached in his shirt pocket and handed me another piece of paper. "Here's my home number. Call me if you get in trouble. And for God's sake, limit your time down there at night." Now *he* was ordering.

A week later, Hannity met me again to report what he had found. His ruddy face looked tired and troubled. He hadn't found anyone who had seen Pygmy in the last week. The boy seemed to have disappeared. Hannity had discovered several youngsters with the same street name, but one story he'd heard seemed to fit the kid I'd seen. None of it was confirmable, but according to housing project lore, shortly after Pygmy was born, both of his parents had been arrested and imprisoned. In those days LAPD regularly rounded up the adults in a household and left the children at home alone without telling County Child Services—it wasn't their job. There was no record of Pygmy's birth or of the county ever coming to get him. No one seemed to remember if he had a real name. The tiny boy had been passed among relatives, all gang members. When they disappeared to prison or the cemetery, he got handed around some more.

On top of everything else, was Pygmy a feral child? My stomach roiled with fear that the gangsters had either moved him out of the county or worse. I was sick with guilt for not overriding Fred and snatching Pygmy away from his tormentors that day in the restaurant, even though it could have gotten all three of us gunned down. On the verge of tears, I asked Hannity to keep looking and to pump all of Southeast's arrestees for information about him. The captain agreed and then touched my arm. "Connie, this is not your fault. They often remove child surrogates who pose any real threat of turning on them." He meant to help, but that was not the thing to say to me at that moment. I lost it. My hand shot to my mouth to stifle my howl of anguish, but nothing could stop the burst of tears. He stayed with me until I regained my composure and then left to head back south to his command.

Against Hannity's orders, I resumed looking for Pygmy.

Back at Fred's bungalow a few days later, I pressed him to tell me if there were other "l'il assassins" out there. My cross-examination of Pygmy in front of Fred's armed opponents had rattled Fred, but he seemed as angry about Pygmy as I was. My earlier doubts about the source of his rage evaporated. Fred had flaws, but he fought to protect kids and had pushed hard to make the older gangsters lay off all kids sixteen and under. I began by asking him a stupid question. "Fred, what choice do the younger ones have about joining Grape Street or Bounty Hunters?" I asked, ignoring the middle-schoolers milling around. "I mean, can they say no? What happens if a kid tells the recruiters, 'No, I won't join'?"

Fred started talking to some teens at a checkers table, appearing to ignore my question, but I could tell he was deciding whether to answer honestly or to spin it. He barked some orders to Black about the drill team's practice schedule and dispatched Molotov and Insane to the campus office for more supplies. Five minutes later, he cleared everyone else out of the bunker. We were alone, and he dropped his game face.

"The answer is, in a lot of 'hoods, it depends on the gang. I chose to bang. No one forced me. But here in Jordan, Nick, and Imperial, it ain't about a choice . . ." He paused, frowned, and began chewing his lip. Shaking his head, he sighed and resumed. "I wasn't ever going to let anyone like you see this, but . . . if you really want to know, you should see it. So let me show you what their choice is."

He retrieved a VHS tape from a locked drawer and walked over to the television. As it cued, Fred teed up the story. "Crip recruiters had checked a fourteen-year-old boy a few months ago; cornered him in a school bathroom and ordered him to join Grape Street. He tried explaining that his mother wouldn't let him, that he was a church kid who just wanted to play baseball and go to the Boys and Girls Club. They came back for him the next day. He told them no again. The third day the recruiters handed him this tape."

The screen flickered on. The grainy black-and-white video brought flashbacks of the King video, but this would make the King beating look like a Disney trailer. The screams of a girl were the first sounds, followed by grunting. The camera caught the back of a man's bobbing head and her contorted, screaming face. He was raping her. He got up, and other male arms held her down as another pulled his pants down, took his place, and began raping her anew. By the third man, her screams had become guttural whelps and howls. The tape had another four minutes of more gangsters raping the child, but Fred saw that I could not watch beyond the third and turned it off. Tears streamed down his face. The girl was the little sister of the fourteen-year-old who had just said no.

"There were seven of them altogether. They made her brother watch this tape and told him that the next time he said no, they would rape his little sister again—and then kill her. He joined that day."

I got up, stumbled down the bungalow steps, and vomited.

The triumph of excruciating evil was roaring in my ears. We—all of us—had left a helpless eleven-year-old girl, a hapless fourteen-year-old boy, and tiny Pygmy in the malevolent hands of predators. In this kind of abyss, the questions quickly sink into the obscene: How many thugs can violate an eleven-year-old before she dies? How long does it take a fourteen-year-old to destroy himself for triggering his baby sister's gang rape? How many killings can a nine-year-old do before losing his soul? What civilization locks kids into a basement run by fiends?

But that afternoon the question blaring loudest in my head was: *Where the hell was I when these children needed a wall between them and these monsters?* They should have had to kill me first before reaching a single kid. They should have had to mow down a whole army of good people before reaching the little ones. There was nothing that could excuse my leaving children in such conditions. Nothing.

Child soldiers, warlords, rape as a weapon, epidemic violence, ethnic cleansing, human trafficking, rule of the gun—Serbia? Sicily? Mogadishu? The Congo? No. Someone needed to tell Hollywood's celebrity ambassadors that every third-world atrocity they could want to engage was all right in their backyards, in the kill zones of L.A.

After I'd met a nine-year-old assassin and viewed that hideous tape, my mind stalled. Not just over the utter horror of what had befallen them and the fire-ravaged Zuniga family but also over my own blindness. I had failed to detect these kids, never mind save them. The appalling threat of rampant violence had snagged my attention, but not so the dangers of isolation and abandonment. And not yet the other threats in their ecosystem, especially the failed schools we pretended were improving.

To reboot, I retreated for a few days to the Hollywood Reservoir, my hidden refuge tucked in the folds of fir-cloaked hills, where daily I race-walked to think and keep sane. It was time for another internal come-to-Jesus meeting.

Where was the "fierce urgency of now" that King died demanding? I demanded of myself as my sneakers pounded around and around the jade-green water. As civil rights lawyers, we had failed to declare an emergency—no, *bellow* a war cry—that safety and education must happen now. Without safety, there *are* no other civil rights. Without freedom from violence, there *are* no other freedoms. And without viable education, there is no self-determination—and no way up. Without these, the lifelines of the twenty-first century, liberty's promise is a lie. A lie we enabled with gestures of charity, court victories that delivered partial remedies, and pilot programs that offered them the illusion of opportunity and us the delusion of decency.

After ten miles, the anguish receded and clarity slowly set in. We felt no urgency because the people who mattered were safe. We saw no emergency because Pygmy was not our child. It was not about facts or law or morality. It was about power: the political will to extend basic opportunity to their communities. And it was about the moral courage to face the fact that we had written the poorest of the poor out of the American script.

As I sorted through the shattered shards of my soul, the way forward emerged.

Ending this epidemic of violence—and the conditions that spawned it—had to become job one. In Fred's world, I had touched too many children marked for two kinds of death: the death delivered by gun-wielding thugs, and the "death at an early age"[14] delivered in the classrooms of our worst schools. Pygmy, the Zunigas, and the unnamed kids linked to that gang-rape tape (whom I decided to call the Jackson kids because they needed to have a name) had died from both. Our unconscionable comfort with their destruction had to end. Our tacit tolerance of their disappearance down the greased chutes of dropout factory schools and into prisons or joblessness had to end. These failures doomed their well-being and that of our nation. In our poorest neighborhoods, both were happening on a massive scale.

From the start of this venture, my lens on Fred's world had been distorted by extremes. I had packed the shootings, ER visits, and other crises into intense and totally unrepresentative epiphanies. While most children in Watts struggled to grow in the depleted soil of poverty, few suffered the extreme plights of Pygmy, the Jackson kids, or the Zunigas. But nothing about my skewed view changed this bottom line: Twisting children into assassins, gang-raping them, and killing them with impunity should not be remote possibilities anywhere. Period.

These atrocious traumas stemmed from a spectrum of individual, cultural, and institutional failures. It was easy to blame the tiny number of gang parents, but the multitudes who tout civility yet glorify predators share that blame. From Wall Street's Gordon Gekko to the Godfather, our prurient worship of violent power belies King's values. It also undercuts essential efforts by families, schools, and religious groups to seed a healthier culture. Beyond individual responsibility, we failed to fix the schools. And our failure to make viable jobs more common than jail cells destroyed far more families than gangs. If the entire community of Watts were gang-free and behaved like paragons of virtue, there would still be too few jobs, too few good schools, and too little before- and after-school care for kids to thrive.

In Watts I was seeing the results of our collective failure to heed King's most important command: to put out the fires of inequity raging in our basement. Well, for forty years, smoke jumpers like us had been fighting the fires of entrenched inequality in courts and legislatures. Guess what? Becoming firefighters was not enough.

The destruction of the Jacksons and the Zunigas happened in spite of major legal, legislative, cultural, and political progress since King's death. It happened in a city led for eighteen years by an African-American mayor and in school districts run by my friends. Those of us luxuriating in the American penthouse could no longer hear the despair of our poorest children or challenge our friends on their behalf.

This much I knew: The death of opportunity and the spiral of downward mobility in hot zones are not only bad, they are dangerous—the kindling for riots and growth hormone for gangs, both of which eventually will reach those of us thriving in the safe zones.

When Martin Luther King Jr. set out to save America's burning house, he did not intend that Watts become Bel Air, just that for those willing to climb out of the cellar, there be a staircase, and that children like Pygmy not suffer conditions so dangerous they cannot survive or learn.

We failed to heed King's warning then. And we failed to heed it after the Watts riots in 1965 when the McCone Commission called on us to end the "spiral of despair": the vortex of hopelessness seeded by joblessness, education malpractice, cultural disintegration, and political isolation that aggravated tensions with the police. Instead of reversing the spiral of despair with viable neighborhoods, L.A. built skyscrapers, golf courses, and mini-malls, while the Crips and Bloods built a spiral of destruction.

Almost thirty years later, the riots triggered by police abuse of Rodney King had left swaths of South Central Los Angeles in rubble, and it looked like the city would sleep through this wake-up call, too.

As I wrestled with what had happened to Pygmy, the Zunigas, and the Jackson children, I could see the city's limp response to the riots unfolding. If the biggest race riot in American history hadn't galvanized Los Angeles to end the spiral of despair, what would?

L.A.'s inertia did not excuse my obligation to end what had doomed these kids.

From where I stood, transforming Watts was nowhere in sight, but the path to securing basic safety for its kids was. Such a mission would not be accomplished primarily through Fred and his gang workers: No one in power followed ex-gangsters, no matter how noble they had become. While I wished that our fractured allies in the civic and faith-based sectors commanded the strategic clout needed for long-term strategies, reality said otherwise. Term-limited politicians also ignored demands for long-term solutions that exceeded their short-term election cycles.

But no politician ignores a police chief. Given the absence of an effective progressive political movement or enough savvy grass-roots organizers, this mission would have to be accomplished in part by harnessing the unrivaled political clout of police. LAPD and the sheriffs had sufficient power to force "musical chairs" politicians and feckless school leaders to face the crisis and stick with the long-term fixes. In L.A.'s spinally challenged political culture, police backing would be essential. With it, we could clear the way for ending the spiral of despair, to turn what *is* into what *should be*.

Circling the Hollywood Reservoir that week did not give me all of the answers. Far from it. But my rounds clarified the vision. And it horrified me. We had more chance of winning the lottery than winning LAPD cooperation. In the city's mounting power struggle with the Blue Grip since the riots, the department seemed to double down on defiance. Especially after June 1992, when voters, in their only response to the King beating, slapped the first term limits on the chief of police and installed the inspector general as LAPD watch-dog. The only reason I dared to imagine harnessing police power was that I had seen the determined goodness of our police clients and blue angels. And the only reason I dared to feel certain that was the right strategy was because Martin Luther King Jr. had said "the place to start . . . is . . . especially [with] community police relations."[15] If the good cops defeated the Graveyard cops in the battle for LAPD's soul, the strategy stood a chance.

I reached the reservoir gates and laughed. In two days we would be filing our next lawsuit against LAPD. The only partnership we had with LAPD was as dueling gladiators in court. Even there, we would win most of the fights, but we seemed to lose the contest for LAPD's soul. I was about to get two very dramatic out-of-court lessons in just how far we had to go, the first of which happened in the countdown to the second Rodney King court verdicts.

Chapter 11

GOOD FRIDAY

Within weeks of the April 1992 state court acquittals of the four officers charged with illegally beating Rodney King, federal prosecutors had slapped them with federal criminal civil rights indictments. Almost a year later, the federal jury was nearing a decision. This time, with the trial held in downtown Los Angeles, guilty verdicts stood a better chance, but LAPD was taking no chances. Bitter about accusations that it had been AWOL during the first post-verdict riots, the department was determined not to get caught with its badge down again. In response to a provisional notice that the jury might be approaching the end of its deliberations, LAPD had prematurely issued a verdict countdown alert, canceling vacations and pre-positioning police to crush any post-verdict upheaval.

It was late on April 9, 1993, Good Friday, and most of the LDF office had emptied out. I was still at my desk when my phone rang.

"Lady Lawyer?" From that honorific title, I knew he had to be Grape Street. And this had to be serious. They never called me at my office during the day.

"Yes. Who is this?"

The caller told me not to mind who it was. He was calling to sound the alarm. In the countdown to the verdict, he reported, cops were acting "crazy," riding four strong, brandishing rifles out cruiser windows and blocking off 108th Street with concrete barriers near LAPD's fortress-like Southeast Division headquarters. The caller continued his ominous description: officers in riot gear masks, tape covering their name tags, and snipers on the roof of the station, all of which, he concluded, signaled to him a conspiracy by LAPD to use the countdown as cover for rounding up Grape Street and killing them. He ended with a warning: "You need to tell the police that we ain't fittin' to go down like that—there's gonna be a lot of dead cops if they come up in here. A whole *lotta* dead cops, 'cause we jess ain't goin' down without no fight."

Snipers, blockades, roundups, rifles—I scribbled as fast as the pen would go. I asked him who had told him all of this.

"Ain't no one *tole* me nothin'," he retorted. "I *seen* it maself. Jess tell 'em—stop this shit or they gonna die." He hung up.

I dialed Hannity. "Just got a heads-up from Grape Street," I told him. "They think you're prepping for war with them. Say you've got riot gear, face shields, street barriers, roof snipers—what's going on?"

Hannity sighed. "Parker Center ordered us into emergency countdown, top alert, and full riot gear. We got reports that gang members were going to bomb the station, so we put snipers on the roofs."

For a moment I was speechless. "Captain—you're kidding. *Bomb* the station? With what? Crop dusters? Ben, this isn't Colombia, at least not yet. They don't have airpower! What are you doing? You're panicking them. You're about to trigger the very thing you're trying to avoid."

I paused to calm my voice. Men stop listening when they hear the "girl voice," the tone of high-pitched, escalating plaint. I could hear Hannity straining to listen.

"Let's back up for a minute," I continued in a steadier, lower pitch. "What plans do you have for the Easter barbecues this weekend? Have you talked to Fred Williams or other community leaders?"

Hannity asked slowly, "What barbecues?"

He had forgotten it was Easter weekend, when the parks filled with families, many gang-related, for big cookouts. Riot-pumped cops and groups of tatted-up black men with fires—an inauspicious combo for any weekend and a disaster-in-waiting for this one.

"I'm coming down—now," I announced. "You are meeting with Fred. Order your officers to let me past the barriers—and tell them not to shoot me."

I tossed the phone into its cradle, reached Fred, and then raced out the door. I had to get both sides to stand down.

On 108th Street, nameless officers behind face shields stopped me at the barriers, but not for long. Via radio, they confirmed their captain's orders to let me through, and I crawled slowly through the barricade. I glanced up; snipers with scope rifles were indeed on the roof. Whipping my tin can of a car into the watch commander's parking space, I got out and marched into Southeast Division. Fred arrived, bristling alertness, his bald head, boxer's build, and baggy pants triggering anxious looks from the officers behind the front desk. Fred shot me a look that said, "Dammit, I'm only doing this for you." Despite his discomfort, he showed Hannity his best—level-headed and full of street intelligence. He laid out the panic caused by police preparations and told Hannity that he could help calm the situation if the cops stood down. Frowning, Hannity weighed Fred's credibility and his words. He had to be considering that not only would he disobey Parker Center, he'd be riding shotgun with an ex-gangster and a civil rights lawyer who sued his department every chance she got. Fred, sensing Hannity's dilemma, offered up his own in commiseration. "Look, man, this ain't good for neither of us, just for the community and your officers."

That did it. Hannity extended his hand to Fred. "Okay, let's go get this done right." They exchanged numbers, drew up a to-do list, and we fanned out to complete our tasks.

Hannity removed the snipers, ordered his officers out of riot gear, put the name tags back on, unbarricaded the street, and reassigned everyone to foot patrols over the weekend, excluding all new academy grads whose only exposure to black people had been *The Cosby Show*. Fred communicated the stand-down to Grape Street and Nickerson and got them to pull back on their counterattack preparations. Beginning that evening, Fred took the captain and a few of the more enlightened patrol officers to each park, introduced them to everyone they ran into, and later escorted the officers to the family barbecues—the exact kind of community interaction the Christopher Commission had recommended but LAPD had tossed into a bonfire. In the end, everyone came through. I watched Hannity and Fred operate like old vaudeville partners on joint foot patrols, schmoozing the neighbors and the cops into a calm cooperation.

The verdicts came in a week later, announced quietly on Saturday morning, April 17, and they triggered nothing but relief: Koons and Powell were found guilty on all counts of criminally violating Rodney King's civil rights. With that, a few of the twenty-seven cops responsible for the brutal beating of Rodney King finally would pay some kind of price.

The rest of Easter weekend passed without incident, thanks to an exhausted Hannity and Williams. I chuckled at the unlikely duo and the macho bickering they needed to mask their mutual if grudging respect. But I had to shake my head. If not for the dumb luck of Grape Street's phone call to a meddlesome civil rights lawyer, a dedicated ex-gangster, and a risk-taking captain, LAPD had been well on its way to detonating another public-police blowup. The safety of the country's second-largest city once again had been imperiled by intemperate police action, and had been saved by quickly flipping to the community policing that the department had flatly rejected. At least now we knew what it looked like when it worked. The first glimmer of partnership with LAPD had peeked through.

The following Tuesday I smiled at one of my phone messages, an anonymous four-word missive: "Thanks. I owe you." Hannity did not owe me. Almost another year would pass before I again took up his standing offer of help, and got my second and most harrowing lesson in how far we had to go in winning the war for LAPD's soul.

Never did that goal seem more unattainable than the night I saw firsthand confirmation that the gangsters brandishing guns were not the only predators roving the streets of hot zones. A few wore badges.

It was early morning on a moonless night and I was sound asleep when the phone rang. On the second ring, my eyes dragged open and squinted at the red numbers on the clock. A bleary three A.M. bled through the darkness. Barring the Nobel Committee or a drunk telemarketer in Japan, nothing good ever came from a three A.M. phone call. I sat up to jog my brain into gear. *Has to be another shooting. Who was it this time?*

"Hello?" I moaned.

"Connie, Connie . . . It's Fred."

He sounded anxious but not injured. At least this time it wasn't Fred.

"Fred . . . what's wrong?"

"I really need you to do something. I mean, I hate to pull you into this, but really, you *have* to do this."

He seemed to realize that his stumblingly ominous opening was not the way to begin a request at three in the morning. He took a breath and hit restart. He asked if I remembered a shooting about a year ago in which a young Crip had killed a fifteen-year-old pregnant bystander and then fled from the police. I did. Fred explained that Jamal (not his real name), the shooter, wanted to turn himself in to LAPD.

"Good for him," I said. "What do you need me for?"

I wasn't exactly awake, but Fred wasn't making sense. Jamal was a surrendering homicide fugitive. Given their sky-high pile of unsolved murders, LAPD should have been throwing a red-carpet parade for him. Was Fred back on crack?

"Nah, nah, Connie, you don't understand," he countered. Stammering slightly, he explained that if I didn't escort Jamal into the station, the cops on Graveyard shift would shoot him dead in the street before he could turn himself in.

Now I was awake. Though Fred was not high, I still wasn't buying it. "What in the hell are you talking about?"

"No, no, li-listen, Connie," he pleaded. "Jamal has a fifty-thousand-dollar warrant out on him. He k-killed two people in a wild shoot-out. He's got no support in the community 'cause he killed that girl. He escaped from LAPD and, like the fool he is, shot at the police while fleeing. I'm *telling* you, LAPD—Graveyard—don't let shooters like that make it to the station."

My dearth of synaptic activity at three in the morning did not explain my difficulty in processing what Fred was saying. Even though I knew there were cops who endangered officers they viewed as traitors or threats, I still resisted an ex-gangster's charge that LAPD had death squads. This was not Guatemala. Nor were we in backwoods Mississippi.

"Fred, where are you?"

"At the phone booth across from Jordan."

"Give me the number. I'll call you back. I need to check something out. If I don't call within fifteen minutes, call me back." I made sure he had enough change for another call and fumbled for a pen and a piece of paper. Fred hung up. I threw on a robe and slippers and headed for the kitchen to fetch another number from my briefcase. I dialed. It was 3:20 in the morning.

"Yeah?" a groggy baritone growled.

"Ben?"

"Who is this?" He was not happy.

"Captain, it's Connie . . . Rice. I'm sorry to wake you, but—"

"Where are you?" He had snapped awake.

"Home."

"Oh." He sounded relieved. He must have imagined me calling from somewhere in Southeast.

"Fred just called. He's trying to bring in a homicide fugitive. But he's insisting that *I* bring him in to keep Graveyard from hunting him down. I told Fred that was absurd—I mean, he can't be right, but he sounded so convinced—I just wanted to—"

He interrupted my incoherence. "How much is on the warrant?"

Why had he asked that?

"Uh—fifty thousand," I replied.

"How many did he kill?"

"Two, including a pregnant teenager."

"Can he claim support from politicos or respected local leaders?"

Had Hannity been on the same line with Fred and me?

"No . . . but—"

"When he fled, did he shoot at LAPD?"

I felt my stomach dropping. "Yes," I mumbled.

Silence. For what felt like minutes, Hannity said absolutely nothing.

"Ben?"

"You had better bring him in."

My spine went cold. There was no mistaking what he had said. A captain of the LAPD had just confirmed his awareness of execution squads. I stared into the darkness.

The phone rang. I jumped. When had I hung it up? Fred! I had forgotten he was waiting.

"Hello?" I answered.

It was Hannity. He did not elaborate on our earlier exchange. He just said, "On second thought, I had better bring both of you in." Before I could respond, he barked instructions.

"I'll meet you at your office in one hour. Tell Fred to get Jamal out of South Bureau and up to your office. Tell him to move fast—but not too fast." He hung up.

My descent into shock would have to wait. I reached Fred at his pay phone and instructed him to get Jamal downtown to my office quickly but carefully. Forty-five minutes later, in the office kitchen, I fed Jamal some cereal and made sure that he understood the consequences of turning himself in. Scared, penniless, and tired of running, he looked less like an armed menace than a cornered waif. He was seventeen and his life was over. I told him not to say anything until he had talked to the criminal defense lawyer I would find for him that morning. He stood, offered his hands to Captain Hannity for cuffing, and we left.

At five-thirty in the morning, the four of us rolled out of LDF's parking lot onto Olive Street and headed down to Watts in a caravan. Fifteen minutes later, Jamal walked into Southeast station. Alive.

The parallels between corrupt cops and gang members never struck me more starkly than during that night's exchange. The deeper insight that escaped me then—the overlap between gangs and the rest of us—came later from Dr. Deborah Prothrow-Stith, a Harvard professor of public health policy and a pioneer of treating violence as a disease. She switched on this lightbulb for me during her fascinating description of the duel between Alexander Hamilton, one of this nation's founding fathers and its first secretary of the treasury, and Aaron Burr, the country's third vice president.

In July 1804 these two aristocrats dueled to Hamilton's death. From his diary, we know that Hamilton agonized over the many reasons not to fight. He did not want to duel so soon after his son Phillip had died in a duel three years earlier over a forgettable slight. If Hamilton died, he would leave his still-grieving wife a widow and his family a mountain of debt. Besides, dueling was illegal and condemned by God. Moreover, Hamilton admitted that he did not feel enough animus toward Burr to warrant the fight. Nonetheless, he concluded that he had to go through with it: *The honor of his family required vindication.* If he declined the challenge, his community standing would fall so low that he would not be able to function, and his wife would lose her own social standing and thus her respect and love for him. He felt there was no choice but to heed society's expectation. He got up the next morning, dueled, and died.

How many times had I heard gangbangers swear they didn't want to kill but disrespect demanded it? The honor of their 'hood demanded an answer of death. Wasn't the gang code a coarser version of the elegant code of the duel? Dueling eventually faded out of fashion, but only after women rejected it as the ultimate act of romantic devotion and more sophisticated norms of problem-solving overtook it. Gang experts advise emulating this dynamic: Offer youth better options and help girls decide to reject violent street-gang members. Succeed in doing this, and half of street gangs would be out of business tomorrow.

We were not as different from them as we needed to believe. Yet we reacted to gangs and the pockets of extreme poverty in Watts like India reacted to Dalits. We contained America's untouchables behind the thin blue line, where they stayed jobless, hopeless, and dangerous. We were in denial about the fact that our safe zones depended on the savage inequalities of their kill zones. My quest required harnessing police power, but it also depended on unwinding this deadly codependence.

As the era of LAPD chief Daryl Gates faded behind us, the time for his most ardent opponent also wound down. Shortly after the federal convictions came down in April 1993, Mayor Tom Bradley announced the end of his twenty-year reign over Los Angeles. The King riots had been a bitter episode for the proud, dignified man who had made history as L.A.'s first black mayor. As an embattled career officer in LAPD for twenty years prior to becoming mayor, Bradley had carried his fight with Chief Gates and LAPD into city hall, only to have the same arrogant agency that had bedeviled his policing career tarnish the end of his political career.

I barely knew the mayor, but he knew my role in the civil rights community, and he had called me in June 1992 to proudly announce his selection of Philadelphia's black police chief, Willie Williams, to replace Daryl Gates. I didn't know what to say. LAPD would destroy Williams; a lone outsider with no preparation for the Blue Grip had zero chance of leading LAPD. I suggested that he consider Bernard Parks, the brilliant black LAPD assistant chief who was sufficiently ruthless to rein in LAPD's growing defiance. The mayor told me never to mention Parks's name to him again and hung up. Willie Williams arrived a week later amid banner headlines and jubilation in the black community, unaware that LAPD command staff had already decided he had to fail.

I had no idea which grenade pin my suggestion of Chief Parks had pulled, but my mistake did no lasting damage. A few months later, Bradley appointed me president of the city's board of commissioners for the Department of Water and Power. I took this unlikely assignment to learn the politics and mechanics of changing a government bureaucracy from the inside. Too often the bureaucracies put under the court orders we'd won had no clue how to rewire themselves to deliver what we wanted. By learning how to run a city-owned utility, I mastered city politics and an advanced level of inside strategy.

After Bradley stepped down, Richard Riordan, a wealthy Republican businessman and philanthropist, won the mayor's race in June 1993. He beat his Democratic opponent by vowing to crack down on crime, particularly gang violence, and to hire three thousand more police officers. I remember the glossy brochures emblazoned with his campaign slogan: TOUGH ENOUGH TO TURN L.A. AROUND.

From where I stood, we needed strategies smart enough to solve the problems, and programs comprehensive enough to reverse the spiral of despair. Throwing a few thousand more paramilitary police on the thin blue line and declaring more wars was unlikely to solve much of anything in Bel Air and likely to aggravate a lot in Watts. The war on gangs had racked up an impressive body count but had left the gangs stronger, more unified, and in control of ever more territory, including every housing project and park they claimed. Law-abiding neighbors feared the gangs and the police equally, and all of their nonviolent neighbors being sent to prison for drug use and low-level drug dealing were just learning how to become better criminals and less eligible for the area's dwindling jobs. The war on drugs had been even less effective than the war on gangs, producing no decline in drug use but inflicting on underclass communities crushing incarceration rates for nonviolent drug crime that got prosecuted much more rarely in wealthy white enclaves like Malibu. A poor black kid faced up to a fourteen times higher chance of being prosecuted for marijuana possession than a white kid, and everyone knew the devastating racial impact of the hundredfold higher sentences for crack versus powder cocaine.

By far the worst blowback from the "tough on crime" obsession comes from the devastation of mass incarceration, the saturation jail-and-fail strategy of locking up so many members of a community that more of them go to prison than to college. To be clear, I am never talking about violent criminals who need locking up, but the 70 percent of people in prison for nonviolent drug crime. We have arrested an inexplicable two thirds of underclass black men. Mass incarceration has effectively criminalized whole communities. In one of the most moving encounters of that decade, a young man from Books Not Bars stopped me in a hallway and said, "You know back in your day, when you was fightin' Jim Crow? Well this jail shit is *my* Jim Crow." I was so elated with his incisive analysis that I didn't even care that he thought I was eighty years old.

Michelle Alexander documents this youngster's epiphany in her brilliant book *The New Jim Crow.* Alexander's book shows how mass incarceration has revived the same systematic discounts in freedom and exclusions from employment, jury duty, housing, voting, public benefits, and social status that my great-grandparents suffered under the original Jim Crow. Ex-convicts too often can't get a legal job, serve on juries, qualify for housing, get welfare, or vote.

From all of this police and prison action, you'd think Watts would at least have derived the benefit of ubiquitous public safety. Hardly. With eight thousand unsolved murders, in 1993 South Bureau remained outlandishly dangerous and lawless. No surprise there. "Tough on crime" was never meant to protect the Jackson kids. It was meant to protect the sensibilities of voters in communities on the right side of the thin blue line, and the seats of the politicians rallying votes by waving the bloody "tough on crime" banner.

In the early '90s, legislators sounded like they feared killer toddlers. Hysteria over crack cocaine had politicians warning voters about addicted infants—predators in Pampers—who surely would become super-predators as teenagers. As a result, we criminalized poor kids of color through insane actions like calling police to arrest a five-year-old who threw a tantrum in school and rejailing a thirteen-year-old for carrying a Magic Marker that police viewed as "graffiti paraphernalia." What chance did rational, never mind transformational, policy stand? None. The only transformation going on during those years was turning nonviolent drug addicts into violent ones. In the hot zones, we had allowed 50 percent unemployment to become entrenched, criminalized the available local economy, arrested and removed 55 percent of the men for nonviolent drug offenses, then acted appalled to find families with no fathers and women with no gainfully employed husbands.

Watts had had enough of tough. It needed to counter the gang mind-set. It needed jobs. It needed schools that worked. It needed universal child care, mental and health care. It needed healthy food. It needed green space. It needed compassion. Above all, it needed the rest of us to stop projecting our fears onto their community.

The first step to all of this was safety won with police who did not target the community but protected it.

Losing LAPD reformer Mayor Bradley to LAPD enthusiast Mayor Riordan inevitably undercut Chief Williams's mandate and removed the wind from the sails of our court victories and the Christopher Commission report, but only to a point. Despite our political differences over policing, our new Republican mayor reappointed me to the Department of Water and Power. Since I was one of four Bradley commissioners whom Mayor Riordan kept, and the only one who also was suing him, he'd always greet me with "Now, Connie, are you with me on this one—or suing me?" Eventually, we'd become fast allies on education and energy, and Riordan would generously fund our work through his foundation. But we remained opponents on police reform.

After several articles on our police abuse, lead poisoning, and voting rights cases, in 1994 the *Los Angeles Times* published a profile entitled "Debt of Honor" with a big picture of me in a pink pantsuit with Robert and Kevin sitting behind me.* In addition to our

---

*To view the article, please visit www.powerconcedesnothing.com.

reputation for aggressive litigation, blunt talk on radio, and suing our friends in office, I had also begun weekly appearances on Bill Rosendahl's local television shows, *Local Talk, Week in Review,* and *Beyond the Beltway,* which covered politics and policy analysis. Under Justine Lewis's tutoring, I honed my sound bites and learned the alien world of hair, makeup, and greenrooms, where, over the years, my conservative opponents on TV, Joel Fox, Bobbi Fiedler, and Arnie Steinberg, became my friends.

In the span from 1993 to 1995, I was splitting my fifteen- to twenty-hour days among our police dog-bite cases, our new sex discrimination case against LAPD, running the city's Department of Water and Power, preparing a landmark transportation case to protect bus riders, working the streets with Fred, and helping our boss, Elaine Jones, the first woman to head LDF, raise money.

I hate raising money. Gang wars, renegade cops, prison riots, and nuclear plant mishaps were doable, but not fund-raising. I'd have preferred retaking the bar exam to the excruciation of finding honorees, designing programs, signing entertainment contracts, and selling tickets. Nonetheless, in 1993 Elaine charged Bill Lee and me with producing LDF's Thurgood Marshall Lifetime Achievement Awards dinner—in Hollywood, no less. I would have to rub my awkward elbows not only with L.A.'s elite but with Hollywood royalty. We were honoring two fabulous figures, Harry Belafonte and Sidney Poitier, and the dinner, on November 17, 1993, was the hottest ticket in town.

When the date finally arrived, I was dispatched to escort Mr. Belafonte and his wife, Julie. I feared disappointing both. Playing Girl Friday had never been my strong suit. I should have saved my worry beads. Harry jaunted down the wrought-iron stairs of his hotel, took one look at my intense face, wild hair, and Coke-bottle glasses, and became fascinated with the creature seated before him. He pulled up a chair and, in his melodic rasp, asked me from where did I hail and what it was that I did.

Five hours later, I had taken him through my nomadic path into gangland, and he had taken me from Paul Robeson to Nelson Mandela. I had found manna from heaven. He was just broaching the topic of Fidel Castro when Julie descended in her evening gown and inquired whether the two of us had any intention of attending the dinner. We reluctantly hit the pause button and got ready for the evening.

Harry was smitten by the gang work and broke out in disbelieving delight when I told him that Fred and the guys would be at the dinner: "*Gangsters* at a high-society Beverly Hills gala—I love it!" he exclaimed. After he glad-handed on the red carpet with Mr. Poitier, we slipped away from the wall of cameras, and I took Harry over to meet Fred and his crew. To their amazement and the horror of the event director, Harry pulled up a chair and parked himself at their table. They regaled him with tales of their truce and truancy work. The event coordinator had to drag him away to accept his award with Mr. Poitier. In what I would learn was his trademark of lifting up local leaders, while at the microphone, Harry spoke at length about the truce, and he had Fred, Black, and the team stand for an ovation during his acceptance remarks. At the exhausted end of the evening, he found me again and asked me to cancel whatever I was doing the next day. He wanted to see Watts and their work for himself.

The next day we entered Jordan Downs from Grape Street on the west side of the complex. Within minutes, wafts of "Day-O! Daaay-O! Daylight come and me wan go home . . ." echoed through the courtyards. The older residents were greeting him with off-key strains of his signature song, but at least twenty youngsters also instantly recognized Harry Belafonte. He laughed and talked as the children and women of Jordan Downs swarmed around him, clamoring for his autograph and the touch of his hand. For me, observing the power of celebrity was something new. Sure, I loved watching certain movie stars, but I found the irrational worship that people showered on strangers who touched their fantasies fascinating and baffling. As I watched Harry wade through the throngs of thrilled admirers, it struck me that his influence spanned four generations. The great-grandchildren of the women who had fallen in love with him two generations ago knew his face, his name, and his songs.

After I'd lived near Hollywood, the Mecca of Narcissism, I found

it hard to avoid the conclusion that fame warps and that superstar-
dom warps absolutely. But over the subsequent years of watching
Harry in the rituals of celebrity, I concluded that its elixir had less
control of him than he had of it. Harry loved the engagement, but
more for the chance to touch and elevate the lives of others than for
the veneration of self.

This view crystallized with diamond clarity a year after we met,
during his filming of *White Man's Burden* in L.A. Harry's shooting
schedule was preventing him from joining me at a conference of
global poverty strategists meeting in upstate New York at the end
of the week. He called late one afternoon midweek and told me to
pack a bag and meet him the next afternoon on the tarmac of the
Burbank airport. Although I didn't see how, he said we were going
to the conference. I waited on the tarmac, as instructed. A Rolls-
Royce pulled up: John Travolta was driving, and Harry was sitting in
the front passenger seat. I got in, Harry introduced me as the "real
white man's burden," and I tried to greet the chuckling Mr. Travolta
as if getting into Rolls-Royce sedans were something I did every day.
He floated the Rolls over to a white Gulfstream. Harry was borrow-
ing Travolta's jet for a twenty-four-hour whirlwind turnaround that
would allow him to attend the conference without disrupting the
filming schedule. Aside from vigorously thanking Mr. Travolta for his
generosity, Harry paid zero homage to all of this bling. And once we
were on the plane, he spoke not one word about the glamour of film,
movie stars, or their jets, and nothing of the palaces, royal châteaus,
and private islands to which he had held the keys.

With the long flight ahead of us, we resumed the poolside conversation that had never ended. He plunged me into the astonishing
panorama of his political life, a sweeping saga that spanned the cruel
cane fields of Jamaica, Harlem's rough streets, Mississippi's terrain of
terror, South Africa's Robben Island, and the killing fields of Cam-
bodia and Rwanda. He poured out the gems he had culled from a
pantheon of mentors who rivaled any Justice Hall of Fame: Eleanor
Roosevelt, Fannie Lou Hamer, Ella Baker, Bayard Rustin, Mahatma
Gandhi, Bobby Kennedy, Malcolm X, César Chávez, Rosa Parks,

Nelson Mandela, Kwame Nkrumah, Stephen Biko, and of course, Martin Luther King Jr. After five numinous hours, I wondered, had there been any major struggle of the twentieth century with which he had *not* been involved?

This is why, eight years into our relationship, I completely forgot that Harry Belafonte sang. While planning an awards show to celebrate the tenth anniversary of the Watts gang truce, I earnestly asked him, "Now, whom do we know who can do the music?" Without missing a beat, he lifted his eyes heavenward and, in his honeyed rasp, roared in relief, "THANK GOD! She is actually CAPABLE of saying something STUPID!" We laughed for ten minutes at my blunder. As a little girl, I had listened to his music on my dad's record player, but my world with Harry had been so wrapped around our passion for social justice that I had completely forgotten he also was a world-class musician. In our ongoing conversation about social change, I had mistakenly thought his music had nothing to do with his magic. In my mind, it was his passion for human dignity, the vast span of political history he had lived, and the poetic genius with which he expressed his vision.

I first saw his combined political and musical gifts that afternoon in Jordan Downs, when Harry offered to say a few words to Fred's volunteers. Half of Grape Street must have crammed into the Cross Colours bunker to hear him. Harry took the floor and told them that years ago, as a fatherless teenager, he, too, had associated briefly with a street gang before being rescued by the greatest American of the twentieth century. Paul Robeson had snatched Harry from a Harlem street gang, plopped him into a drama troupe, and taught him to leverage art into politics. He remembered the ingenious baritone, athlete, and visionary telling him, "Get them to sing your song, and they might listen to your ideas."

"Paul Robeson made me join another gang," Harry told the spellbound Crips. "But instead of petty crime, this one was dedicated to perfecting its dramatic productions and music."

From that moment, he had them. Harry Belafonte had been like them but had escaped and made something spectacular of a long life.

He took them through conflicts in Angola, South Africa, Northern Ireland, and Namibia, linking their truce work to the freedom fighters and peacemakers he had seen around the globe. He talked of King and of men like Nelson Mandela who had put their lives on the line to win freedom and end conflict. He talked of King's concern for prisoners and men like them. And he cracked them up with the tart quip that King had muttered after a particularly useless summit of bloviating pastors: "Give me ten convicted felons over five hundred ordained pastors any day, and I'll get done a whole world of good."

As they filed out of the bunker uplifted and refortified, Harry asked Fred to hold back his inner circle. He needed to find out who they were. Why had they joined the gang? What had been missing in their lives? Had they done time? For what offenses? How did the idea of the truce get started? What was their vision for their turf? Harry's eloquence intimidated professional speakers, and to these men and boys who did not express emotion easily, his questions were daunting. Fred started with his story and prompted some of the others to respond. A few mentioned keeping the truce going as a vision. But most remained silent, especially about what they'd done time for—they didn't want Harry Belafonte to hear about armed robbery, assault with a deadly weapon, or murder. Harry switched gears and asked what was missing in their lives. After none could find the words, Fred said: fathers and men like Harry who could show them a better way to be men. After that, the others opened up, answering with their flat affects of aborted grief and suppressed trauma, lifting their masks, trusting him with the intimacy of their pain but describing it in terms of what they could not feel.

I was watching lost sons confess to a newfound father.

Chapter 12

THE NEIMAN MARXIST

I hated to see Harry go, but Bill and I were deliriously happy to get the awards dinner done to Elaine's satisfaction and return to real work. By early 1994 Bill had noticed that my irritable state of agitation had not subsided, and he asked me what was wrong. I confessed to him my growing impatience with the complacency of my black middle-class colleagues: the good souls who still tried to help, pursuing charity and limited projects that saved a few but challenged none of the policies that, if changed, could impact many. Most had joined the rest of the country in pretending the underclass—the poorest of the poor—could be ignored. They understandably recoiled from the violence, and a few admitted they had given up, with one weary civil rights leader finally telling me, "Connie, those are not our kids."

I shared the longing to enjoy prosperity free of obligation. But the job was not done. King died after winning only the first phase of the civil rights revolution—the quest to end racist brutality and legal segregation. The second phase, the realization of equality and universal opportunity, was still under way.[16] If the black establishment didn't stand up to demand opportunity for the poorest kids of all races, how did we carry out this second phase, never mind win the last phase, fully integrated equality? My politically savvy allies were right that, without an effective political movement, we would never end the entrenched misery of severe poverty—or halt the relentless drive of regressives to shred the safety net and end upward-mobility programs for the poor. But with strategic leveraging, I knew we could seriously dent and dislodge both.

My colleagues at LDF and in other civil rights law firms were some of the few who strategically confronted the plight of the underclass and understood that it endangered everyone. But that didn't mean they understood my unorthodox street ventures in Watts.

In early 1994, for the first time, I told Elaine at a staff meeting in our L.A. office how I had met a nine-year-old assassin. Ignoring my colleagues' startled looks, I argued that Pygmy's plight meant that LDF's entire docket should be reorganized to take aim at the family, cultural, institutional, spiritual, political, educational, legal, and economic failures that had led to his unspeakable fate. Elaine got what I was saying but looked at me like she wasn't sure I knew what lawyers did. Everyone else's eyes seemed to glaze over. Other than me, what lawyers were going to add to their insane caseloads some crazy civic mix of gangster grooming, school takeovers, community building, and criminal justice reform?

It would not be the last time I'd fail to persuade my colleagues to wrestle the third rails of the kill zones or tackle the yawning indifference between our worlds. Bill nonetheless appreciated that I was chasing something important, and he urged me to keep at it, even as he decided to get me some help. "You need someone who thinks like you," he concluded, and suggested I have lunch with Molly Munger and speak with her about joining our office.

Well, that was an easy request. Molly and I had worked well together before Fred's clothing-design dispute. In our first case, in which she was co-counsel from her law firm, we'd won a settlement against the biggest housing developer in Orange County for refusing to rent to interracial families. But I did not want Molly to leave her prestigious partnership at Fried Frank to come to our tiny nonprofit office that didn't even have legal secretaries.

We met at the pool bar of the Bonaventure Hotel, where John Malkovich almost killed Clint Eastwood in the movie *In the Line of Fire*. I spent three hours trying to talk her out of it. No woman who had battled her way to the top of her class at Harvard Law School and into one of the first partnerships in a downtown law firm should chuck away that kind of hard-won status, money, and resources. I warned that coming to LDF would be like leaving a luxury cruise liner for a trawler with no lifeboats. That it would bankrupt her, as it had me, and that if she started running around with yours truly, she would lose her considerable social standing—people would stop coming to her New Year's Eve party. Besides, her father would never forgive her. Molly's dad is the fabled Charles Munger, head of the Munger, Tolles & Olson law firm, and lawyer for the even more fabled Warren Buffett. I continued for another ten minutes with the mounting parade of horrors.

Luckily, she completely ignored me. The '92 riot had shaken Molly, and as a former federal prosecutor, she was livid about LAPD's lawlessness, intransigence, and lying. She had become determined to work full-time on getting L.A. out of its rut, even if it required her to make a drastic career change. She had made up her mind, and the only thing worse than telling me no was telling Molly "don't." She joined LDF-L.A. that winter. And in changing the course of her career, Molly chartered the most important partnership in mine.

As a woman with a steel trap for a brain, a passion for racial reconciliation, and a bloodhound's nose for corruption, Molly would have been a gift to any civil rights legal team. But her greatest gifts to me were abiding friendship, ridiculous generosity, and, as a sister workaholic, the ability to make me take a break. She'd say "enough already," and within minutes we'd escape to the Biltmore Hotel for high tea, followed by a frenzy of shopping or decorating. Very few knew that two commanding litigators like us were spree shoppers who, on a whim, could dissolve into reveries over bolts of peony-rose chintz or, in half an afternoon, buy nine pairs of new shoes each.

Our worst outburst happened the fall of 1995 in Manhattan, when we extended a New York LDF meeting into a shopping blitz. Within six hours we had indulged ourselves at the best breakfast place, a famous teahouse, shoe stores, clothing boutiques, makeup salons, and all eleven floors of ABC Carpet & Home. We topped off our extravagant playdate by taking my brother Phil, then the head of Brooklyn's Kings County emergency ward, and Molly's opera-singing friend Nina Edwards and her sister, Lisa, to dinner and to *Stomp*, Savion Glover's Broadway tribute to tap. Unaware that our exuberance had set off alarms in the financial world, we later learned that a credit card monitor had woken Molly's husband, Stephen English, at eight-thirty A.M. PST, to warn him that there had been an *extraordinary* amount of activity on his credit card, *in New York City*. Steve deadpanned, "I guess that means they got there safely."

Molly and I returned to L.A. the next day loaded down with the spoils of our invasion. On the flight back, I shook my head over the sad truth that, at one level, I really was a Neiman Marxist. The pitiful extent of my economic ideology was that everyone should have the chance to earn enough for life's basics and to experience the joy of buying shoes at the Nordstrom Half Yearly Sale, if they so desired. I agreed with President Kennedy that we should end severe poverty and engineer upward mobility in a way that only required the rich *to get richer than the rest of us at a slower pace.* How my opponents could call this pathetically incrementalist, capitalism-preserving, shopping spree–inspired outlook as radical, was beyond me. It was an insult to radicals.

There was one other woman I had met in 1993 who would inadvertently begin to play a bigger role in my life after Pete Wilson won reelection as California governor in late 1994.

As a registered independent, I had not voted for Governor Wilson, although given the Rice tradition of voting for the party of Lincoln, it would not have been outlandish to have considered it. My grandfather William Rice so staunchly believed in Lincoln's legacy that he proudly planted his Cleveland neighborhood's only GOLDWATER FOR PRESIDENT sign on his front lawn, so upsetting my grandmother that she banished him to the guest bedroom until the election passed. But since the '70s, the GOP's Southern strategy of sheltering white civil rights opponents had it looking far more like the party of Strom Thurmond than of Lincoln.

Barely aware of California state politics, I didn't even know from which of the many wings of the GOP Wilson hailed (libertarian, practical problem solving, paranoid fundamentalist, business protection, kill government, military *über alles,* or the David Duke wing). I had assumed that his becoming governor a second time would have little immediate impact on me or our cases. I was wrong.

Wilson had ridden to a second term on an ugly anti-immigrant platform and Proposition 187, an unconstitutional ballot measure to deny public aid and education to unauthorized immigrants and their children. In early 1995 I was pleasantly surprised when Chandra poked her head into my office to announce that the governor's office was calling. The woman on the line introduced herself as Governor Wilson's judicial appointments secretary. I thought, *Oh, of course— every governor would seek suggestions for judges from LDF.* I even had ready a ranked list of smart to brilliant law professors, litigators, and other reasonable Republican lawyers arranged by court. I began giving the secretary the names. We were doing fine until we reached the law professors I had saved for California Supreme Court vacancies. The woman stopped me. "Oh, I'm sorry, Dr. Rice, the governor has to save the highest court for those who really, uh, uh—came through for him during the campaign. I'm sure you understand."

I didn't. "You mean he doesn't want the top scholars for the top court because he has to give it to lawyers who gave him a lot of money?" I asked, thinking, hadn't the man just won reelection campaigning against affirmative action for not being merit based?

"Oh—uh, well, I certainly wouldn't put it like that," she responded, slightly startled, "but we'll certainly take a look at the candidates you've suggested for the lower courts. Thank you, Dr. Rice." She hung up.

I wandered down to Molly's office, where she was doggedly teaching herself the DOS keystroke commands required by our ancient computers. She looked up, and I explained the puzzling call.

"*What* did she call you?" Molly asked.

"She said Dr. Rice."

"Connie!" Molly exclaimed in exasperation. "The woman wasn't calling for *you*, she was calling for Condoleezza! That didn't occur to you?"

It really hadn't. In the black community, where anybody with a graduate degree was regularly addressed as "Doctor," I also was occasionally called Dr. Rice. In my arrogance, I had thought it wholly appropriate for the governor to seek advice about judicial appointments from the state's best lawyers—which, of course, included me.

"Oh," I said stupidly.

This was the first time I had been officially confused with Condi. I again silently thanked Mom for overriding Dad's bid to also name me Condoleezza, a family name he'd always liked. I had met Condi for the first time two years earlier, in 1993, after delivering a keynote speech for a minority lawyers' conference at Stanford, where Condi had just become provost. As I made my way to her office, a group of Stanford law students cornered me. They complained about the fact that I was related to Condi, and they lobbied me to get her to reverse some tenure decisions she'd just made. I suggested they challenge the provost's decisions through the proper channels and added that we were more alike than they imagined.

I knew this because we came from the same mold. My dad, who cherished his relationship with Condi's dad, had reported on her exploits since I could remember. When I was competing in swim meets, Condi was competing in ice skating. While my brothers and I were striving for straight A's, Condi was skipping grades. While I received honorable mention at a University of Illinois piano competition, Condi was on her way to becoming a professional pianist. The newspaper articles about her were in the same box as the newspaper articles about us. Photos showed that in the years before my wisdom teeth closed mine, the two of us had the same Rice gap between our front teeth that my first cousin Carolyn and aunt Vernice had, too.

I left the Stanford law students and walked across campus to meet the second cousin who'd been a presence throughout my life. She was the exceedingly poised, self-assured, and contained woman I'd imagined. With me, she was warm, welcoming, and curious about the close relationship between our fathers. In subsequent meetings, more similarities emerged. We had both inherited the Rice loner gene. We escaped by doing what we loved—playing piano for her, doing Tae Kwon Do for me, and shopping and exercise for both of us. We were overly close to our parents and emotionally remote. We were driven, self-sufficient, results-oriented, and professionally demanding. We had no patience for groups, dithering, or incompetence. And people feared our decisiveness. Although few ever saw our softer sides, we had them. She was more social, but with close friends, I could bring the house down telling stories.

Our differences also emerged. She was a woman of deep Christian faith. I was a non-belonger whose spirituality was much closer to an Einsteinian awe for the mystery of what exists. She was a rising star in the Republican Party who accepted their economic bent toward a less regulated private sector and the market's invisible hand. I sued too many Democrats to belong to any political party and did not care if a good idea came from a Demublican, a Republicrat, or a Communist. The only sworn enemies on my list were the violence, structured inequality, and lack of opportunity that blocked upward mobility for my clients, no matter how hardworking or morally correct they were. I also had no faith in the rationality of markets. Markets were as irrational as people and needed regulating to prevent greed from destroying the economic system. For my clients, there was no invisible hand, only an invisible fist that pounded them into deprivation. Politically, Condi and I differed, but I remained confident that our mutual respect for complexity, facts, and solutions would more often than not trump the increasing tilt of the Republican Party toward ideological rigidity.

That proposition would face many more tests in the years to come. In 1995 and 1996, however, Condi quietly defied Governor Wilson to oppose his measure to end affirmative action, Proposition 209, and helped Molly and me in the statewide NO ON 209 campaign by clearing the way for us to win the support of General Colin Powell.

In 1996 I really could have used a crystal ball, because our next joint venture would have to wait through thirteen years of unimaginable calamity, confrontation, and change in our separate worlds. For Condi, this period of time included moving to the White House and onto a global stage. For me, this critical stretch proved to be the last in our battle for constitutional policing. It began with insights from our court cases that set me on an unorthodox journey with LAPD that would usher in changes far beyond anything a court could touch.

As someone who loves cats, I expected to learn little from suing LAPD over its use of dogs. Our canine (K-9) cases against LAPD and LASD police dog handlers, *Lawson v. Gates* and *Silva v. Block,* however, changed my mind about our fanged friends and profoundly changed my approach to police reform. Reverend James Lawson, the great architect of Martin Luther King's nonviolent resistance army, and Reverend William Epps, the pastor of the venerable Second Baptist Church, had put their black churches on the firing line as organizational plaintiffs in those cases to halt cops' misuse of police dogs. As for our big sex discrimination case, *Tipton v. LAPD,* I had greater expectations. Led by the indomitable LAPD detective Terry Tipton and her implacable colleague Sergeant Myrna Lewis, our brave women officer clients and the male cops who had defended them sacrificed their careers to clear the minefields that LAPD set to demolish women officers. All three cases were politically and socially significant.

At first, the best thing about these cases was that I got to work with Carol Sobel and Barry Litt. For Barry, a quietly tenacious man with a razor-sharp mind, law was a means to the power that we needed to do justice, but unlike me, he also made money. As with Bill Lee, it was dangerous to underestimate his kind demeanor. Barry ruled in settlement negotiations with a dogged insistence that our opponents face facts, with a detailed mastery of the record, and with a superior understanding of the law and politics of a case. His skill in reading people and seeing five moves ahead on the chessboard made him formidable—and victorious in cases he was supposed to lose. Over the years, Barry would end up being my closest mentor.

I had picked an equally great mentor and a friend in Carol Sobel, a sublimely talented ACLU litigator. She taught me the unique skills needed to represent women police officers and how important it was to know the "*Peyton Place* Factor"—the sexual liaisons among LAPD officers. "If you don't know who has slept with or coveted whom," she'd warned, "you'll never figure out what's really going on in LAPD." I saw how right she was in a situation that I'd have sworn was driven by race discrimination but was actually a retaliation battle between two male officers who had competed for the love of the same female cop. Who knew?

Carol did, and she offered the added benefit of being hilarious. Doing a case with her was like working at Hollywood's Comedy Store. Short, elegant, with wise gray eyes and a beautiful shock of white hair, she looked like a kindly, if stylishly shod, high school teacher, an impression that was only partly right. Her heart was bigger than Texas, and given her talent, her ego should have been similarly sized, but she was selfless and humble. She matched these qualities with grit, courage, and fierce will. Carol also was about the only person in L.A. with whom I regularly yakked on the phone. We talked about our cases, but more as friends; and I had found a sister shoe diva who could do an intervention when I binged. We required ourselves to issue "Imelda Alerts" after all excessive shoe purchases.

Led by Paul Hoffman, then the head of litigation at the ACLU of Southern California, our crew of civil rights litigators teamed up with police-dog mavens Robert Mann and Donald Cook, an eclectic duo who had tried hundreds of K-9 cases in state court and had shown that LAPD's sixteen dogs bit an amazing 80 percent of their suspects and hospitalized an astounding 37 percent. In contrast, the entire police force hospitalized fewer than 2 percent of their arrestees. How did sixteen dog handlers rack up an 80 percent bite rate and put nearly twenty times the suspects into the emergency room? Every week LAPD dogs unnecessarily mauled suspects, ransacked yards, bit bystanders, and killed people's cats on the way to a takedown. If for no other reason, I had to do this case for my black-and-white tomcat, Jaws, a kitten waif I'd bottle-fed and hand-raised since his birth and Meesh's passing in 1990.

In spite of their skill, Cook and Mann had lost for two reasons: the unappealing profile of their clients, but above all, the Rin Tin Tin or Lassie factor. The latter could be seen when LAPD's handsome German shepherds padded into the courtroom, hopped into their seats at the defense table, and adorably caught a ball tossed by the officers. The jurors melted into puppy love and the case was over, especially after Rin Tin Tin was followed into court by the budding gangster sporting his teeth marks.

We changed strategies. We took the dogs and juries out of the cases, lumped the individual cases into a class action, and put on a dry statistical case before an even dryer data-oriented judge. It worked. Once the judge saw the ugly story told by the aggregated bite rates, hospitalization rates, bad deployments, and a videotape of officers cheering as a dog viciously mauled an unarmed black kid, he told the department's lawyer that she would be wise to settle the case. Settlement usually signaled the end of a case and pending victory, but for me, the K-9 negotiations proved to be an eye-opening beginning.

I had done policy settlements before, but this was my first session in which lawyers hammered out the money that a client should get for physical and economic damage. From law school, I knew what the calculation for damages required. The more highly educated and paid your client was, the higher the damages award for her losses would be. However, I was not ready for the emotional impact of hearing estimates of human worth for clients like ours. Over and over the wretched assessments rattled out: no high school, no GED, no military service, black, Latino, male, a history of crime and drug use but no history of work, and low to no prospects of employability. The bloodless discounting of their worth hit me hard. For the first time, being the only African-American lawyer in the room hurt. I wanted to halt the session and force the formula to calculate the cost our clients had borne for growing up in a kill zone, the value of drumming them out of bad schools into the streets, and to estimate their worth as fodder for the state's $8 billion prison industrial complex. I wanted to recalculate employability in hot spots where 50 percent unemployment is the norm and legal jobs don't exist. I wanted to tally the cost of brain damage from lead and chemicals dumped in their playgrounds by unregulated companies.

But I sat in masked sorrow because there was nothing in a damages settlement that could undo the unfairness of the formula or of the structured inequality built in to their neighborhoods. I kept quiet because this was the only way we would get a small measure of justice for clients who otherwise had no leverage over misconduct by police and their dogs. We were doing our jobs, what law school trained us to do: Defend your client's interest within the system. The battle to undo these ravaged realities belonged to another arena that I needed to master quickly.

The second eye-opening epiphany from these cases redirected my journey through the world of policing. It came from the officers of LAPD's K-9 Unit. Up until the settlement, I had not considered the dog handlers as individuals, only as a unit that allowed some of its members to misuse the dogs against suspects in cruel and sadistic ways. But when several handlers asked to be put in charge of changing their unit, we listened. They accepted our challenge that if the bite and hospitalization rates dramatically dropped, they could determine how it got done. In less than half a year, both rates plunged. The 80 percent bite rate dropped to 12 percent and the hospitalization disappeared to under 1 percent. They did it by using shock collars to retrain the dogs to find and circle rather than find and bite. (Up until then they had trained the dogs to *expect a bite of a human being* as the reward for finding the suspect!) They revamped handler training and agreed to psychological profiling, and when three handlers tested as sadists, they were promptly drummed out of the unit (but not out of LAPD). The changes were sweeping, swift, and sustained. There was no way to know it in 1994, but ten years later, when I called Donald Cook to see if the bite rates had reverted upward, he reported that not only had the 90 percent plus reductions held, but that he and Robert Mann no longer did police dog bite cases; there were too few victims.

When I saw how quickly the officers had muzzled their dogs and changed their own behavior, the lightbulb went on. Police could change when they wanted to change. They needed help, but let them do it on their terms, and they could do it quickly and permanently. From that point on, my thinking about how to fight for humane policing began to shift to an inside strategy. But we had several bends in the road before I'd get the chance to switch direction and work with LAPD instead of suing it.

In 1997, right before he declined a second punishing term as LAPD's first post-riot chief, an embattled Willie Williams asked to meet at the LDF offices to discuss our LAPD sex discrimination case, *Tipton v. LAPD.* Once seated at our conference table, the chief set right into a blunt rant about an "intransigent" LAPD that illegally "submarined" female officers in ways that reminded him of his own struggles as a black officer in Philadelphia. Nothing in Philly, however, had reached the "single-minded viciousness" of LAPD, he complained.

Williams was not the first command officer I'd heard lament his inability to protect female cops, but he was the first chief. LAPD's sabotaging of Mayor Bradley's choice of Williams had turned out worse than I'd predicted. My mind flashed to the sad 1995 *L.A. Times* photo of Williams standing outside of a bolted door to the SWAT office, demanding that the Centurions on the other side open up to admit the first qualified woman officer. They had told him to get out of their building.

Williams had come to our office to announce that he was reversing a finding against one of our black female lieutenants whose command had been torpedoed by hostile white male sergeants. Now, when the chief of a police agency that you are suing becomes your witness, this is a major victory, even if he is on his way out the door. I assumed that Williams's effort to settle our sex discrimination class action had done us and the next chief a great favor. There was no need to do anything but thank him and wish him well in his new life.

Two months later, on August 12, 1997, Mayor Richard Riordan appointed former assistant chief Bernard Parks as LAPD's new chief of police. The Parks era had begun.

I had always found Bernard Parks compelling, despite our disagreements. I understood his opposition to our lawsuits on behalf of LAPD police clients. In Parks's view, you took a bullet before you made the department look bad; all officers, including black cops, should tough it out in silence, as he had. I also understood how hostile factions within LAPD had targeted him for destruction after he became one of the first black watch commanders, but he had outwitted his rivals and advanced impressively into leadership of LAPD's most powerful units. Parks skillfully gained control over LAPD's Internal Affairs, ran the elite Metropolitan Division, and soon racked up too many achievements, secrets, and favors to be challenged. When he became chief, I was still figuring out what to make of a brilliant black cop who denied the existence of racial profiling and had campaigned to reinstate Daryl Gates. That was water way past the bridge, and at first I bet on Parks's ability to bend LAPD's defiance into compliance with the Christopher Commission's mandate for community policing. Chief Williams had not made a dent in LAPD's unbowed hide, and the department, a ticking time bomb, needed a stern master.

Given all of the other work to do, I assumed that Parks would want to settle *Tipton* after Chief Williams's acknowledgment of mistreatment and findings of sex discrimination. I should have known better than to assume facts not in evidence. Within six months, the new leadership declared war on all litigants and nullified everything Chief Williams had said to us.

Barry, Carol, and I had a ringside seat to the new team during a key *Tipton* settlement conference held at Parker Center after Parks's private law firm had failed to derail our case. Ten minutes late, a phalanx of stern-faced brass filed into the chief's conference room. With their midnight-blue, almost black uniforms bristling with badges, guns, and batons, and with their militaristic and hostile demeanors, they made a dramatic entrance. The judge's eyes widened in surprise at this display of incivility, but the three of us found it juvenile. I had to hit Carol under the table to ward off the wisecrack quivering on her lips.

After twenty minutes, the chief had not appeared, so the judge turned to Barry to address the first issue of the session. Before he could get through the facts of the first case, a deputy chief interrupted. "Chief Parks does not accept the premise that your clients suffered any discriminatory actions."

A second deputy chief chimed in. "Chief Parks also rejects the contention that your cases state sufficient grounds upon which to demand changes in LAPD policy."

A commander piped up with another "Chief Parks says" statement, and on down the line they went, demolishing every point that Chief Williams had conceded. I looked at Carol and scribbled a note about a Greek chorus, to which she jotted, "No—court of Torquemada." Then Chief Parks, forty minutes late, swept through the door at the northwest entrance of the room and assumed his seat at the top of the U-shaped table. The judge brightened and welcomed him, but the chief returned no greeting to His Honor and looked straight ahead in disdain.

The blue choir resumed its refrain, speaking for Chief Parks as if he were not in the room. Carol cut the officer off and remarked that the chief's belated entrance probably negated the palace guard's need to continue with the third-person pronouncements on his behalf. She then turned to Chief Parks and, noting that this was not the Vatican, asked if there was some reason we could not address him directly.

The brass choir froze, and the judge paled. Chief Parks stood and left the room. The session was over.

Barry later received a request from the chief's office that future

negotiations exclude Carol and me. We laughed for five minutes at
the idea of ever complying with this absurd request. That night Carol
called me with a scheme to increase our "command presence" by
pinning all of our old medals, pins, and ribbons from swim meets,
karate tournaments, Girl Scouts, and her husband's military service
onto our suit jackets. The next morning I tried to keep a straight
face as she marched through security with medal fruit salad pinned
to her blazer.

That would be one of our last moments of levity with LAPD.
After months of pointless hand-to-hand combat, we eventually settled *Tipton,* a case that should have ended when Chief Williams left.
Had the confrontation with the new LAPD leadership ended with
our cases, I would have chalked up the department's hostility as the
price for the invaluable removal of the "hunters"—the graveyard-
shift outlaws who had tangled with Sergeant Reidel and Captain
Hannity. Chief Parks's firing of the hunters was important enough to
overlook all hostility, but not important enough to ignore reversal of
the Christopher Commission reforms.

Unchecked by Mayor Riordan or police commissioners, LAPD
openly undermined Katherine Mader, the first inspector general. The
voter-approved IG position was one of very few reforms enacted in
response to the King beating. But, in my view, the department had
submarined Mader as relentlessly as it had our female LAPD clients.
Officers who entered her office reported being required to explain
what they were doing there. Staff for the IG were denied access
to information and investigations. Brass challenged every request
and action the IG sought to take, and the chief openly disparaged
the office. By November 1998 LAPD pushed for Mader's firing on
grounds that she had exceeded her authority.

I was furious. Where were all the civil rights leaders to defend
the one check on police power that we'd won? Why were the City
Council members and a majority of the police commissioners roll-
ing over like lapdogs? On the morning of the "hearing" in City
Council that would ratify her removal, I went downtown to sit with
Mader through her kangaroo-court dismissal. Outside of the hear-

ing room, I ran into Parks. I told him that the voters of Los Angeles had approved the creation of an inspector general and that he had no right to overturn their decision. He looked amused for a second, then replied that the voters did not run LAPD. When it came to LAPD, he said, "I am the law."

As he receded down the hall, "I am the law" reverberated in my head. Cold rage plunged me into a dark silence. We couldn't even force LAPD to obey the laws passed in response to their abuse of Rodney King.

In his first year, Parks had done a great service firing many of the worst officers. But he also had gutted the Christopher Commission mandates, iced the inspector general, and deep-sixed the remedies in our cases. It felt like an iron door was closing, that in overtime, we were losing the fight for the LAPD that Jesse Brewer, Hannity, Sergeant Reidel, Terry Tipton, and Myrna Lewis had sought.

Bernard Parks had joined the Blue Grip chiefs who equated themselves with the law and placed LAPD beyond civilian control. These were mistakes that, in my mind, negated his right to lead LAPD.

Chapter 13

BO TAYLOR AND THE
PREDATOR TRANSFORMATION
BUSINESS

The inside strategy for LAPD would have to wait until after Parks released his iron grip. In the meantime, we would continue our gladiator tango with LAPD in court and grooming our army of Serpico cops willing to challenge unconstitutional policing. There was plenty else to do, including our landmark bus riders case that was putting over $1 billion into the bus system, and finding a new partner for my exploration of gangland and its nether orbit of the prisons.

By 1996 I had lost Fred Williams. The last time I saw him was in late 1995. An LAPD officer called me with a terse warning to quickly get Fred out of the county, but he had already left California. Even though disruption from arrest, eviction, and job loss could strike at any time in his world, the abrupt ending to our partnership bothered me. I wished him safety from whatever threat he'd had to flee, and I began to disengage. Without a gifted street Sherpa, my exploration of gangland had to end.

I half hoped that Fred's replacement would never appear. Three of our big cases had reached critical stages, and it would have been a blessing to skip the street work in Watts. By late 1995, in our case against the MTA for gutting the bus system on which L.A.'s poor relied, we'd just maneuvered the agency into settlement talks by getting the U.S. Department of Transportation to withhold MTA's federal rail money until it settled our case. Like a junkie in withdrawal, MTA wanted immediate settlement talks that would take up a lot of time from Kevin, Robert, Bill, and me. At the same time, Carol, Barry, and I were at the height of our discovery battles in *Tipton,* and Molly was pulling me into meetings to gear up for battle against a man named Ward Connerly, who wanted to usher in the Age of Aquarius by abolishing affirmative action with Proposition 209. Exiting the emotionally draining world of gang intervention would have been a welcome break. But I didn't have the heart to leave Black, who said he still needed my help. And then one day I found Fred's successor, a man whose game had advanced way beyond truces, midnight basketball, and handing out turkeys at Thanksgiving.

Darren "Bo" Taylor exploded into my life at a high-voltage meeting called by California state senator Tom Hayden in 1997 to introduce midcity and coastal gang intervention leaders to potential supporters. I didn't know any of the other attendees, a mix of advocates like me and middle-class or wealthy supporters from Hayden's Westside district. During the fourth speaker's anemic expression of "concern" about the plight of L.A.'s gang zones, Bo shot up out of his seat and shouted, "Look, I'm sorry, y'all, I just can't sit here and listen to this bullshit no more." He proceeded to vividly cuss us out for accommodating the killing like it was some "fucking wallpaper" on our dining room walls. His outburst shook up the room. I was intrigued. His rage, while rash in that setting, struck me as rational. His broadside, if brutally honest, had been sanely delivered. And his dedication seemed genuine. He had thrown a grenade. Since so many of my best relationships started with confrontation, I picked it up and tossed it back.

After he calmed down, later in the meeting, I challenged him to articulate specific needs and listened to see if he passed the test. He squared his bald-headed and blockish bulk in front of me, locked his big angry eyes on mine, and glared, but after Grape Street, I was immune to gangster bluster. I glared back, and he pointedly detailed the safety needs of the children, mothers, and grandmothers in his war-racked neighborhood west of downtown L.A. He argued that without jobs for the men, in or out of gangs, there couldn't be any hope of things getting better; without activities for the kids, they'd get in trouble, and without intervention, the violence would escalate. He had answered with the proper indignance at having to pimp his community's need to dilettantes who benefited from its plight. Every passionate word out of his mouth had focused on the people he served. Every proud demand had been on their behalf. He had sought nothing for himself.

I had just found my next ambassador.

From that crackling confrontation, our partnership took flight. It was clear from our balky beginning that he would be every bit as vexing and exhilarating as Fred. Bo, short for "Bozo," his childhood nickname from an aunt who thought her spunky little nephew's unruly hair and big ears resembled the clown's, had none of Fred's calculated gloss. He was kinetic—bubbling with high-octane energy and a friendly, almost playful volatility. When angered, he could seem a hair trigger away from detonation, but he was solid, without the instability I always feared from Fred when he slipped back into his addictions. Bo, a Muslim, did not take drugs and did not drink. He was bullheaded, but his word was his bond, he did what he said he was going to do, and he was fiercely protective.

Bo was not so much charismatic as he was magnetic. He was charged with contradiction: a peace broker who wielded menace; a desperately driven rescuer of children with too little time for his own; a hard taskmaster who was deeply humble; an uncanny detector of danger who could not protect himself. Bo was a man-child, a manic-obsessive adult and a wonder-filled youngster rolled into one. By the end of our journey, I could say without caveat of any kind that of all the gang workers I knew over twenty years, no one gave more of himself than Bo.

For Bo, the work extended far beyond street patrols, cease-fires, and keeping children busy and away from gangs. He had no patience for the brain stem bluster that passed for thinking in gangland. It had taken me years of watching Fred operate in Watts to reach a conclusion that Bo had known from the beginning: that averting shootings was an important short-term tactic, but long-term success in ending gang violence depended on ending the thug mind-set. A guru in the business of "predator transformation," Bo spent a lot of time reprogramming banger behavior by teaching the reasoning and self-control that normal people get before kindergarten: think before you act, choose right over wrong, consider the time before you do the crime, count to ten and deescalate confrontation, resist provocation, restrain destructive impulses, take responsibility for your misconduct, reach for positive thinking. "Turn negativity to positivity," he used to say. He taught these skills as the lead instructor of a course with the dry title of "Amer-I-Can Life Skills Curriculum." The course, developed by psychologists at the behest of football legend Jim Brown, was a kind of Gangsters Anonymous that aimed to break addictions to impulsive destruction and expose them to the ABCs of rational thought, self-control and a vision of advancement that replaced the cult of death. But it worked because of Bo's passion for their salvation and the love he and the other instructors offered to men seeking a second chance.

If Bo had to pass my test, I had to pass the test of his employer and mentor, Jim Brown. Four months after our first meeting, Bo presented me at Jim's mountain-ledge home above Sunset Boulevard during one of Jim's regular gatherings of Amer-I-Can workers. Jim knew who I was and greeted me with a girded grace and respect that he probably reserved for strangers of consequence. He was not someone you would ever call friendly, but he seemed guardedly intrigued by what he viewed as my bid to enter his world. After Bo paid homage to Jim as the man who had saved his life, Jim asked me questions. I remember thinking during my responses that this was a formidable man who dominated off the playing field, too. As he triangulated the risk and benefit of my involvement with Bo, I scanned my host. Time had weathered his taut physique, and he strained for the fluid ease of his youth but settled for a stiff, acute dignity. I was looking at a physical genius, one of the world's extraordinary athletes—the best running back in the history of football, and football wasn't even his best sport. Though injuries of yore had slowed his gait, nothing had diminished his flinty intellect. Jim asked how I had met Bo. What had brought me to this work? Who else in Watts had I worked with? What did I see? When did the NAACP get interested in men like Bo? By the end of his questioning, he seemed satisfied that I was there for enough of the right reasons and posed no threat to whatever he needed to protect. He signaled his approval to Bo, and the Amer-I-Can drawbridge lowered. Jim ordered someone to refresh my drink and stiffly strutted over to a group of men awaiting his attention on the other side of the patio.

I sat back in the cabana chair, enjoyed the breathtaking hilltop with its panoramic view, and thought about the men milling around Jim. Most were cut from the same cloth as Fred and the men of Grape Street, with the same bristling brawn, macho dignity, and street vibe. Each had fought hard to be there. Gang members invited into Jim's orbit had to humble themselves into accepting the disparaging but accurate designation of "predator." They had to claim responsibility for the damage they had inflicted on themselves and everyone else, and they gained Jim's slightly less harsh designation of "former predator" only after years of proving themselves to him. I did not need to befriend or even like Jim to respect what he had done for the men strolling around his garden, talking in his living room, and playing chess on his patio. He had extricated them from the streets and molded them into respectability, and they had gladly paid the price of self-transformation and loyalty to join his church of entrepreneurial self-reliance. There was no way to know whether Jim's quo ever matched their quid. It was nonetheless clear that he did not just talk about stanching the loss of black men to nihilism. He did it every day, with real human beings. Man by man, it had worked with at least the men in that backyard. That was good enough for me.

After my vetting, I met others in the Amer-I-Can constellation of ex-convicts and ex–gang leaders: Big Ship, Looney, Sleep, K.T., Melvin Hayward, Stan Muhammad, Jorge Avalos, Skip Townsend, Jeff, Roc, and many others. They had arrived as exes but had emerged as men. With Bo steering the way, his teams spread the gospel of gang-free living and violence-free manhood by teaching the Amer-I-Can curriculum in prisons, schools, and the streets to inmates, addicts, gang members, and anyone else who needed to hit the restart button.

I started rolling with Bo, which meant moving throughout the city of L.A.'s nearly five hundred square miles into the much larger L.A. County and eventually across the country. His network stretched way beyond his neighborhood and, rare for this world, included interventionists from the veiled and tangled world of Latino gangs, such as Nane Alejandres of Barrios Unidos, an extraordinary community builder from Santa Cruz. Bo took complaints about his wide span in stride, calming folks who got upset when he crossed boundaries and went beyond his turf and legit reach. But with Bo, there would be no retreat, only expansion. He was an interventionist without borders.

Bo also was Amer-I-Can's leading acolyte, spearheading the teams of instructors who taught the group's Gangsters Anonymous life-skills course. Jim had made inroads with county officials to teach the course to inmates in jails and prisons, but sheriffs' deputies had resisted having ex-cons teach anything in their prisons. That was where my help came into the picture as I added my voice to Jim's efforts by enlisting Assistant Sheriff Lee Baca's help to extend the Amer-I-Can program's shelf life in the county prisons.

After hitting a stone wall with LAPD's new leaders, I had built up my relationship with Baca, whom I first met in the early '90s during our lawsuits against the Los Angeles County Sheriff's Department. The riot-prone LAPD may have commanded more of our atten-

tion, but with more than fourteen thousand deputies, LASD was the
second largest law enforcement agency in the United States. With
four thousand square miles to patrol, it had by far the nation's biggest urban police territory this side of Alaska. As karma would have
it, in 1998, right after I bought my mountainside bungalow, Lee Baca
unexpectedly won the race for L.A. County sheriff after the longtime incumbent, Sherman Block, died five days before the election.

Lee Baca was a strange character for law enforcement. Unlike
Captain Ben Hannity, who was a self-reformed old-guard cop, Baca
had never been part of the warrior cops. He was an unorthodox
thinker, a lone ranger with fierce loyalty not to the group-think of
beat cops but to his core principles, tenets that any missionary could
embrace and any self-respecting warrior cop of the '70s would torch.
Baca, it turned out, was a humanitarian maverick with a gun. This
unlikely cop had just taken the helm of the law enforcement agency
with a jurisdiction that had LAPD's city turf smack in its middle.
With Baca newly at the helm, things were about to change in the
LASD, starting with his invitation to former adversaries like me to
join his team of advisers. I gave him my numbers and told him to call
whenever he needed help, day or night.

Two years later, in 2000, he did. It was just after five in the morning, but I recognized his voice immediately. My brain went to the
race riot that had broken out that week at L.A. County's Pitchess
Detention Center, Baca's sprawling prison farm that housed inmates
doing county time and many others on their way to trial or to state
prison. I knew the situation must have deteriorated badly for him to
call me this early. He had not slept in the two days since the riot, but
his voice was alert and tense. He was calling from Pitchess. "Yes, it's
Lee Baca, Connie. Sorry to wake you like this, but I need your help."

He knew I'd been following the racially charged events at Pitchess.
He confirmed that things were getting worse and said he still had
badly injured African-American inmates barricaded and held hostage by Latino inmates. They wouldn't release them to the ambulances. He asked me what I was hearing that he might be able to use.

It was a strange question. How could my fifth-hand intelligence help the sheriff? But maybe it could. The prior morning, the *L.A. Times* story had described the barricaded room in which two unconscious black inmates lay stashed between two bloody mattresses. I had dropped the paper and called several experts to see what they knew. The consensus was that the violence had been ordered by a contender for the helm of the Mexican Mafia prison gang, or Eme, for the Spanish pronunciation of the letter M. The order supposedly had been issued to show a contender's power to stir chaos. Another contact who watched the prison-street connection agreed that it was an Eme kill order, as if this were something surely everyone knew. I knew nothing about the power struggle they referred to, but all agreed that one of the candidates vying to head the powerful prison gang had issued an order for all California Latino inmates to attack and kill black inmates and guards. Any Latino prisoner who failed to heed the order could expect severe punishment. Another added that the order was thought to have come from a federal prison in East Texas. When I asked how he got this information, he said, matter-of-factly, the prison grapevine. I had no idea how to evaluate this information, but they all reported it as if they believed it was true.

The sheriff asked if I knew who could go in and get this thing reversed. I warned him that if he met with the people who did know, his deputies would turn against him, and it might cost him reelection.

"Inmates are dying up here," he snapped angrily. "I don't give a damn about getting reelected. Get these people to me." He hung up.

I dialed Bo. I asked him, how did a Mexican Mafia kill order get reversed? He told me not by us but by real rough characters he didn't think I was ready to meet. I asked him to bring them to my office, and he told me only if I followed his lead. That would be easy, since I had no idea what had to be done.

By seven-thirty that morning, a panicked guard called me in my office, and I raced downstairs. Standing behind Bo, glaring at the guard, was the most menacing bloc of tatted-up, bald-headed, buffed-up, pirate-looking ruffians I had ever seen. One of them had a ruby-and-green dragon tattoo scaling his thick neck and bald head, with the dragon's red tongue slithering down his nose. I couldn't take my eyes off the forked tip that flared over his nostrils. Bo and two hard-core Rollin' 60's Crips whom he kept on call for dangerous forays were the only blacks in the largely Latino crew. For whatever reason, they had answered Bo's call for help. I calmed the guard and greeted them like Molly had greeted Black years earlier.

After a careful Kabuki dance, the men explained how to respectfully beseech the prison gang hierarchy to lift the kill order. If they helped, there could be absolutely no coordination with the sheriffs, and they had to be free to do what was needed. The sheriff agreed to let Bo's SUVs of hostage negotiators into the prison. Four hours after Bo's teams entered the besieged terminal, the barricaded attackers released the injured inmates to the ambulances.

Late that night, Sheriff Baca called to convey his gratitude and say how impressed he'd been by Bo, Jim, and the Latino negotiators. He said that Bo and his Amer-I-Can team should be in his county prisons every day, teaching and mediating. I reminded the sheriff that approval of the Amer-I-Can contract was once again stalled. Within a week, Bo was back at Pitchess, ready to teach the Amer-I-Can life-skills program.

Bo's professionalism overcame the resistance of the guards, and Leon, Melvyn, Big Ship, Jorge, and the other Amer-I-Can instructors began helping Bo lead classes of thirty-five to fifty super-maximum prisoners to shed the behavior of predators and learn the thinking of men. They studied a spiral-bound "Life Skills Curriculum," memorized its principles, and applied its lessons to their lives. They learned to dissect their predatory acts, intercept predatory impulses, think about the consequences of their actions, and use reason and restraint. They practiced their new civilized outlook and conduct in the dorm where they lived together during the course. Above all, they shared their fears and fiercely supported one another.

At the end of each course, Bo and his team held a graduation ceremony. The graduates first listened to encouraging words from guest commencement speakers. Bo then called up each graduate, the assembled listened to him say what he had learned, and Bo handed him a diploma. At the end, the graduates dived into pizza that Bo had brought in from outside. For the first year, I suspected that a lot of them had taken the course just for the chance to eat real pizza, but as the number of graduates grew, the reputation of the course as a life-altering opportunity spread. The Amer-I-Can course was becoming a phenomenon at Pitchess.

At the fifth graduation I attended sometime in 2001, it became clear why. By then I was used to a multiracial roomful of super-maximum-security inmates sitting on folded chairs. Some of these men had already been convicted of murder, robbery, or other serious crimes, and others awaited trial, but all sat respectfully without ankle shackles or hand restraints. Several deputies stood in the back, but not enough to control that room. They knew they would not need to. The students clapped and cheered as Bo brought each of them up to the front of the room to haltingly or eloquently explain how the course had changed his life. Each had learned how to think about the consequences of his actions. How to turn negativity to positive action. How to deal with feelings without getting frustrated. How to respect himself so he could respect others. How not to lash out in pain. How to ask for help.

All of this was par for an Amer-I-Can graduation, but what happened during a ceremony in 2002 was not. A Latino inmate, terrified of public speaking, got up and struggled through his hand-scribbled remarks, but then he put down the tattered paper and spoke from his heart. He said that he had never graduated from anything and that this ceremony would be his first recognition for doing something good. He then said he needed to do something and thanked a deputy by name for bringing him an extra blanket and a hot-water bottle when he was really sick but the infirmary was too full to take him. "You didn't have to do that, man, and I know you paid a price for showing me some kindness," he said, choking back tears. The room burst into clapping, including, for the first time, the deputies standing against the back wall. Then the deputy who had just been thanked unexpectedly took the podium and, in an emotionally clouded baritone, thanked the inmate for having the courage to acknowledge his kindness in that kind of room. The room again burst into applause—for a guard.

As they applauded, I looked to the back of the room for Lieutenant Moak, the ranking deputy whose icy command ruled Pitchess. Moak was a hard, reserved deputy who had not wanted the Amer-I-Can course—or me—in his facility. He had relented when Sheriff Baca stood him down. I slipped next to the compact, intense lieutenant and quietly asked him which side had changed. Without turning to face me, he whispered back that both cultures had changed.

"Before," he continued, "that inmate could never have publicly thanked our deputy for bringing him that water bottle; his homies would have taken him down a stairwell and stomped him senseless for showing gratitude to one of us. And worse—I hate to admit this, but it's true—we deputies would have taken that deputy into the lockers and beaten him down for showing kindness to a prisoner. Both sides changed."

I was struck less by his honesty than by his tone, one of quiet reflection. Moak's eye watered, and he dabbed it with a tissue. I next asked him how he knew the course was the cause of the change. He said because ever since the course, on his days off, he could finish eighteen holes of golf without being called back to the prison for a lockdown.

For Moak the case was closed. Bo's leadership of the Amer-I-Can team had changed the behavior of the inmates. The startling part was not that the team had delivered their instruction, as promised, but that they had won the acknowledgment of the guards. After that session, Moak attended every graduation.

Two years later in 2004, as the lieutenant readied to retire, he asked to speak at the last Amer-I-Can graduation he would attend, a milestone that Bo relished. Bo introduced the stiff disciplinarian known for disliking inmates as an especially honored guest who needed no introduction. As the inmates politely applauded, Moak took the podium, nodded his acknowledgment of Bo, and cleared his throat.

"Thank you, Mr. Taylor," he began. "I've been a corrections deputy for over twenty-five years. You all know where I come from and how I see things. So you also know this podium is nowhere I would expect to be." The inmates chuckled. He continued, "But I've watched these classes for quite a while, and I've wanted to say some things because of them. You might see me wiping this eye a lot. It's not because I'm crying. It's because, after an inmate shoved a shiv into it, the tear ducts water uncontrollably. After I got attacked, I didn't just lose some of my sight, I also lost all respect for inmates. And as my anger grew, I began to think of convicts as less than human. I let my injury blind me to their humanity." He paused, looked out at the riveted room, swallowed, and touched his glasses before saying, "I was wrong."

The room fell silent. Bo stood and began a sober clap. Then the graduates, their blue jumpsuits marked SUPER MAXIMUM SECURITY filling the room, stood and clapped with meaning. Not long ago they'd have expected to hear the trumpet of Gabriel before ever hearing those words from Lieutenant Moak. They sat back down.

Moak continued. He said he had also been wrong to oppose the Amer-I-Can course. For two years, he had watched Mr. Taylor and his instructors come into Pitchess and conduct themselves professionally, with dignity and respect, and he had also watched this class and prior classes conduct themselves with honor. After they graduated, he had seen many of them carry out what they'd learned— stopping fights, teaching respect, and leading other prisoners to act right. "Best of all," he said, "I've seen you respect my deputies and treat us fairly. So now I know you can change."

He cleared his throat and dabbed his eye again before continuing. "So, Mr. Taylor, thank you. And because she has sued our department for so long, I strongly disliked civil rights lawyers like Miss Rice, and for a long time did not want her in my prison, either." The class laughed and looked my way. "But I know differently now. I've learned about this lady. Now I understand that even when I disagree with how she does it, she always fights for what is right, and she never stands down no matter what the cost to herself." He then turned to face me. "I just want to say, Miss Rice, you are a hero of mine."

The inmates again rose to their feet. Not for his recognition of me

but for their recognition of his courage and how far he had come. As
the chorus of cheers grew, I thought, my job risked nothing. Moak
risked his life daily doing his and had just risked everything else to
reveal his soul at that podium. There was a hero in the room, but it
was not I. Moak dabbed again with his tissue, but this time it was
both eyes. The clapping thundered, not just for the transformation in
him but also for the change in themselves. I turned to view the room
in its pandemonium, and for a moment I let myself feel deeply happy.
Redemption. Reconciliation. Transformation. This is what it should
be about all of the time, not just in fleeting moments of magic during
a graduation ceremony.

There would be an even more powerful graduation. It came after Bo
and Jim decided to add white prisoners to the black, brown, and Asian
students. The Amer-I-Can course was the only interracial oasis in a
prison system structured around racial gang segregation. Their decision meant members of the white supremacist Aryan Nations would
deconstruct their faults in the presence of the black, Latino, and Asian
prisoners they were supposed to dominate. To me, it sounded like a
good way to blow everything up. But in Bo's skilled hands, it worked.
He called after each session to report how extraordinary the intense
revelations had been as inmates from the different tribes confronted
one another over the mutual racial fear and hatred, but doing so with
the common purpose of tearing down the walls and starting over. I
just wished he had been able to film it.

   After the last class, Bo called to say that the ringleader of the
Aryan Nations had asked to speak during the graduation ceremony.
This I had to see. I rode the forty miles north to the prison with
Bo and joined James and Debbie Ingram, two stalwart supporters of
Bo; Gina Belafonte, Harry's daughter; and other regular Amer-I-Can
graduation attendees. Bo led us past the library, farther back in the
prison, to the cafeteria. Jim Brown followed us in, and radio host
Steve Harvey joined him as this graduation's celebrity guest. Finally,
the moment came. I watched in fascination as a burly, chipped-

toothed white inmate with the build of the Michelin Man rocked up to the podium. He gripped its sides with meaty hands, stomped into a dramatic stance, looked defiantly out at the audience, and shook his head in pantomimed disbelief. He whistled and then launched into what sounded like the middle of a sermon.

"Wow. Wow," he exclaimed. "I'm here to testify and, and, ya know, nobody could have told me this would happen. NO-BODY," he shouted. He said that before taking the Amer-I-Can course, he had been "a stone-cold hater." Pointing to his tattoos, he said, "Y'all know what this spider means. See this tear? You know what that means, too." He touched the spots on his body with the tattoos signifying different kinds of killings. "I was raised a hater. My daddy hated, my brothers hated. Hatin' is all I knew. It's what we did. But see, I know somethin' different now. Now I really know. This shit . . . this shit *here.*" His voice crescendoed as he held up the Amer-I-Can course book and shook it in the air. "This here shit is the shivvy— this has totally blown open my mind—turned it total around. Listen to me, I am telling you: I don't hate nobody. I don't *need* to hate anybody. When I get outta here, my daddy ain't gonna believe the change in me. He won't even know me. Because of this shit here, I can say every last one of you in here is my brother. I love all you motherfuckers. Black, brown, yellow, white. I ain't a hater of nobody now. NOBODY!" he yelled.

The room exploded. A pumped and astonished Bo hurtled to the podium, straight into the former Aryan's arms. The two men held on to each other and rocked back and forth, the epicenter of the stomping, whooping pandemonium shaking the rafters above. Guards came running into the cafeteria with batons drawn but stood in confusion at the scene before them: men hugging, yelling, and stomping in joy.

It did not stop for five minutes. I sat in the rip of emotion, searching for the false note, the ruse, the con of this over-the-top performance. As he rocked in Bo's arms and Bo in his, I decided to enjoy the fact that the feelings of the moment were real. Once again, I had come to see a graduation and witnessed human transformation instead.

Bo lived for these moments. To a true believer, they were not merely stunning hallmarks of an effective program but harbingers of a new day. To men who saw failure in the mirror, the sessions of wrenching self-critique had opened the path to self-respect. But as exhilarating as the moments had been, I thought they were, at most, testaments of momentary hope, tragic glimpses of what could be if only we wanted rehabilitated people more than we wanted an $8-billion-a-year corrections system that created more violent felons.

Sadly, Lieutenant Moak's initial resistance to rehabilitation was the norm. Deputies at Pitchess later sheepishly confessed that they had secretly amassed four years of data on Amer-I-Can graduates with the intention of using it to discredit the course. To their surprise, the numbers showed that the course improved inmates' post-release outcomes. Less than 12 percent of the Amer-I-Can graduates violated probation, and those who did took three times as long to do so. That was in contrast to over 60 percent of the other Pitchess prisoners reviolating within a year of release. So why weren't courses like Amer-I-Can mandatory and universally available? Because no one's job depended on men *not* returning to prison. Because the prison industrial complex made more money when more men were locked up.

For all of its inspiration and glimmers of short-term success, the course was not a harbinger of permanent transformation. How could it be? It was a three-week session with no resources for tracking its graduates or providing them with jobs or the support to sustain their new mind-set. Moreover, most of the super-max graduates were on their way to serving sentences in California prisons that were gang-run penal colonies known for 70 percent recidivism and brutishly increasing the criminality of their inmates. But after he'd buried two hundred friends and family members felled by gun and gang violence, who could blame Bo for seeing a ray of hope as the sun of a new day?

If Bo cleaved to these moments of graduation triumph, I had two of my own that vindicated my entire decade and a half of helping the people who strived against the trauma and violence of gangland. The first occurred in the last week of October 2000. Bo, sounding strangely officious, called midweek to ask that I come to a "very important" meeting that Saturday afternoon out at the Furama Hotel. "Now, you sure you'll be there?" he asked for the third time. "Jim needs you there, Connie, this is really very important." Annoyed at the repeated calls, I replied, "Yes," but I was thinking that unless they were announcing the end of all gang violence, there was nothing that could possibly justify a thirty-mile slog across town on a precious Saturday to attend a meeting at a one-star hotel all the way out at the airport. By Thursday, Big Ship, Looney, and Sleep had also called to ensure my attendance. I threatened not to come if one more call came over my phone. That Saturday, I grumbled the whole freeway drive out there, slapped the car into a space, and trudged up the stairs to the meeting room. I swung open the double doors and stopped in my tracks, stunned.

A sea of petal-pink tables with a white rose at each seat flowed across the breadth of a yawning ballroom. At the front, above a raised dais that stretched across the stage, hung a huge banner that read in gold letters: TO THE WOMEN IN OUR LIVES, THANK YOU FOR LOVING US WHEN WE DID NOT DESERVE TO BE LOVED.

At the tables across the ballroom floor sat hundreds of women in their Sunday best and the long gowns of Muslim dress, amid dozens and dozens of buzzing, rambunctious, happy kids.

Bo, dressed up in a suit, had reached my side, giddy with delight at my stunned state. "Hey, fellas, we finally made her speechless!" he called to Looney and Big Ship, who were on their way over to the entrance, too. Responding to the unspoken question on my face, he explained. "Connie, this is our appreciation celebration for all the women. Everybody's mamas, grandmamas, baby's mamas, wives, mistresses, daughters, nieces, aunties, sisters—and our lawyers, too—is here. We're thankin' all y'all that saved our lives, for stickin' with us through thick and thin and helping us survive to get where we are today. And we knew you, Madam Attorney, would be the hardest one, so to get your ornery ass here, we told you it was a meeting." He high-fived Looney and then bear-hugged me to whisper in my ear, "For real, Connie. Without y'all, we'd all be dead."

I bit my lip and hugged him back. What had gotten into them? Who put this idea in their heads?

They led me to my table and my white rose, and for the next four hours, the most amazing event I've ever seen unfolded. After eating, it began with twenty burly, buffed, hat-wearing, gold-chain-adorned men in suits. Each stood and gave an amazing confession. Each asked for forgiveness. Some asked their wives to forgive them for the beatings, the betrayals, the abandonment, for not being good husbands, for going to prison. One man in a red suit and matching fedora told his wife that he had abused her because she was just one more thing in his life that made him feel he wasn't a real man when he couldn't provide for her, couldn't handle the kids. That, he swore, had been nothing but a piss-poor excuse for his weakness. He knelt before her and vowed never to hit her again, never to get arrested again, and thanked her for standing by him when she should have been done with him. A huge man in a three-piece yellow ensemble explained to the audience that he did not understand women or how they thought, that he always said the wrong thing and felt stupid when he couldn't keep up with his wife, who was smarter than he was. Another told his mother that he would not have made it back on his feet without her and asked his daughters to forgive his leaving them for prison. Scores more stood to give similar testimonials, freed by the magic in the room to drop the masks and armor of machismo. Only one unwittingly broke the solemnity with a sincere promise that he would do as his girlfriend asked and not shut her out, would learn to talk about his feelings and the issues bothering her, but he had just one plea: "Baby, please, please, just don't ask me to talk about this shit during the football game!"

We all cracked up.

The confessions and professions of gratitude went on for two hours. There was not a dry eye in the room. Jim Brown, who'd had his own problems with domestic turmoil, had played a big role in this event. He, Bo, and the other men on the dais then presented plaques of appreciation to some of us, and after that the great vocalist, composer, and diehard Bo Taylor fan James Ingram sang his classic hit "One Hundred Ways." The room swooned.

This celebration had been solely the idea of Bo and the other men from Amer-I-Can. They had done everything themselves, from the pink tablecloths and the white roses to the banner. I congratulated as many as I could, hugged Bo, and headed for the double doors at the room's edge. Not quite sure what I had witnessed but very sure I'd never see it again, I paused and held the door to look back at the lingering families one final time, to take in once more the banner, the roses, the men, the women, and the joy. What a milestone. They would never be feminists, and most would slip up or fall back, but they had taken a dramatic step up the right road. Satisfied that it really had happened, I closed the door on the warm magic of that ballroom.

Walking downstairs to my car, I thought back to my allies' anxious objections to this work. My feminist friends especially had feared my choice to aid men who seemed wired to hurt women. It seemed at best a waste of time, at worst a betrayal. But I saw it differently. As professional women, we might face discrimination, but as underclass black men, they faced annihilation. I told my friends that the women of Jordan Downs had asked me to help their men, and I had gambled that if I stood in the breach against their annihilation and stayed the course in helping Fred, Bo, and the others change the violence, eventually, a few would change themselves. For at least one evening, in a ballroom of pink, my bet had been paid back in aces.

Once at my car, I placed the plaque and the rose on the front passenger seat, got behind the wheel, and wept.

Before the Furama event in 2000, gang intervention seemed to gain only a creeping acceptance with mainstream leaders and a few police officers. After the event, for whatever reason, the momentum quickened, and far more seemed willing to run the risk of working with ex-gangsters. So much so that when Harry Belafonte decided in 2002 to celebrate the tenth year of the Watts gang truce, Cardinal Mahony joined him, Sheriff Baca, and Chief Bratton to cohost a gala. The awardees were truce leaders, Tom Hayden, the Wellness Foundation, County Supervisor Mike Antonovich for championing the Amer-I-Can program, and John Dovey, the progressive prison warden of the California Institution for Women, a women's prison where I had taken Harry to visit and where we had recorded their prison choir.

In the year it took to plan and carry off the gala, Bo, Gina Belafonte, Debbie Ingram, James Ingram, Ms. Shabazz, and a whole team of us spent a maddening amount of time lining up sponsors, music, and money. We designed a beautiful award made out of melted bullets shaped into the Sankofa bird of redemption. I was squeezing this planning in between a pitched battle over reappointment of the chief of police and our ongoing police and bus rider cases. At one late point in the year, I burst into our conference room as Bo was reading over a script, and in panic over the lunacy of what we were doing, I asked how in the hell were we going to fill a ballroom with gangsters from rival races and warring sets and keep anyone safe? Bo told me to calm down. Security was *his* job, and he had it "under control."

"You think I'm gonna have anybody acting up in front of Harry Belafonte and Danny Glover? If any one of these niggas even thinks of pulling some shit, I'll *kill* the motherfucker."

I told Bo that murder to provide security at the Urban Peace Awards would be a little off message. I got my law partner Steve English to buy a catastrophic event rider to our corporate insurance.

When the night arrived, the packed event went off without so much as a shoving match. After Japanese Taiko drummers pounded the hall with their primordial call, Father Greg Boyle opened the evening with a prayer of tears for the inconsolable grief of a mother burying her gunned-down child and of shame for our unconscionable indifference to the hopelessness that fuels *la vida loca*. He touched the hearts of everyone in that amazing room full of the unlikely allies from every tribe and profession that, since 1991, we had built to fight the violence. With former and current gangsters in tuxedos, cops in uniform, and clergy in robes, we successfully celebrated the tenth year of the Watts gang truce that Fred had been fighting to enforce when I met him at the beginning of my journey to learn gangland. There would be just one other incredible encounter that ended in epiphany and light.

On April 24, 2001, Jim invited Harry and me to visit his Beverly Hills home during one of Harry's frequent trips out to L.A. It was early evening when Harry and I arrived at Jim's home. Bo and thirty or so other Amer-I-Can men were waiting to see "Mr. B." again. Up to that point it had not been a good day.

Harry and I had returned from visiting a state prison—an ugly, lethally crowded pen of fetid dormitories and cells crammed full of restless black and brown men. The place looked like the hold of a slave ship. With the caged misery still roiling in his mind, Harry stood before the gathering, acknowledged Jim, and then took the room back to the beginnings of the modern civil rights revolution. He recounted how he and other Negro World War II veterans had returned to the U.S. fresh from liberating Europe and shutting down the horrors of Auschwitz. As tested soldiers, they found themselves unable to any longer stomach the segregated repression they had left behind for war. Black soldiers determined that, after fighting for European liberation, they could no longer accept subjugation in their own country. And after white men in Georgia dragged a returning Negro soldier off the bus and gouged out his eyes, there was no turning back. "When we came back, the fight for black liberation was *on,*" Harry said to his rapt audience. He explained that it was a strategic movement fought on every front—by Jackie Robinson in the dugout, Thurgood Marshall in the courthouse, Paul Robeson in the playhouse, Rosa Parks at the bus stop, Fannie Lou Hamer in the DNC, Martin Luther King Jr. everywhere, and legions of Americans from all races marching for justice under Gandhi's rules for strategic nonviolent resistance.

"At every turn, we had to plot and strategize—there were no accidental heroes," Harry told them. "Rosa Parks did not just *happen* to be on a bus and all of a sudden get too tired to move for a white passenger." She had been carefully selected, he explained, trained, and deployed, and the community had been trained to follow through with a punishing boycott designed to bring the segregated bus system to its knees.

One of the pivotal lessons, one of their core principles, he said, was that they never gave the other side what it needed. "We always deprived them of what they needed from us to force our participation in our own degradation. If they needed passengers to fuel a racist bus system, we walked. If they needed our patronage at their racist segregated stores, we boycotted. If they needed our inferiority, we met them with dignity. If they needed our violence, we confronted with peaceful protest."

Then he spun it all around into the most profound of challenges to the men in that room. "Now, it took us three hundred years of struggle to free ourselves out of European shackles. Many sacrificed mightily for that freedom. Many, many died. Many, many more suffered. And through it all, we never willingly ceded that which the slaver needed to keep us under his boot. So when I see an entire generation of us *back* in cages, *back* in chains, it is unacceptable. I—I cannot accept it. I simply will not accept it. How *dare* you willingly put yourselves back into chains! How *dare* you let them trap you back into cages! You make a mockery of the sacrifices paid for your freedom. People died so you could be free—and you throw that away? You never, *ever* give your oppressor what he needs to oppress you. What *today* do they need to shackle two thirds of black men? Two things: your stupidity and your criminality. It is unforgivable that you freely give them both. You have the power to deny this mass incarceration obscenity what it needs for its cages—our brown bodies! Deny this demonic system the fuel it needs. You have the power to shut it down tomorrow. Use it."

I was staggered by the power of his words: *We never, ever gave our enemy what he needed to oppress us.* They had landed with the force of blows. Breathless, I slipped a glance around the tense room. Did they understand what he had just said? Was it too harsh for them to hear? The tears in their eyes said they understood. I looked around again. They had been moved by his indignation, stung by his rebuke, and riveted by the idea that they had the power to starve the prison beast. Bo stood up in silent tribute. The others followed. Jim stood, too. Relieved, I took a breath and watched as once-lost men clamored over two of their fathers.

After Harry finished his talk, the meeting melted into clusters buzzing about Mr. B.'s "heavy" message. As the men fanned out onto Jim's hillside patio, I, too, headed outside to its panoramic vista, sweeping from the twinkling Pacific to the San Gabriel Mountains rising behind the downtown skyline. As I took in the full moon rising over the mountains, and the orange-pink sun slipping into the ocean, a heavy hand tapped my shoulder.

"Lady Lawyer?" I turned and could not believe who was seeking me out. It was Roc, a walking wall of a man who, in all these years, had never addressed me directly beyond respectful nods of acknowledgment. He was one of the many men in that world who had accepted my presence but never spoken a word to me.

"Roc!" I blurted, almost falling over and failing miserably to disguise my surprise.

"Can I say somethin' to you?" He towered over me as I regained my wits.

"Yes, of course."

"Thank you." He tightened up and drew a deep breath, as if readying for something important. "I just wanted you to know that I am not the predator you met ten years ago. I have evolved, and I am now fit to address people like you and Mr. Belafonte. Before now I was not good enough to talk to you. But now I am a peacemaker."

My heart burst. This giant man's silence had been purposeful, and unlike so many others, he had lived in thought and humility to find a new way. Over badly suppressed emotion, I told Roc that he had always been fit to speak to me and that he should be proud of how far he had come. From predator to peacemaker was a long arc of change—a long journey.

"I am proud to know you," I said. "I'm just really happy that you feel you can now talk to me."

Roc pursed his lips to suppress the impact of my words and nodded his acceptance of my respect. I pursed mine in a smile, nodded back, and for the first time in decades, I thought of an exchange with a migrant worker's kid long ago in a tin-roofed shack outside of Phoenix.

Chapter 14

THE ADVANCEMENT PROJECT

In 1997 my mentor, co-conspirator, and linebacker Bill Lann Lee brought our long partnership to a close. He told Molly, Kevin, Robert, and me that he wanted to become the next assistant attorney general for civil rights in the second Clinton administration. Crestfallen, we nonetheless dived into preparing our irreplaceable friend for Senate confirmation with everything from testimony to hair mousse.

Bill was right. It was time to move on. He deserved to move up to the political front lines, and those of us he was leaving behind in the trenches needed to create a more nimble organization with a bigger toolbox. The civil rights establishment seemed exhausted—stymied by the polarized politics and unable to keep pace with technology or change.

Bill's imminent departure for Washington meant that my time at Thurgood Marshall's law firm, my professional home for nearly twenty years, was coming to an end. I would never lose sight of the debt we owed: Without LDF, the vastly more just America we took for granted never would have happened. We would always stand on the shoulders of LDF's great lawyers. I hated to leave the venerable grand dame of civil rights, but the work ahead exceeded what venerability could carry.

Frontline civil rights work in the twenty-first century required actions that no organization carrying the legacy of Thurgood Marshall should take. It was bad enough that in our bus riders case, Bill, Kevin, Robert, and I had sued members of LDF's own board of directors and a former LDF lawyer.[17] But if our colleagues and friends in office continued presiding over policies that mindlessly dropped the poor from the script, we would have to sue more of them, not fewer. Moreover, if the Zunigas and the Jacksons were to ever get put back into the American Dream, we would have to remove the worst leaders from office and take over the institutions that were too incompetent to be sued. This was what twenty-first-century civil rights would require vis-á-vis our friends. Our regressive opponents seeking to repeal the last century of human progress and to excise slavery from history, reason from discourse, and reality from policy, would receive even less cordial countermeasures.

Of course, coercion would be our last, least used choice—and done separately from the foundation-funded work. First we would talk to seek real solutions. But not for long. I was done with my friends' penchant for endless discussion, actionless conferences, and timid tinkering with incontinent policies that hurt poor kids. I was ready to infiltrate opponents, take over the levers of government, and seek to do more with unlikely allies. I wanted to use technology to marshal data, raise money, empower folks to solve their own problems, and expand the inequity mapping that had helped win our $1 billion school construction case, *Godinez v. Davis*.

If this new organization did half of what I envisioned, my New Year's Eve party invitations were about to dwindle to just one: Molly's.

In this new organization, we'd need to do more than vindicate rights won in the 1960s civil rights revolution. We had to push for fresh recognition of the innate rights, freedoms, and responsibilities that are the stepping-stones for the "unalienable rights" enumerated by our founders in the Bill of Rights, the Declaration of Independence, and the amended U.S. Constitution. We had to establish the "unalienable" right to safety,[18] vest the "inviolability" of freedom from violence, and launch the "most necessary and most important rights" to viable education and employment.[19] These rights are not listed in our founding texts, but they shoulder every line of those great documents. Indeed, the founding fathers stated that life, liberty, and the pursuit of happiness are meaningless without safety. It makes no sense to proclaim a right to life but have no right to be safe; to assert rights to liberty and the pursuit of happiness but have no opportunity to achieve either. In family law, most states end parental rights and remove a child to a safer home under a standard called the "failure to thrive." We needed to establish for all children the right to thrive—to be safe, sheltered, fed, clothed, healed, loved, and educated. Dr. King, a founding father of post-slavery America, called these notions a "revolution of values." He challenged us to elevate human well-being above avarice and corporate excess to create a "people-oriented" capitalism that a just and widely prosperous society requires.[20] Our job was to revive Dr. King's doctrine of basic human rights.

My other, related goal would be to show how tacit destruction of the underclass inevitably leads to middle-class endangerment.

After Bill heeded the call to go to Washington, D.C., one of the best legal teams in the country parted. Kevin left for a Westside law firm. Robert joined the National Resources Defense Council. Molly and I teamed up with Penda Hair, our colleague who headed LDF's Washington office, to form a new policy and legal action group called the Advancement Project. Molly named it for the only word other than "people" that we liked in LDF's long name: the National Association for the *Advancement* of Colored People Legal Defense and Educational Fund, Incorporated. Molly and I would lead the Los Angeles office, and Penda would head up the Washington, D.C., office. Luckily for us, after listening to our kitchen-table planning of this new venture for six months, Steve English, the same man who calmed credit card companies whenever Molly and I went shopping, volunteered to leave his law partnership at Morgan, Lewis & Bockius to become our managing partner. He knew that Molly and I would never make the trains run on time. For the tougher jobs that required lawsuits and campaigns, Steve, Molly, and I also formed our own law firm, English, Munger & Rice.

I left LDF for the Advancement Project and my new law firm at the end of 1998. I was forty-two years old and feeling good about our new venture and my life. My fast gait had slowed a bit, and all-nighters at work now took a toll, but my mental age was still twenty-seven, the birthday I first felt complete and fully content with the woman returning my gaze in the mirror. It would be from a new platform, but every day would still give me the privilege of working with the best people to finish what Martin Luther King Jr., Thurgood Marshall, and a whole slew of prior pioneers had started.

A few weeks before the move out of LDF, I spotted Cookie waiting to wheel herself across Ninth Street. My heart sank. She was a toothless glassy-eyed shadow of the sly, bodacious woman who accosted me on my first day at the L.A. office of LDF eight years earlier. I thought that as we started a new chapter, she was fading and probably would not last much longer on L.A.'s squalid downtown streets. There was so much to do just to deliver the basics and a decent chance.

This was why we created the Advancement Project. We needed bolder strategies, wider reach, and deeper impact to change systems. For that we required more than a law firm and more than a think tank or talk tank. We needed an "action tank"—and a bigger toolbox that included technology. The vision for the Advancement Project was to clear the way for every child to have a fair shot at achieving her potential. We would not stop at vindicating the basic rights underlying the promises of equal treatment, life, liberty, and the pursuit of happiness; we would engineer them. Our mission is to generate upward mobility by making the basic opportunity systems work without bias and with enough competence for folks who want to advance themselves out of poverty to do so. And if that required taking over dysfunctional bureaucracies and political offices, we would do so.

While keeping tabs on Bo and wrestling with a resurgently insular LAPD, Molly, Steve, and I turned to the second evil bedeviling hot zones: the cemeteries we called public schools. Education malpractice was where the Advancement Project in L.A. first picked up the baton after leaving LDF.

I had been waiting for a long time to storm this particular Bastille.

The failure of hot-zone schools had first hit home when Chandra was forced to teach an office intern, who was ranked third in her class at Jordan High School, how to alphabetize. The student had taken every honors course at her school and had studied hard, but no one told her that the courses had no college-prep content. And no one had told her that her 3.8 GPA in the Los Angeles Unified School District (LAUSD) was the equivalent of a C- in Malibu. We paid taxes for this tawdry education fraud that deceived children. Now, *this* warranted new criminal statutes: first-degree theft of viability— with aggravating circumstances.

My first day in Watts had confirmed the dismal state of hot-zone schools. Fred Williams and Black could read and write, but every other young man I met from Grape Street had been drummed out of the LAUSD and sent to the even worse county prison schools, where illiteracy was the norm. The LAUSD, a colossal bureaucracy with a $10 billion budget, buried the futures of more children than San Francisco had residents. And our friends were running it.

The hand-painted banner that hung across the back wall of Fred's bungalow behind Markham Junior High School had exclaimed in star-spangled green and purple letters, EDUCATION IS THE KEY! I remembered how earnest Fred had been, standing in front of it and reading the slogan out loud like a Pledge of Allegiance. Anywhere else, his display would have seemed absurd; the banner, a cliché. But coming from the minds of gang members, the slogan struck me as profound. Those who had aborted their own education for crime had ended up pushing school as the only rescue line out of *la vida loca*.

Superb schools that not only educate but also enrich the community can reverse the unholy trinity of despair: violence; ignorance; joblessness. Good public schools, like the ones my mom attended, can catapult a family from sharecroppers to medical doctors in one generation. But catastrophically failed schools like Markham Junior High catapulted far more into prison than medical school. A third of Markham's students and a quarter of its teachers suffered Civil War levels of PTSD, half of the kids would drop out, and four of the remaining kids might end up prepared for a four-year college.

This kind of perennial failure was not just unconstitutional, it was the engine driving the prison industrial complex. The naked nexus between failed education and the country's vast prison network was clearest in the states that based projections for prison beds on the number of seven-year-olds who could not read. Who knew their lives were over by second grade?

I did not need statistics and studies. I knew the children who paid the price of our failure to keep them safe and learning at high levels. I had known them all of my life, from migrant workers' kids in Arizona to subway serfs in the Bronx and now Fred's kids in Watts. I knew what happened to them. I knew the options they did not have, the odds they were unlikely to beat, the ugly ends they were more likely to meet.

For these kids, Los Angeles public schools were, at best, conveyor belts to nowhere and, at worst, greased chutes into the abattoirs of prison. In fact, L.A. County schools, the dumping-ground schools of last resort for the criminally convicted and expelled LAUSD students, were designed to operate more like prisons than schools. Over the past seven years, Molly and I had participated in several civic school-reform efforts that had no ability to penetrate LAUSD's culture of aggressive mediocrity and chronic failure. As with taking on LAPD, avoiding this fight was no longer an option. The civil rights question of the twenty-first century was not whether the few poor kids who qualified for college got to attend UCLA or UC Irvine. It was whether kids in the kill zones had an environment safe enough for learning and schools rigorous enough to give them viable options in a global information economy.

When our LDF boss, Elaine Jones, had asked us in 1996 why her L.A. lawyers had no lawsuits against the abysmal Los Angeles public schools, I responded, "Because we would win."

I was not being sassy. All you had to do was look at the pile of court settlement orders thicker than a phone book to see that winning a lawsuit was no magic bullet. The only court order that mattered would be one ordering a viable education for poor kids, but obeying it would exceed LAUSD's ability.

It wasn't that we hadn't considered a lawsuit. I had been all hot to trot about a legal theory of education malpractice. Schools like Markham, with 3 percent of students proficient in math, 11 percent proficient in English, and perennial dropout rates of 60 percent, had to be violating *some* kind of professional standards. But the courts had declared that the field of education had too few standards on which to base liability for malpractice. How could education have no standards? My mom was a teacher, and she had the highest standards and expectations for performance. You had no choice but to learn in her classroom. I could see her now, sitting at the kitchen table poring over papers well past midnight, giving her students everything she had.

Courts alone did not have the power to fix the problem. Desegregation, equal funding, minority representation on school boards, special education rights, access to honors courses, skewed distribution of qualified teachers, racial tracking, unfair discipline, language acquisition, disabled-student access, gifted-child rights—each theory had successful legal champions, but none of these cases had fixed a dysfunctional school.

The army of folks wrestling for decades over improving education astounded me. Hundreds of foundations, corporations, commissions, boards, and associations obsessed over improving education. They raised money, threw conferences, offered training, conducted research, championed new models, sponsored partnerships with public schools, and rang alarms. *A Nation at Risk,* the latest of the clarion calls that some national commission seemed to issue every decade, had sounded the alarm yet again: Fix the schools or lose your future. We had plenty of smart people worrying and warning about education failures.

There also was no lack of ideas, as seen in the alphabet soup of reform fads—TQM, LEARN, LEAP, LAMP, all community efforts to help schools educate more effectively. We certainly suffered from no shortage of touted remedies: Magnets. Charters. Vouchers. Classroom-based budgeting. School-based management. Raise taxes. Reduce class size. Get rid of unions. Return to vocational ed. Get rid of school boards. Fire teachers. Fire administrators. Evaluate teachers. Grade parents. Bring back paddling. Deny diplomas. Give schools away. Train principals. Lengthen school days. Mayoral control. Raise expectations. End tenure. Punish parents. Educate parents. Pay kids to achieve. Fix families. Pray.

With all of this activity, why was education still so broken? Correction: Why were schools for *poor* children so broken? Upper-middle-class kids in the best public schools fared quite well, routinely ending up at Stanford and in the Ivy League.

When we started our education work, my knowledge about the conundrum of public education merited an "educable mentally retarded" classification, one of the lower academic tracks into which LAUSD placed the majority of black boys and increasing percentages of Latinos. I needed someone to show me why the problems at L.A. Unified were so intractable—and then figure out a way to get inside and start fixing them.

I found her at Martin Luther King Jr.'s legacy organization, the Southern Christian Leadership Conference, on Western Boulevard in South Central L.A. Genethia Hudley-Hayes stood five feet two inches tall and, when quiet, could be mistaken for a nice, cute little brown lady. When not, she struck terror in everyone around her. Genethia had started her career as a teacher, but LAUSD fired her after she refused to dumb down her teaching material and then told her principal that he needed a brain transplant. She made education reform her life's work, becoming a curriculum specialist and then education projects director for the SCLC.

Genethia was a human flamethrower. Her brain clicked like a switchblade, her will bowled over blowhards, and her sharp tongue could wilt Velcro. I adored her from the moment in July 1992 when she upended a meeting at my LDF office, physically moving the poor man who had placed himself at the head of the table from his seat and proceeding to assign tasks. Fifteen minutes later, the meeting ended, and she corralled me into a corner, took my arm, screwed her sharp little face into a question mark, and honed in. "Come here, you. I'm Genethia Hudley-Hayes. Just who the hell are you, and why am I just now meeting you?"

I laughed and thought, *Is this my office or hers?* She ripped on: "I saw you sitting over there, all quiet, looking like you've never in your life seen such a group of fools. You are absolutely right, they *are* walking exhibits of *The Miseducation of the Negro,* but you need to watch that bright little face of yours in these damn meetings. Now answer my question, where the hell did *you* come from?"

We went to lunch and never looked back.

In Genethia, I had met my doppelgänger. She cussed more, but not by much. She was bolder, and suffered fools even less than I did, but we shared a worldview and a bias—that there is a superior gender and we were members of it. Genethia is the only person I know whose attachment to her parents mirrors mine and whose passion for finishing Dr. King's work exceeds mine. She also was the only black leader who pressed as hard for Latino advancement. When too many of our colleagues were silent, she loudly opposed the unconstitutional Proposition 187, which barred unauthorized immigrants from all public services, including health care and schools. I will never forget her commanding me to join her in the fields to pick strawberries with Latino farmworkers after members of her SCLC board complained that, as the head of a black organization, she was focusing too much on Latino rights.

"These Negroes have pushed my last Jesus nerve!" she bellowed. "I am doing nothing *but* Latino rights from here on out, *y estoy hablando nada sino español.*"

She began addressing the SCLC board members solely in Spanish, boycotted the board's annual retreat, and went to pick strawberries with farmworkers. Within a month, the board had surrendered.

It took no time for Molly and me to join Genethia's orbit of determined women, or as one man complained, those "wolf women." Phyllis Hart, Cynthia Robbins, Dorothy Pozner, Alice Duff, Phyllis Louie all ran or worked for nonprofit organizations determined to fix schools for the poorest kids.

Over the years, Molly and I had learned education warfare at Genethia's sharp elbow. So by the time we launched the Advancement Project and English, Munger & Rice, we were ready to help when an enraged Genethia summoned us to help her take over the school board and oust entrenched incumbent Barbara Boudreaux. Genethia had confronted Boudreaux over her vote to stop documenting how many kids were taking the courses required for entrance to University of California colleges. Boudreaux told Genethia that if she wanted a say in the matter, she had to first take her seat as a board member. We joined forces with Mayor Riordan and took not only Boudreaux's seat but two others.

Genethia installed herself as LAUSD school board president in 1999, fired the superintendent, hired former Colorado governor Roy Romer as the new LAUSD superintendent, and ordered us to help Romer create a school construction enterprise to build 150 new schools needed to end the severe overcrowding that shortened the school year, blocked all academic improvement, and doomed one hundred thousand kids to sitting on floors and windowsills with no desks, no lockers, and no access to restrooms. The district had failed to build schools for thirty years.

This massive mission involved: filing and winning *Godinez v. Davis,* our $1 billion lawsuit that ended the state's unfair school construction bond distribution system; leveraging the *Godinez* money to help Romer jump-start LAUSD's school construction; wrangling Republican support to pass $30 billion in school construction bonds; backing Romer's hiring of retired Navy engineer Captain Jim McConnell and his platoon of talented Seabees to head the building program; helping Romer and the Seabees create a quasi-independent school construction authority; neutralizing the racial and union politics to keep the Seabees safe from board stupidity; and for nine of twelve years, blocking the politicians from squandering the construction money with their politicized micromanaging. Under this model, Captain McConnell's construction system built more than 140 beautiful schools, on time and on budget; completed over $3.7 billion in school repairs; and won more than eighty private-sector awards for excellence in mega-construction management.

This ten-year battle to construct schools that we waged while Genethia and Romer tackled instruction is a five-diamond blueprint for how to get big stuff done when bungling bureaucrats, inept politicians, sclerotic unions, and powerless people cannot get it done. By the time I left the building enterprise in 2011, we and our military builders (eventually, we added Air Force and Army engineers) had ended multitracking, ended busing due to overcrowding, and given every student a seat in a neighborhood school. It was an astounding feat.

But in 2000, as we began this work, Bill Lee was two thousand miles away, settling into his job as the nation's new acting assistant attorney general.[21] He may have thought he'd left L.A. behind, but Bill was about to finish what the Christopher Commission had started nine years earlier in response to a taped beating seen around the world.

Chapter 15

TAKEDOWN

S ince the removal of LAPD inspector general Mader in November 1998, Chief Parks had achieved a robust comeback for the old, arrogant, and insular LAPD. As the chief crushed the department under his masterful control, he also blocked external interference and rebuffed all outside reformers like us. My hope for collaboration withered. And since Mayor Riordan and the president of the Police Commission were enthralled with Parks's impressive command, there was no one to counter LAPD's withdrawal. Nothing short of a neutron bomb was going to loosen Parks's iron grip.

The first detonation went off on September 8, 1999. I opened my *Los Angeles Times* with the rest of Los Angeles to read that Rafael "Ray" Perez, a former LAPD CRASH gang officer in Rampart Division, had pleaded guilty to drug charges and, under oath, disclosed that he and dozens of fellow officers had routinely framed suspects, stolen drugs, planted evidence, fabricated probable cause, lied in court, and physically abused suspects. It would later be revealed that to cover their crimes, Perez and his cronies had fixed investigations, arranged the deportation of witnesses to their crimes, and forced rookie cops to commit crimes. Worst of all, in 1996 Perez had illegally gunned down an unarmed gang member, lied to cover it up, and then committed perjury to send the man to prison for twenty-three years.

It was a stunning litany of criminal misconduct by an officer from the same gang unit that, nine years earlier, had threatened Sergeant Reidel for stopping the Russian-roulette torture of a gang member in Southeast Division.

If Perez's allegations were true, the scale of the abuses, the impunity with which the abusers acted, and the protection they had commanded put this corruption at a nine on the Richter scale. This crisis dwarfed the King beating. It was one thing for LAPD to provoke a $1 billion riot after an outrageous beating of a single suspect. It was an entirely different matter for gangster cops to frame suspects and torpedo the integrity of the entire Los Angeles criminal justice system. Had a gang of outlaw cops just jeopardized hundreds or even thousands of criminal convictions? This time LAPD may have crossed a line that threatened the elite, not only the poor and powerless.

Parks responded by quickly suspending twelve lower-level officers and dismantling the Rampart CRASH unit. It would not be enough to contain the damage. Allegations that outlaw cops possibly had corrupted hundreds of trials triggered the kind of sweeping investigations that ensnared everyone in the criminal justice system. A corruption scandal of this magnitude would rock the foundations of LAPD. No one would be safe from scrutiny, not even the chief of police. The end of Bernard Parks's reign had begun.

Perez's allegations touched off a lollapalooza of tangled investigations of what everyone was calling the "Rampart CRASH scandal" or just "Rampart." The criminal justice machinery lurched into reaction against LAPD officers. The county district attorneys had to create teams to investigate potentially tainted convictions, and get ready to release any prisoners convicted on evidence fabricated by CRASH officers. Other teams had to investigate the dozens of police crimes that Perez had divulged to meet the condition of his plea bargain. As the paranoia set in, special task forces dived into figuring out if dots connected CRASH corruption to a bank robbery by an LAPD officer associated with Perez. Another unit investigated missing cocaine from the LAPD's evidence locker, as well as a clique of cops rumored to be linked to Death Row Records and hit squads. This was *L.A. Confidential* on steroids.

Before long the Los Angeles FBI and the U.S. attorney joined the DA's investigations. The Police Commission woke up and asked a group of outside lawyers to do an independent investigation of the scandal. Trying to outpace the avalanche, Chief Parks had already launched a board of inquiry to investigate what he called the "Rampart incident." More important than L.A.'s five-ring circus of investigations was that Perez's explosive testimony had landed like a mortar in Bill Lann Lee's Washington, D.C., office at the United States Department of Justice. Perez's confession had gutted the grounds for his DOJ office's prior decision to suspend federal takeover of LAPD.

Seeing no role to play, I settled in with the rest of L.A. to await the results from the criminal probes and civilian investigations. I had plenty to do, what with *Tipton* mediations, supervising bus system improvements in the MTA case, and, on my own time, helping Genethia Hayes explore a race for school board. On March 1, 2000, Chief Parks unveiled his 362-page report on Rampart. It characterized the fiasco as an isolated incident and narrowed the blame to Perez and his rank-and-file CRASH cronies. While it noted significant failures in supervision at the division level, it largely exempted the highest levels of LAPD management from any culpability and ignored the culture and attitudes that had spawned the corruption and shielded the misconduct. Unfortunately for LAPD, the report of the board of inquiry did not even begin to quell the furor. It did, however, prompt a very unlikely call to me the week following its release. I had difficulty believing who was on my line.

"Connie, this is Ted Hunt," said a gruff voice, as familiar to me as chalk on a blackboard. Hunt, a stout bulldog of a man with crystalline blue eyes, was the head of the Police Protective League (The League), the police union whose leaders had bedeviled our female and minority officers and once thrown me bodily out of its headquarters. Before I could utter a syllable, he rushed to admit that, given the League's mistreatment of me and our clients in the past, I had every reason to refuse his call. But, he added, "I'm just hoping you'll look past our history. Because we need your help."

I was having trouble processing the "asking for help" part. It was as believable as Bull Connor calling Martin Luther King Jr. for help. He thanked me for not cursing him out. I offered to cuss him out later and asked him what was up. Hunt was livid about the scapegoating of rank-and-file cops in the chief's report. He considered it the latest abuse of officers during the panicked "cover brass ass" investigations. He wanted to know if I would help Erwin Chemerinsky, the genius constitutional law professor from USC, conduct an independent investigation of the Rampart CRASH gangster-cop scandal on behalf of the Los Angeles Police Protective League.

I was momentarily speechless. Hunt filled in the silence with an urgent pitch. "Connie, do you know how bad things have to be for the League to ask the city's leading liberals for help?" he asked rhetorically. "We *have* to have at least *one* investigation that the rank and file trusts to say what was the culpability of the upper ranks for letting Perez run wild. To tell you the truth, I fear there will be no LAPD left to fight over by the time this last blow plays out. We're at the end of our rope. What Parks isn't wrecking, Rampart will finish. What do you say?"

The irony of the League—which had terrorized our clients for years—bemoaning intimidation, Machiavellian traps, and persecution was rich. He would not have wanted to hear my assessment that LAPD was reaping what it had sown. Parks had turned LAPD's mean, Inquisition-like, paranoid, arrogant, and ruthless culture back onto itself, and now they were eating their young with the same Torquemada zeal they had used on the black community.

Nonetheless, Hunt was right. The board of inquiry report begged for a credible rebuttal to its simplistic "blame the grunts" conclusions. Erwin Chemerinsky was the one to give it. Erwin would show the full range of culpability for the scandal, especially at the top, and he would level a ruthless review of the League's own responsibility. If

Erwin had agreed to do this inquiry, and he wanted me on his team, there was no question what my answer would be.

But I would have said yes even if Erwin had turned the League down. I knew from our black, Latino, Asian, gay, and female officer clients that, under Parks's investigatory zeal, the department tottered on the brink of disintegration. My job was to help save it from the abyss, even if that required joining an arch-opponent like Hunt. The only thing worse than a racist and brutal LAPD was no LAPD.

Dire straits produce strange allies.

Erwin Chemerinsky, to me, was the conscience of Los Angeles. He was a compassionate renaissance man and scholar who used his great brain not just to teach the law of the United States Constitution but also to advance its promise in the real world. He was scary smart and the only person I knew who naturally spoke in outline order and full paragraphs. To carry out the League's request, Erwin refused any payment, insisted on total editorial control, with no prior review or approval, and joint presentation—League leaders could read the report and appear at our press conference but could not ask for changes. Erwin then convened what had to be the most liberal group of lawyers since witnesses appeared at the McCarthy hearings in the 1950s. He invited Samuel Paz, who had filed and won as many police misconduct cases as Johnnie Cochran; Paul Hoffman, the ACLU's director of litigation; and Laurie Levenson, Erwin's equally brilliant criminal law counterpart at Loyola Law School, who had become a familiar face on television as a commentator on the O. J. Simpson trial. To round out the panel he added Carol Sobel, my comedic friend and co-counsel, who wisecracked about the Magnificent Six working for the cops who would beat Rodney King all over again tomorrow.

Parks's board of inquiry report had concluded that the Rampart CRASH incident was about a few bad apples. We helped Erwin make the case that the barrel, the tree, and the entire orchard also were rotten. The mistreatment of suspects by Rampart CRASH officers was not a rare incident but a widespread practice tolerated by supervisors. Based on our analysis, Erwin concluded that CRASH corruption was the inevitable by-product of an LAPD culture that celebrated outlaw cops, rewarded excessive force, and used intimidation against the public and its own officers. He also called for something that had not yet happened for the biggest scandal in LAPD history: a completely independent investigation by an entity that was not involved with LAPD.

The League's gamble on engaging us had paid off in one way: They had a credible report by unimpeachable adversaries to refute management's relegation of blame to rank-and-file gang officers. But the Chemerinsky report, released on September 11, 2000, also leveled harsh criticism on the League. From the uneasy faces of the union's leaders standing next to Erwin during the press conference, one could tell it had been an ambivalent victory.

Looking across that lineup of awkward allies, however, I had no ambivalence. If it's done with enough skill, a powerful report written *with* your opponents and used aggressively to drive an unexpected agenda could, for a short while, paralyze the naysayers, shine a spotlight, correct the focus, reverse the inertia, and elevate policy over politics. The Chemerinsky–Protective League report had not been just a countervolley in a blame fight. It had created the unlikely alliance with Ted Hunt and the League that would be a much bigger turning point in the quest for constitutional policing than even my epiphany with the K-9 officers. The League's Praetorian Guards, while still hostile, had cracked open the castle door—enough to ask for our help. But that inch would be enough for me to eventually push it wide open with the battering rams of campaigns to come.

Our joint venture with the League was over. Fallout from Rampart, however, was just getting started. There were tons of dull agency reports to come, but the public had far more entertaining fare to watch: the twists and turns of the CRASH officer criminal trials, indictments of additional LAPD officers, charges of sexual escapades in the Rampart civil grand jury, reversed convictions that freed inmates, dueling press conferences by politicians, public blowups between the district attorney and Chief Parks, spats between the FBI and LAPD over investigations, Mayor Riordan's firing of hard-charging police commissioner Gerry Chaleff, and the arrival of a new district attorney, Steve Cooley.

Of course, the public had no idea that this L.A. circus was the sideshow. The main act had been unleashed in May 2000 by the big guns from the United States Department of Justice in Washington, D.C. After determining that LAPD had failed to achieve promised reforms, the DOJ's Civil Rights Division, now led by Bill Lann Lee, filed suit and demanded that LAPD and the city submit to a federal consent decree and federal court control of the department for at least five years.

To Mayor Riordan and Chief Parks, this was a declaration of war. How could a department that had proudly dismissed compliance with Supreme Court cases possibly accept federal court control? It couldn't. The mayor and the chief flew to D.C. in May 2000, determined to stop Bill and the Civil Rights Division. Riordan and Parks begged everyone from Janet Reno to Bill Clinton to force DOJ to withdraw the lawsuit that would put a federal judge in charge of LAPD reform. It did not work.

In September 2000 the Los Angeles City Council voted to submit to the DOJ consent decree, ending the efforts of the mayor and the chief to avoid federal receivership. The Los Angeles Police Department was forced to submit to the jurisdiction and control of the United States District Court for the Central District of California, and Judge Gary Feess, a former lawyer for the Christopher Commission. I could not have been prouder that the man who had placed the Blue Grip under this extraordinary federal control was my former partner at LDF, the acting assistant attorney general for civil rights, Bill Lann Lee.

That same November, a jury handed down guilty verdicts for three more CRASH officers, and the 2000 presidential election ended in a tie. Over the Thanksgiving holiday, I watched the constitutional drama unfold on the television in my mother's kitchen as she cooked our week of feasting. Like the butterflies of Madagascar or the swallows of Capistrano, I had not missed my annual pilgrimage home in twenty years. It was the one time I took off my armor and relaxed. I was home and safe. I remember pumping my fist as Al Gore mentioned our codirector Penda Hair's name in an NPR radio report on his battle to get votes counted in Florida. Penda, a voting rights expert who headed the Advancement Project's D.C. offices, had dropped her own Thanksgiving cooking and raced down to Dade County to collect sworn statements from upstanding black voters who had been illegally designated as felons and removed from the voter rolls by a Republican unit dedicated to that task. Removing voters and limiting vote counts was the only way for them to win a tie.

The only thing that went well that holiday was seeing my parents, now in their seventies. They were healthy, feisty, and fussing with each other. My dad had retired from the Air Force and his post-military jobs at United Technologies and Pratt & Whitney. My mom, ever her sunny, upbeat self, was still substitute teaching high school and had not slowed down a bit. Her life revolved around Dad, her kids, students, friends, siblings, and now her three grandchildren. In 1996 my brother Norman, an anesthesiologist, had married Rosalind, a sharp and stunning woman who loved sports and had a knack for business. Their first child and my second niece, Ashley, a vivacious and clever girl, made her way into our lives a year later. Her brother, Ryan, a gregarious and multitalented kid and my first nephew, had arrived four years after that. They had settled in Dallas, where Norm ran his own highly successful medical practice.

Phil had joined Harvard's medical school faculty after a long stint running the country's second-biggest emergency room, the Kings County regional trauma center in Brooklyn, New York. He had one child, a smart and beautiful daughter, Kristen Nicole, who inherited her aunt Connie's shopping gene and Imelda tendencies. Phil lived in Needham, Massachusetts, a forty-minute drive from our parents, and he watched over their health and made sure they were okay.

Back in Connecticut, Dad had found a gorgeous wooded reservoir where he walked several times a week. During that Thanksgiving visit, I went with him on his walks, and we talked more than I ever remembered. He shared memories of his childhood in Birmingham, working in the print shop, almost not surviving a burst appendix at age four, and moving to Cleveland. We watched the owls, ducks, and swans, and he said how proud he was that I had lived my life on my terms and become what he never had: "totally and completely free." He was slowing down, but not too much. He told me he was buying a condo in Tampa, Florida, to escape the depressing isolation of Connecticut winters. He and my mom would spend most of the winter there, and then Mom would come back up to New England before the heat set in. But Thanksgiving would always be in the main "headquarters" in Connecticut.

By the time I left to return to L.A., the Supreme Court had selected George W. Bush as president, and Al Gore had conceded. Condi, one of Bush's top advisers, was on her way to the White House, and a much different Department of Justice was about to take the helm, but not in time to save LAPD from Judge Feess's control. Bill Lee would close the consent decree deal right before winging it home to California. Enforcing the LAPD consent decree would be up to the district court in Los Angeles—and us, L.A.'s police reform community. The activists who would not drop the quest for good police had a whole new ball game to play and would soon have a new mayor who would at least understand that LAPD had turned its back on the Christopher Commission mandate for community policing.

In 2001 Richard Riordan's second term as mayor was coming to an end, and two familiar political figures had made their moves to succeed him that July. I endorsed Council Member Antonio Villaraigosa, who had often been an ally in our fight for urban peace and better schools. The majority of African-American leaders, however, backed the city attorney, James Hahn, whose father, County Supervisor Kenneth Hahn, had often gone to bat for the black community. He was remembered and revered as the politician who had greeted Martin

Luther King Jr. at the airport after Mayor Sam Yorty refused to meet
him. As city attorney, James Hahn had been my opposing counsel
for ten years, and he'd always struck me as a thoughtful and decent
prosecutor, more concerned with justice than with scalps for his belt.

During the campaign, I'd wondered whether either candidate
would be able to rein in Chief Parks, who was still hell-bent on bucking the DOJ federal consent decree. The next mayor would have to
decide whether or not to renew the chief's contract. That decision had
been very much on my mind the winter of 2000 when Mitzi Grasso,
the woman who had replaced Ted Hunt as head of the Police Protective League, asked me to meet for lunch. Mitzi got right to the point.
The League was endorsing Hahn with one demand: that he not reappoint Parks as chief of police. Where would I be on that issue?

I ate my soup while I decided whether to trust her with an honest answer.

Mitzi, a petite Jodie Foster–like blonde, was strategic and grounded.
The gun she packed was big, but her real weapon was steely determination. She had taken over the League to get one job done: oust
Parks. And she knew that if the department's "white Neanderthals"
led the charge, it would be too easily dismissed as a racist ploy by
the union. As I watched her cool eyes, the oddity of a black woman
lawyer and a white woman cop contemplating the removal of a black
chief of police struck me as strangely remarkable. I told Mitzi that
neither Hahn nor Villaraigosa had any intention of denying Parks a
second term, and if they tried, the black elite would eat them alive.
The Jaws of Life could not pry Parks out of the chief's office, and
I doubted either candidate had the stones to do it. Mitzi, however,
did and needed to know that I would publicly throw down to get
another chief.

Parks's words "I am the law" came rushing back into my ears, and
I knew what my answer would be. I told Mitzi that if the next mayor
found the guts to deny Parks a second term, my support would be
public and loud enough to give the mayor racial cover.

I left the lunch, betting myself three things. First, that Mitzi Grasso
would be a reliable ally in any foxhole. Second, that if the removal

fight happened, I would be standing alone against an onslaught from the African-American elite. And third, that no new mayor was going to take down L.A.'s most powerful figure, the chief of police.

I won only the first two of those bets. But my last hunch wasn't far off the money.

In June 2001 James Hahn won the runoff election by six points, with a big assist from black voters. In the first months following his July inaugural, Hahn met with Chief Parks several times to tell him he'd be reappointed once he agreed to fully comply with the consent decree and carry out Hahn's vision for reforming the department. The new mayor, however, was on a futile quest. Throughout several tense negotiations and a series of brokered interventions to bring the chief around, Parks steadfastly refused to accept the mayor's conditions. But before the last act of "Can This Chief Be Saved?" played out, we would have to survive a national cataclysm that put many of the freedoms we took for granted in the gun sights of fear.

Like most, I remember the events of 9/11 with haunting clarity. Sleep had been elusive for me the previous night. By two in the morning, I had given up and switched on the dulcet tones of BBC Radio, finally drifting off a half hour into *The Interview.* Three hours later, my half-awake ears vaguely processed the singsong smoothness of an NPR voice noting that a plane over Manhattan had apparently hit one of the Twin Towers. *Must be a small commuter plane or a mistake,* I thought groggily; lower Manhattan was a no-fly zone. At least it was twenty years ago, when I was in law school interning in Tower Two for the New York attorney general. I'd slipped back into light dozing for a spell when a news bulletin punched through my semiconsciousness. It had been an airliner. I sat straight up. Airliner? I listened for a moment more and bumped my cat, Jaws, off my arm to grab the television remote. CNN was in the full-throttle chaos of emergency coverage, so I muted it, turned up NPR, and watched numbing images of billowing smoke burgeoning from one of the

Twin Towers. It was ten minutes before six in the morning, Pacific Standard Time.

A minute later, the phone rang. It was Dad telling me to wake up and turn on the TV. I asked him what we were seeing. He said the country was under attack and that we needed to get ready for more hits. I stayed on the phone with him and thought back to the Twin Towers bombing eight years earlier. This had to be an extreme comeback of that attack. I had been sure that homegrown murderers had attacked the federal building in Oklahoma City; I was equally sure that in this attack, the perpetrators were from overseas. They had attacked the towers before and homegrown extremists these days rarely attacked Wall Street.

Our screens filled with footage of the chaos—emergency vehicles, hundreds fleeing through cascading ash and smoke in the lower Manhattan streets I used to walk. From the dark smoke pouring out of the blackened void near the top of the tower, I knew that the hit spanned dozens of floors and hundreds had to have died. *My God,* I thought, *weren't our offices on the seventy-eighth or eightieth floor of the South Tower?* I did not remind my dad of that fact. It was just after six, and he was telling me what NORAD should be doing—"They should be scrambling the F-16s! And not over the damned Atlantic Ocean—this is an attack from domestic airspace, not from the Soviet Union—and those idiots in the Pentagon will be watching this on television—they're going to get hit next."

It was even worse than he feared. A moment later, we both gasped as the screen showed the sickening sights of a second plane plowing into the upper floors of the North Tower, spectacular fireballs ballooning out of two sides of the building, and the confetti of glass and steel. As the radio reported the possibility of three other hijacked planes, I couldn't quite absorb what I was watching. My dad was yelling—"Scramble the F-16s! Scramble the damned F-16s!"—and then he left the phone to Mom. The country he had spent his life defending was under attack, and the veteran soldier was instinctively commanding forces to defend her. Twenty minutes later, a plane hit

238 POWER CONCEDES NOTHING

the Pentagon, just as Dad had predicted. We later learned that staggeringly brave passengers had downed a fourth plane into a Pennsylvania field. After Dad returned to the phone, we watched a bafflingly huge bubble of gray smoke tumble down the first tower, neither of us understanding that it was the first of two incomprehensible collapses that would wipe the World Trade Center towers from the face of Manhattan.

My overriding emotions were anger and sorrow. I thought of my time in lower Manhattan and the people with whom I had worked in those towers. Of Phillip's years working across the river in Brooklyn at Kings County Hospital. I thought how Condi's world had just been blown up along with those planes. I put out of my mind the blowback of arming mujahideen in Afghanistan, a venture some experts were saying had sown the seeds of this catastrophe. The thing I'd dreaded most was rewarding the attackers with the fear they counted on—and the Pavlovian overreaction to acts of terror that could drag this country back to the dark place of internment camps and mindless retaliation.

I did not need to understand what we had been watching that deadly morning to know that the world in which I had drifted to sleep the night before was gone forever. Time henceforth would be marked before and after September 11, 2001. Nothing was going to be the same. Not even LAPD.

Like the rest of the country, I spent the months following the September attacks closely monitoring the national response to the trauma. After making sure that the Muslim community in L.A. had defenders, I returned my attention to the mounting drama over the chief of police's fate. While the vote to reappoint the chief belonged first to the Police Commission, the mayor's announced opposition to Parks would largely determine their action. Time was up. In late January 2002, Hahn tried one last time to get Chief Parks to promise to carry out the mayor's reform agenda. Parks reportedly dared the mayor not to reappoint him, and Parks was told that his first term as LAPD's leader would be his last. On February 4, 2002, the mayor informed a small group of prominent African-American leaders that he would not support Bernard Parks's bid for a second term as chief of police. Within a day, newspaper accounts made it seem like every elected official, civic leader, and pastor in black L.A. was up in arms.

This level of uproar on behalf of a man who had blindly defended LAPD struck me as strange. But the fury was not about Parks, whom few really knew. It was about elite leaders' embarrassment at having their one campaign demand ignored.

Now that Hahn had decided to remove the chief, there was no question what I had to do, and it meant going against my friends, colleagues, clients—and almost every African-American leader. The same sensation of swelling disaster that I'd felt upon hearing the King verdicts had resurged. Only this time the storm would break directly over my head.

I took a breath and dived in.

First I called Janet Clayton, the editorial-page editor at the *L.A. Times,* and told her I was drafting a piece supporting Parks's removal. Janet understood that I was the only African-American with any expertise in policing who would publicly oppose him. Within a week of Hahn's announcement, my editorial ran prominently. The piece was a litany of reasons the chief should not be reappointed, starting with the facts that ten years after the Christopher Commission, LAPD was reeling from a gangster-cop corruption scandal, under federal court supervision, and no closer to accepting community policing or civilian control than Mullah Omar was to adopting feminism. The article's real value was that it gave Mayor Hahn the racial shield he needed with the elites of every nonblack community. If a leading black civil rights lawyer who specialized in police reform backed the mayor's decision, the fight was not about race.

I did not stop with the *L.A. Times.* In addition to my regular appearances as a panelist on Bill Rosendahl's weekly cable news programs, *Local Talk, This Week,* and *Week in Review,* I put myself on ten radio shows and five television news programs to make the message stick. For two months, I kept up this media blitzkrieg, debating anyone who wanted to argue for Parks getting a second term. The chief's defenders had no idea what he had done in his thirty years as a cop. Facts, however, were irrelevant to this fight.

My hat was off to the chief. I had to marvel at how masterfully he refashioned himself into a "race man" and whipped everyone into a frenzy over a job he had tossed away.

Part of the fault was my own: I had not bragged about how our lawsuits that he had opposed had forced LAPD to hire more minority and female officers and promote the few black cops the community trusted. How it was our cases, not LAPD, that had forced the department to dial back its brutality and muzzle its dogs. I had not explained how our work had fixed systems in ways that touched their lives and helped their children get new schools, avoid lead poisoning, and ride cleaner and safer buses. I had failed to earn their trust. Whether because of time, my loner nature, or other shortcomings, I had failed to do what Johnnie Cochran knew how to do—connect with folks so they can understand what you're doing and tell the difference between real remedies and snake oil. Because I had failed to do these things, someone like Bernard Parks could yell "Black man under attack" and win their support. It was my failure, not his.

I was relieved when several black voices besides mine piped up in favor of Hahn's decision. African-American cops had called in to three of the radio shows to support my stance. But those public calls stopped after the officers reported getting reprimanded. They switched to calling privately to give quiet encouragement, as did many of the black public defenders and other lawyers who could not withstand being ostracized from the black community.

The fight quickly turned ugly. After credible bomb threats at the Advancement Project, we upped the security with cameras and door buzzers, and I began checking my car before getting in. Similar threats triggered several cancellations of debates. When Bo found out, he cussed me out for turning down his offer of protection. I told him that running around town with a posse of ex-gangster bodyguards would not be helpful. A woman boldly entering a hostile room alone, I argued, inspired respect. He countered, "Not if she's dead," and hung up.

In early April, there was one last, uncanceled debate in the black community to do right before the Police Commission voted. Reverend William Epps, the head of Second Baptist Church, wanted to show that black L.A. was capable of civil debate and not beholden to the thugocracy that had hijacked the issue. I dressed for battle in my best red silk and gold braid dress with matching gold choker, red pumps with gold piping, and swept-up hair with big gold power earrings. It took an hour to get my war paint right, but I had learned from eight years of watching the makeup artists do my makeup at the Century Communications Studios, where we taped the Rosendahl television shows. Like Elizabeth, I was dressed and painted to rule.

I arrived at Griffith Avenue five minutes before the start time and parked in the space saved for me near Reverend Epps's car. I could hear the crowd in the church. As I strode out of the parking lot, four LAPD police officers came up and surrounded me. I stopped and asked what they thought they were doing. They explained that Chief Parks was concerned about my safety. I snapped that he was concerned about no such thing and that they were to stand a hundred yards away from me. After whipping up all this hysteria, Parks's only concern was that he might get blamed if something happened to me, but I was not going to help him curry favor with the crowd by protecting me. I'd rather get shot.

Reverend Epps greeted me at a side entrance and took me into the church. Standing alone in the well of the sanctuary, I could feel the crowd sizing me up. I looked over to the dais where the four other panelists were waiting. It wasn't fair to call them debaters. I was a trained gladiator who had won a state championship in high school debate and had only gotten better since. They stood no chance against me, not just because I was good but also because they knew nothing about the subject, and two of them had privately confessed they believed I was right. The moderator also supported Chief Parks, so it was really the five of them, plus the thousand people in the audience, against one. This was not going to be a fair fight.

For them.

Part of the crowd began chanting "Save our chief." Reverend Epps stood close by, determined that his regal presence command civility. The entire first floor was packed, and so was the balcony. A thousand people. At eight A.M. on a Saturday morning. Cheering and chanting. For what? I strode crisply up the stairs to the stage, where I swept across to shake each panelist's hand before taking my seat.

In hostile situations like this, there was only one strategy for success: totally dominate and devastate. The format of alternating questions from the moderator and the audience was bound to produce a mess of ignorant speechifying, but it wouldn't matter. I braced myself for the imminent torrent of nonsense and prepared to snatch control of the debate with the first question, which undoubtedly would be for me.

It came from an older woman in a violet dress and matching hat. "Miss Rice, you haven't done nothing for the community, and Chief Parks has. How can you go against a black chief when you are supposed to be a civil rights lawyer and work for the NAACP?"

Applause and cheers.

It was time to take over.

I thanked Reverend Epps for hosting, my copanelists for their friendly opposition, and KJLH for broadcasting the community discussion. I next noted how rare it was for an audience this size to show up anywhere so early on a Saturday morning—and what a shame it wasn't to rally for our kids reading more or to stop gang violence. Next I made them laugh with the observation that as a litigator who had sued every police chief I could find, including Chief Gates, Chief Williams, Chief Parks, and Sheriff Block, I would probably sue the next chief of police, too, whether it was Parks or not.

Turning to her question, I told the lady that yes, I was a civil rights lawyer who had filed major cases worth over $50 million to fight discrimination and police abuse. But I did not back police chiefs simply because they were black. "I back them because they do the right thing," I said, and proceeded to list the reasons that a civil rights lawyer was required to oppose this chief's reappointment. I said that as a civil rights lawyer, I had no choice but to oppose chiefs like Bernard Parks and Daryl Gates, who denied that racial profiling exists, or argued that two thirds of black men get arrested solely because they commit more crime, or opposed our race discrimination cases, when black cops like Mayor Tom Bradley and Jess Brewer had fought to back us. I explained that as a civil rights lawyer, I absolutely could not support police chiefs like Bernard Parks and Daryl Gates, who rejected the Rodney King police reforms.

I paused and asked her, "How can you?"

Part of me knew the debate was over. Reverend Cecil "Chip" Murray called afterward and said he had been so worried about my lone stance in that hostile arena that he had pulled his car over to pray for me. But when he heard my first answer, he switched and started praying for the other side. I cracked up. He praised my performance as having pulled off a miracle.

That was hardly the case. My efforts and that debate were no more than forgettable footnotes in a power struggle among L.A.'s elected elite, the Police Commission, and the LAPD. It was Mayor Hahn who was doing the heavy lifting and who had the courage to sacrifice his political career[22] to make a crucial move of ending the reign of the last imperial chief. I was just a blocker helping clear his way into the end zone.

At their April 9, 2002, meeting, citing a "profound crisis of confidence" in LAPD, four of the five police commissioners rejected Chief Parks's bid for a second term. After a melodramatic speech by the chief before the City Council and a packed audience of the black elite, the City Council vote was twelve to three to uphold the Police Commission's decision not to reappoint the chief.

Maybe now, I hoped, the city could get a police chief we would not have to waste time fighting. A chief who accepted civilian control, believed in community policing, and understood how to use the DOJ consent decree to remake LAPD. We would need him or her to reverse a police culture that punished the Serpicos and celebrated the

Dirty Harrys, and to stop crushing officers who in turn brutalized the public. Maybe then I could return to the lessons of the K-9 case and help officers, on terms they accepted, transition to constitutional policing without brutality, bias, or corruption. After that, would it be too much to hope that the next chief of police could move beyond Whac-A-Mole arrests and stand with us to reduce the violence and the spiral of despair that spawned *la vida loca*?

Had the reappointment fight left me delusional? Maybe so, but after ten years of warfare for humane policing and the soul of LAPD, all of us had earned a moment to hope for a new path.

Chapter 16

INFILTRATION

LAPD had finally hit bottom and was ready to walk the twelve steps to recovery. We had one last chance to get police reform right. Mayor Hahn had cleared the way to pick his own chief of police, but he would not be doing it alone. After a decade of debacles that had begun with Rodney King and ended with Rampart and federal receivership, LAPD needed an extraordinary leader to mend the broken trust between officers and brass and forge new trust between the people and their police. The next chief had to do the difficult immediately and the impossible fairly soon thereafter.

On October 25, 2002, Hahn tapped former New York City police chief William J. Bratton for the job. It was an intriguing choice. Crime had dropped in New York during Bratton's term, but there was ugly racial Velcro sticking to the legacy of "broken windows" excesses that had turned Harlem into a "stop and frisk" police state.[23] The NYPD's sodomizing of Abner Louima and the shooting of unarmed Amadou Diallo illustrated the broken brutality that New York refused to confront.

Nevertheless, my mind was open. Though Bratton's agenda, as I understood it, did not mirror the Christopher Commission blueprint, it would set a strong foundation to achieve those reforms. Bratton was coming to Los Angeles to show that he could simultaneously reduce crime, build trust with minority communities, and get LAPD compliance with the federal court decree. It was a good vision for urban policing, worthy of a chance to succeed—and all of the help Bratton would accept, which at first didn't look like much.

Carol and I watched with mild amusement as he laid down the law in his pronounced Boston brogue, making clear there was a new chief in town and in charge. He demanded a bigger police force, scolded a stunned City Council, and at the same time ordered officers to improve effectiveness in poor neighborhoods. The press swooned, and Bratton shot straight to the top of L.A.'s A-list invitations. I couldn't yet tell what to think of him, but the media had decided he was L.A.'s only political star among a field of dim bulbs.

Behind the barking bluster, Bratton was striving to get his bearings. He found them at an extraordinary press conference that he called seven weeks into his tenure, after an astonishingly bloody weekend of multiple drive-by shootings. I watched a determined William J. Bratton take the podium. Six minutes later, it would be the chief of police of the Los Angeles Police Department who left it. Through supremely suppressed outrage, Bratton listed fourteen killings that had happened over that weekend. He coldly condemned the mayhem and then trained his liquid nitrogen ire on the real crime.

"This carnage," he seethed coolly, "this isn't in Afghanistan. This isn't in Lebanon. This in the streets of the second-largest city in this country. This has *got* to stop. And it has *got* to stop *now*." He blasted L.A.'s complacent and dangerous acceptance of the violence as normal and demanded the city get off its ass and fight for safety in ravaged neighborhoods.

I yelled, "Yeess!" at my TV screen.

No LAPD chief of police had ever called a press conference to express rage over the killings of underclass adults. Just the opposite. LAPD officers still used a radio code, NVNNHI, that expressed their utter contempt for dead and hurt black adults: "Nigger Versus Nigger, No Human Involved." Apparently, the rest of us agreed. Every special law passed to fight L.A.'s endless street killings had been in response to the headline-worthy murders of middle-class white children, college students, very young poor children, or other sympathetic victims. Had victims of the decade's nearly ten thousand gang killings been middle-class adults, the whole country would have declared an emergency and come to a screeching halt. But ten thousand dead underclass blacks and Latinos, many of whom were gang members? NVNNHI.

After an awkward introduction at a Christmas party at the end of 2002, my first formal meeting with Bratton took place at Parker Center in the spring of 2003. I must have been near the end of the list of people with whom he had been told to host a courtesy meet-and-greet. It was a pleasant and pointless fifteen-minute encounter in which he paced around his memorabilia-stuffed office and absently rattled off talking points about his plans. He ended by giving me a blue gift bag with an autographed copy of his latest book and some LAPD trinkets. I looked at the bag and thought, *This man really has no idea who I am,* and laughed at the thought of the Sheriff of Nottingham giving Robin Hood a bag of souvenirs.

Bratton, whether he realized it or not, would need a lot of outside help, but it would take a far more memorable encounter before he was ready to accept it from me. That breakthrough came early in 2003 at Joe Domanick's Annenberg conference on journalism and policing. Joe, the author of *To Protect and Serve,* the best history of LAPD, was journalism's answer to liberation theology. His conference was a combustible jumble of law enforcement leaders, ex–gang members, experts, and activists who appeared on panels before a ballroom filled with journalists. He put me on a panel with an ex–gang member, Sheriff Baca, and Chief Bratton.

This was the first time I got to observe Bratton and Baca interact. The men were circling each other but had signaled a desire for LAPD and LASD to work together, which, absurdly, would be a first for L.A. Both gave boilerplate responses except when Bratton snapped at a question he didn't like. And then Joe pitched the last question to me. "Connie, are there any news stories about law enforcement that you feel journalists have missed?"

I responded ungraciously that we didn't have all night to list the public safety and police stories journalists had missed, starting with the routine murders of poor people that they had deemed too frequent to be news. "So," I quipped, "let me give you the biggest one: How did you miss the cover-up of the biggest police corruption scandal in California history?"

Bratton's head whipped around, and his gaze locked onto me like a laser beam. Surprised journalists in the audience were dashing down notes and darting looks at one another to gauge reactions.

Joe, suppressing a smile, threw me another softball. "What do you mean?"

"The Rampart gangster-cop scandal brought the entire criminal justice system to the brink of failure," I elaborated, "and journalists did not cover that systemic failure. Journalists also missed why the internal investigations failed to go where the evidence led or why the basic facts of the scandal have never been established. And journalists didn't even report on why LAPD never produced the Rampart 'after-action' report that it promised the Police Commission in 2000. No one ever asked for it. That's the tip of the iceberg journalists missed; that's what I mean."

A week later, Chief Bratton was on my phone. By this time, Molly, Steve, and I had moved the Advancement Project to new offices at the corner of Wilshire and Union, on the western edge of downtown. Katrina, my new secretary, a sunny, generous spirit who described herself as "a Georgia peach," popped through the door. She signaled for me to end my current call and handed me a note that the chief was waiting on line one.

His greeting was breezy and familiar, as if this were our hundredth call. He smoothly switched from chitchat to his agenda. He had confirmed my "provocative" remarks at the Annenberg conference about the missing post-Rampart report. He said he needed to make sure LAPD had learned the right lessons, so he would be asking the commission to appoint a group of outside experts to write an after-action, or "lessons learned," report on the Rampart CRASH matter. "I'm hoping that you'll consider leading that group," he said.

The invitation to go inside LAPD had arrived, but I wasn't sure how to RSVP. Five years had passed since the Rampart CRASH scandal broke, and after four major reports, what good could a fifth do? I had brought up the missing after-action report as a glaring example of the sloppy way the L.A. press covered policing, not as a bid to do the report. Done the wrong way, an investigation this late could rip off the scabs of old wounds everyone wanted to forget. Didn't he know that no one wanted the truth of how far the corruption went up the chain of command? Or that there were good reasons why, after several criminal trials, multiple LAPD investigations, DA investigations, FBI investigations, and four major reports, no one had a full explanation of the scandal? I knew these things, but maybe Bratton did not.

I told the chief that an after-action report this late would be difficult to produce. If he wanted it done, he first had to get buy-in from the Police Commission, the Protective League, and LAPD's other factions. And I needed to assess the feasibility of another investigation at this late date. He sounded unaccustomed to getting counterproposals but agreed.

I called in Kathleen Salvaty, our junior lawyer, to kick around Bratton's request. Kathleen was a levelheaded, hardworking young woman, wafer-thin, quiet, and unassuming; her modest demeanor belied an intense dedication and stamina. Kathleen had just helped Molly and Steve power through *Godinez v. Davis,* our school overcrowding case. After the case, she and Steve had taken more than forty flights up to Sacramento to wrangle another $30 billion in school construction bond measures out of our balky state politicians.

Kathleen sat down in a chair across from my desk with a notepad. I complained that the chief's request for another Rampart CRASH report was a suicide mission. The benefit to Bratton was obvious: It

would clear a dirty slate for him and neutralize me—as an adviser,
I could not sue LAPD. Even if there were no benefit for our work,
who turned down Chief Bratton? I told Kathleen to make a list of
my requirements. Just the first five were impossible. The investigation
had to be independently funded and would cost $400,000. I had to
have access to the Police Commission's subpoena power; unfettered
access to all records, including those from Internal Affairs; the sar-
cophagus in which LAPD had buried its Rampart archives reopened;
a unanimous all-present vote by the civil rights–phobic Police Protective League's board of directors to endorse and cooperate with the
investigation. Nothing uncovered by this latest inquiry could serve
as the basis for further criminal prosecutions or discipline. Moreover,
I alone would pick my team, totally control the writing, and publish
whatever we wanted. With Councilman Bernard Parks—in his second career as L.A.'s newest member of the City Council—waiting to
attack anything this new chief did, I wanted the city to provide my
team with full indemnity against all litigation.

Who in their right mind would allow Bratton to give me a license
to hunt with full indemnity? I took one look at the conditions and
assured Kathleen that Bratton would not be able to deliver on half
of them.

It took him a month to satisfy all but the indemnity demand,
which would take months of wrangling with the council to resolve.
But Bratton had won even the League's unanimous endorsement
for the investigation and they agreed to copilot. After Mayor Hahn
raised the money, I told Kathleen my goals for this inquiry: Do a final
scandal scorecard; show that LAPD was still making the supervision
mistakes that had fueled the CRASH corruption; and excavate the
deeper cultural causes of Rampart. In my mind, I was writing for
an audience of one: Bill Bratton. He wouldn't care what I thought
but would value a report that showed him what his cops really
thought. And he would value a clear explanation of how LAPD's
warrior culture and mind-set had seeded Rampart corruption and,
left unfixed, would block Bratton's vision of racially healing "high-
road policing."[24]

I picked a panel of seasoned lawyers. There was no problem with six of them: Edgar Twine, Jan Handzlik, Laurie Levenson, Erwin Chemerinsky, Stephen Mansfield, and Maurice Suh were all prominent lawyers who had done prior Rampart investigations. But some council members went nuts over my inclusion of Carol Sobel, because she "had sued the city." What did they think I'd been doing—and planned on doing again? I insisted on Carol, and Bratton backed me up.

In July 2003 Kathleen and I began an investigation that no one but Bill Bratton wanted done.

Chapter 17

RAMPART RELOADED

An investigation required investigators, an office, and a lot of phones. Kathleen secured furnished office space a few floors down in our building. To direct the investigation, we hired Brent Braun, a retired FBI agent with expertise investigating police corruption. I immediately took to Brent. He was bighearted and earnest yet discerning and hard-eyed, always hunting for things that did not add up. Like a lot of cops, he prized physical fitness and guns, but he was the rare man's man who thought more like a smart woman, networking with everyone, collaborating to get things done, and using his EQ to figure out motivations and how to interact with the right sensibility. In time I would find his judgment and friendship invaluable. We trusted him with everything but especially with hiring the rest of our professional investigators.

Sonny Benavidez, Morris Hayes, Pete McGuire, and Jack Keller, all retired cops from LAPD and the FBI, rounded out the team, but Brent's main partner for the venture ended up being Mike Wolf, a retired LAPD detective. If Brent resembled Elliot Ness, Wolf resembled Dirty Harry. He was barrel-chested, bowlegged, and sported the crew cut he'd had since his military days. They didn't get any more old-boy Blue Grip than Detective Wolf. If you looked hard, however, his decency peeked through his old-guard armor. Brent knew what he was doing. Who would get other cops to talk—a black female civil rights lawyer who had sued their department, or Mike Wolf?

Since I had insisted that League directors copilot the investigation, Wolf would not be the only OG for whom we had to adjust our civil rights sensibilities. To blunt the culture shock, I had urged Kathleen and our intern, Natasha, to practice calming techniques when League officers popped off with offensive statements. "Just stay calm and uncritical—like an anthropologist," I advised. "If you feel the urge to smack anyone, do a silent countdown from ten." The test run of our oddball partnership was a kickoff evening meeting with Police Protective League directors at their headquarters on Eighth Street.

By the end of that first meeting, I had bitten a hole in my lower lip and done five countdowns, the first of which responded to a corker from a League director who was pouring me a soda in the kitchen area attached to their large conference room. Breaking the ice, my host suggested that since we'd be spending a lot of time together, he really needed me to understand why the King beating was a "good beating."

Ten, nine, eight, seven, six, five, four . . .

He was not trying to provoke me. He needed to get this off his chest and was being honest, as I had asked them to be. Kathleen, who had entered the League headquarters looking about as comfortable as a Quaker at a gun show, paled and quietly slipped out of the kitchen to set up her laptop, leaving me to enjoy my host's fresh perspectives. He leaned against the kitchen counter and proceeded to explain how buffed-up ex-convicts on PCP, like King, could explode with superhuman strength, and since "my people" had confiscated the choke hold, the officers had no choice but to Tase and baton him into compliance.

Ten . . . nine . . . eight . . .

My eyes involuntarily widened. He had just rationalized the beating with a King Kong myth of super-strong black ex-cons while blaming "my people"—civil rights lawyers—for ending the barbaric choke hold. I skipped the count and began biting the inside of my lower lip as he went on to elaborate that "officer safety" had required them to keep striking and electrically shocking the prone King. I killed my larynx suppressing the rebuttal bursting in my throat: *What danger could an electrocuted King possibly have posed to fifteen armed cops watching him writhe in agony on the ground!*

By evening's end, I had destroyed my inner lower lip to save the mission. Just as I'd had to talk without recrimination to the sanest of the hard-core gang shot-callers, I would have to do the same with the most reachable of the hard-core leaders of old-guard police. It was stupid to talk to the crazy 1 percent of either culture, but the reachable leaders of both were key to change. If I wanted these veteran cops to say at least some of what they truly thought, they had to trust. Trust the competence of the investigation. Trust Bratton's motives for doing it. But above all, trust us not to use their honesty against them. It was very clear that what trust existed in the League kitchen that evening had resulted from our prior joint ventures: the Chemerinsky report and the ouster of Chief Parks. I had to keep that trust growing.

The League directors consented to our interview-driven research, but they were later surprised when so many rank-and-file officers agreed to talk to our bench of civil rights lawyers. I wasn't. We had Mike Wolf. While standing outside the door of the investigation office, I'd heard Wolf on the phone, cajoling officers to help us.

"I know, I know," he commiserated with a reluctant cop on the other end. "Look, you think I don't know? I'm *working* for her, for Christ's sake. Yeah, she's a crazy civil rights lawyer, but she's a smart lady, and Bratton trusts her . . . Yeah, I trust her—she's gonna tell our side of this damned story, so come on. You should do this."

I believe in mission-based affirmative action.

Wolf and Brent had set up the first interviews with individuals and had conducted them in the standard way of good detectives: who, what, where, why, and when. But we weren't building a criminal case. We needed officers to go way beyond the facts, to open up and give us their unvarnished thinking about the deeper drivers of the scandal. We needed it from too many officers to cover through single interviews. Kathleen and I began thinking about doing round tables but were unsure if officers would talk to us in front of their colleagues. I decided to start with Rampart Division, where the CRASH outlaws had put the Bill of Rights through their wood chipper.

I already had my theory. Decades before scandal ringleader Rafael Perez's rash of CRASH crime, "Rampage Division" had been known for hard-charging, rules-free policing. After gang crime exploded in 1992, politicians screamed for it to stop, and the division's commanders unleashed Rampart's CRASH anti-gang unit. With their gunslinger mentality, it didn't take long for routine abuses to escalate, or for Rafael Perez to descend to drug dealing and theft—lines that most other CRASH officers did not cross.

The new head of the division was Captain Charlie Beck, a twenty-five-year Southeast CRASH veteran whom Carol had deposed any number of times in our lawsuits. While he was more civil than others, he nonetheless was true-blue, old-guard, and steeped in CRASH. I thought: *So much for change.*

When he picked up the phone, Beck told me he had been hoping I would call. He wanted us to see how much Rampart had changed. He promised as much access as we could stand and invited me to his office the next day. While we were waiting in the Rampart foyer, Kathleen had to stop me from attacking an arrogant desk sergeant who yelled at a terrified Latino robbery victim for not speaking English. I thought again, *Old wine in old bottles.* But when Beck came out to shake hands, I could find no trace of the CRASH swagger. The Captain Beck who greeted us was relaxed, smiling, and seemed happy to see us. He was tall and fit but not the over-the-top, bristling buff of hard-core cops. His mustache and hairline evoked the Marlboro Man but without any of the icon's menace. He introduced two of his change agents, Justin Eisenberg, a brainy Spock-like management cop, and Curtis Woodle, a giant, irrepressible Worf-like street patrol cop.

A few days later, Beck convened our first round table. The group consisted of officers who had worked Rampart during the scandal, survivors of Rafael Perez's reign of corruption and the riptide of backlash after the scandal broke. Beck told his officers to speak freely, guaranteed that there'd be no retaliation, and said that he needed them to level with us. The thirteen officers looked as skeptical about his request as they did about us. Beck stayed for our introductory remarks and the first questions.

To the stone-faced officers, Carol Sobel and I explained our goal: making sure the right lessons had been learned from the scandal. Seeing no nodding heads, I tried to tell them how I'd gone from suing police to helping Bratton with the investigation. Carol chimed in with her observations about recent recurrences of the same supervisory failures that had given cover to the CRASH corruption. The officers bought none of it, so we ceased selling and dived in. After halting responses to simple questions, the tension in the room mounted. Annoyed at the silent standoff, I wondered whose bright idea it had been to expect cops who had to survive in a gossip-riddled, vindictive, and mean policing culture to reveal their thoughts in front of other cops—about a scandal they all wanted to forget. And then I remembered it had been mine. Just as we were ready to chalk up the disaster to our own lesson learned, an older patrol officer broke the silence.

"We don't call it the 'Rampart scandal,' like you do," he said. "We call it the 'Perez scandal.'"

The door had opened—a crack. Squeezing through the opening, I asked why. He leveled loaded eyes at me and then attacked Perez as a rogue "criminal with a badge" whose crimes had nothing to do with the good cops at Rampart. Answering questions we had not asked, he moved straight to his feelings about the handling of the scandal—searing, raw betrayal that had been pent up for five years. His emotion unlocked the room, and for the next two and a half hours, all thirteen survivors let it rip.

It was an intensely sad session. The pain from the fiasco still throbbed in their eyes. Tainted by the scandal, many of them had been unable to transfer to other divisions. Their anger over never being asked their views quaked in their voices. They were adamant that LAPD brass had sacrificed dozens of honorable cops ruined by innuendo and guilt by association. The department's kangaroo investigations, they believed, had handed down fixed guilty verdicts. Everyone in the room choked up when one of them recalled how the witch hunts had driven two Rampart veterans to suicide.

By the end of the session, Kathleen and I were drained.

Back at the office, we debriefed with Brent. Both of us were slightly shocked, not so much at what they had said but at the fact that they had said it to us and in front of one another. Their emotional outpouring had been remarkable, and we had captured virtually every word because of our investigation's second secret weapon: Kathleen's transcription-speed fingers. She had attended Catholic schools run by nuns who feared that girls would be limited to secretarial work, so she had taken mandatory typing every year since third grade. Interviewees who balked at the sight of a tape recorder or transcription machine talked freely before a note taker, even one using a computer. One more time, I silently thanked God for nuns.

The group sessions across LAPD's divisions continued for the next eighteen months. We marveled at the rank rawness of the startling confessions. In response to our question about how to fix the trust gap between LAPD and the public, we didn't expect a veteran patrol sergeant to admit, "I'm not sure we want anything fixed, Miss Rice. We just might need the chaos to keep our identity," and have his partner add, "Being an LAPD cop is like being in a gang. We earn stripes, do beat-downs, get tattoos, and back each other to the hilt." Or that a crusty Rampart supervisor would flatly claim that high-level supervisors at the division and downtown openly shielded Rafael Perez: "It was acceptable from top to bottom—Rampart CRASH can do whatever they want to do." Or that on the topic of police lying, we would get patient explanations of it as an essential weapon against an incompetent system: "Connie, what you call lying, we call survival. We tell lie after lie until we don't know what the truth is anymore." Or "If you make a mistake, your career is over—so you lie."

Least expected of all was the stunner from one forty-year veteran
who blithely admitted, "Except for the dope dealing, Perez wasn't
doing anything unusual. Like a backup 'throwaway' gun?" he said,
referring to the police practice of carrying an illegal extra gun to
plant on unarmed suspects they had just gunned down. "When I
came on the department in the 1950s, that was common knowledge." This prompted another reminiscence by two younger officers,
one who said he used to ask CRASH officers for extra dope to
plant on suspects so he could make his arrest quotas: "We'd go up
to Southeast CRASH to see if they had extra dope for the rainy
nights when you needed to make your numbers." And the other,
who chimed in, "Yeah, they swallow the dope or throw it away, so we
beat them up and use our own. They're illegal, they're selling dope,
so what kind of respect do we owe them? That's wrong, but it's how
we thought about it."

I was relieved they could still recognize "wrong." But as the other
officers nodded confirmation of these apparently time-honored tra-
ditions, I could barely mask my alarm. We heard equally revealing
statements across the divisions, but the most extraordinary session
was with seventeen hard-core gang officers in Southeast, the division near Jordan Downs. The group agreed unanimously that society
did not give a damn about underclass neighborhoods, the people in
them, or the cops who risked their lives containing the violence so
that "good" neighborhoods could be safe.

"We know the drill: Protect people in good neighborhoods from
the people in bad neighborhoods."

"We're not paid to protect people in South L.A.; we're paid to
contain them."

"There is a presumption that certain neighborhoods don't count
. . . that certain people don't count . . . [In South Bureau] I can treat
everyone like criminals because it is so dangerous . . . we can excuse
officers when people are treated badly."

After scores of similar confessions, I ceased being startled but
remained worried. The picture was of a troubled and flawed policing
culture that struggled to meet unrealistic political demands. What

worried me the most were the interviews I did with LAPD's best detectives, all of whom stated that they had no confidence in the quality of the average LAPD investigation. What shocked me the most was that not a single gang cop in that Southeast Division room disagreed with us on the big things: The thin blue line was deadly to community trust; for cops to treat the community better, cops first had to stop their mistreatment of one another; and the wars on drugs and gangs were futile.

Given what I knew of past LAPD conduct, the interviews' litany of illegal and unethical practices should have drawn yawns. But hearing it directly from so many officers in matter-of-fact, "this is just the way it is" tones brought on an odd reaction of horror and relief. Horror that what we asked cops to do had made subverting standards the norm. And relief that they were sharing a fraction of the truth in a bid for a better system.

Listening to officers in divisions across LAPD talk about the toll their jobs took was humbling. Reading over a hundred pages of their quotes was overwhelming—and ultimately transforming. It wasn't that we agreed with or even believed everything they said in the sessions. We did not. It was their ardent pitch for us to understand. It was the fear between the lines that changed the game. They feared that we would know they were afraid. That we would not understand why they behaved the way they did. They feared people they neither understood nor respected. Feared that if they reached out, no one would reach back. Feared being badly outnumbered. Feared being left to twist in the wind when "public trust" failed to back them up. Feared losing the facade of power they believed kept them alive. Above all, feared dying for nothing.

Their fears showed me how to end our standoff. We were demanding that they change without understanding why even the good cops felt they could not and, in some cases, would not.

So I learned the right question: "What has to change to make you feel safe enough to police more humanely and end the warrior mentality that led to the Rampart corruption scandal?" They told us: End the lean, mean model of policing that has cops assigned to suppress and contain violence in poor areas and smoke-jump from one emergency to the next. They wanted enough cops, resources, and functioning neighborhoods to support citywide safety that was based on good relationships between police and the public. The best-intentioned of them wanted an end to the spiral of despair that the McCone Commission had identified as the engine of mistrust between poor neighborhoods and the police. They wanted exactly what we had been asking for all along, though their extremists had drowned out the saner discussion. The good cops wanted what Bratton called "public trust policing" and "high-road policing." It was what Captain Beck said he was doing in the revamped Rampart Division.

Given Rampart's history, I could not imagine Beck's infectious optimism reversing those old tides. Breaking the grip of outlaw cops was one thing. Turning community mistrust into collaboration was entirely another. Besides, as scores of interviews had revealed, the vast majority of officers prized career paths to specialized intimidation units like SWAT and CRASH—not community safety and certainly not service. Bratton had told Beck to innovate and turn the division around. Beck was determined to replace intimidation policing with a community partnership that cleaned up the crime-ridden MacArthur Park just east of downtown. To take back the park, they had mobilized the community and made offers that the gangsters could not refuse: Behave and be welcomed; make one grandmother uncomfortable and get ejected faster than anthrax. In four months, park crime had plummeted 45 percent, criminals had left, and families had returned.

We fanned out to test Beck's claims.

The first stop was Angela Sambrano's CARECEN. Sambrano was the preeminent advocate for Central American immigrants, who had no love for LAPD's Rampart Division but had nothing but praise for Captain Beck. She told me to believe it. The police were now polite, even humble, and had sought a real partnership with her. Every mainstream group and business we interviewed echoed Angela's favorable view. One church leader who, three years prior, had testified at a Senate hearing against Rampart CRASH asked if there was any way our blue-ribbon panel could keep the current cops from ever leaving.

Determined to find the clouds in this sunny picture, I met with a group of gang members and local intervention workers to find out how LAPD was really behaving. They started the session with a half hour of horror stories, but it was in the past tense: cops who used to drop them off, sometimes naked, into rival territory and laugh as they got pulverized by their enemies; cops who had provoked drive-by shootings by sending fake messages of assassination orders and threats to their rivals. This was familiar street lore that held a lot of truth. They ended, however, in the present tense, with grudging admissions that they could see the difference.

"Under Beck, we don't see that shit no more," one gang member explained. "He got rid of the assholes—sent 'em to Wilshire. His cops act professional. Don't mean we like 'em any better, but they make righteous arrests and treat us professional."

It was unanimous. Even the gangsters approved of the change. When we visited MacArthur Park, we could see and feel its revival. After it had spent years being a vice bazaar, the drunks, prostitutes, and drug dealers had disappeared. In their place were children and families. Beck had raised corporate funds to fill the park with cameras and lighting, as well as private money to buy new recreational gear and pay for concerts.

What I found impressive was that the changes seemed to hold at night. On one of my test walks in the spring of 2005, I took Beth Barrett, a journalist for the *L.A. Daily News,* for a late-night stroll through the park. We saw mothers with infants in strollers, lone female joggers, elders playing chess, kids playing soccer, families eating on blankets, and couples dancing to music. The money for the lights had yet to arrive; still, not one prostitute or drunk was in sight—at night, in the dark. As luck would have it, however, we exited on Sixth Street to the spectacle of LAPD responding to a deranged naked woman whose incoherent babbling apparently posed a threat so dire it required seven squad cars—of ogling men—to respond.

MacArthur Park was not Disneyland. The streets a few blocks

away bristled with the dark activity that the community had driven from the park. Nor was the recovery of Rampart Division perfect. Indeed, during our investigation, two Rampart officers got caught and punished for planting evidence on suspects, just as Rafael Perez had, and others had started wearing the same hats that Perez had sported with his outlaws. It was nonetheless remarkable to find that Beck and his crew had not just cleaned up so much of the corruption along with the park, they had also changed the thinking of at least some officers.

I was delighted to find that the one place shining a beacon to the future was the division most notorious for corruption. Because Beck had done his own version of community policing, our report could be about a success story instead of a deadly debacle. Our panel's job turned to documenting how this success had happened and how it could be duplicated. The central question of our report and for Bratton and the Police Commission was: Why wasn't all of Los Angeles policed this way? And why didn't all LAPD officers have this mind-set?

The real question I wanted answered, though, was why had Charlie Beck changed?

In some ways, he would have been among the last command officers I'd have bet on to change, and the last to become an actual change agent. Beck's bond to old-guard policing was long-standing and deep. His dad had been a deputy chief under Daryl Gates. His sister was an LAPD detective. His wife, Cindy, was a sheriff's deputy. And he had been a gang cop in South Bureau for eons. Carol, Barry, and I never had any reason to link him with the brutal high jinks of Graveyard, but he had not been a Captain Hannity. As he put it, "There was nothing about me that you would have liked back then—I was as hard-charging a CRASH officer as you could have found." How had a defender of Operation Hammer policing done a 180-degree turnabout?

I asked him.

Without hesitation, he said, "Search and destroy wasn't working." The words hit me. "Search and destroy" was the phrase civil rights lawyers used for law enforcement's decimation of underclass males. It was pioneered by Jerome Miller in his searing book *Search and Destroy*, which documented the targeting of black boys for arrest and incarceration. Hearing it from Beck felt a little like the moment Lyndon Baines Johnson intoned the chorus of the Negro freedom anthem, "And we *shall* overcome."

"It just wasn't working," Beck continued in a contemplative tone. "We had to try something else that didn't make the community hate us."

He said he had finally come to understand that search-and-destroy policing had decimated trust, and without the public's trust, there could be no safety for the neighborhoods or his officers. Like most cops, Beck had policed the way he had been taught, without questioning, without thinking. While the mindless war had racked up body counts for great arrest numbers, it also had wrecked the community and killed the trust that wins the peace. He had come to believe that targeting the community created dangerous blowback. Safety—for residents and cops alike—required helping the community clean up the local problems that seeded crime, like a gang- and crime-infested park.

After what I'd seen and heard, I believed him. But Captain Beck had not mentioned the most compelling explanation for his metamorphosis. I discovered a few months later that he had a daughter and would soon have a son working as LAPD officers on the mean streets of L.A. I was talking to a dad determined to protect his kids. Now, *that* was change I could believe in.

Sitting in Charlie Beck's office during that interview was a turning point. He had collapsed all the years of conflict and wiped the slate clean. A son of LAPD's old guard had chosen to quietly declare his conversion. His intent was clear. He wanted no walls. He wanted trust. He wanted an opponent-ally. Above all, he wanted to start over.

I smiled to myself as Beck's words brought my favorite Thurgood Marshall quote to mind: "We can run from each other, but we cannot escape each other. Knock down the fences that divide. Tear apart the walls that imprison. Reach out: freedom lies just on the other side."[25]

I kept the thought to myself. There was no point in scaring the man off at this early stage.

Somehow we had stumbled onto the elusive Northwest Passage to community policing. And we had found the guide to take us there. Captain Beck had transformed Rampart Division, had transformed how his cops thought, but more important, had first transformed himself.

Chapter 18

CHINATOWN

After the hopeful discovery of the Rampart renaissance and Captain Beck's new policing, everything else in the investigation proved dispiriting. That is, everything except officers' messages following our sessions. After the rough testimony, the "thank-yous" and quiet requests that we return to talk more told me that we were reaching even some of the old guard. My favorite gesture of gratitude came from a gruff, hard-charging patrol cop who stopped me to say that he had named his newest fish Connie because she made the other fish in his aquarium swim in a different direction. And because, he added, she was an angel fish. It was clear that LAPD cops needed outside help to end their isolation, and would need even more help to change their thinking.

The cops were not the only Rampart actors damaged by the scandal. Kathleen, Laurie Levenson, and I learned from a wrenching DA's round table that the toxicity of the scandal had damaged even the prosecutors who put the Rampart CRASH cops on trial for their crimes, as other prosecutors ostracized them and cops undermined their cases. In their rousing session, public defenders came loaded with convincing evidence of a broken criminal justice system riddled with routine police perjury, planted evidence, and convictions of the innocent. Not since my capital punishment days at LDF had the pall of systemic corruption come roaring so vividly into my mind. The rancid record of L.A.'s biggest police corruption scandal pointed to one conclusion: Los Angeles's criminal justice system did not have the minimal integrity needed to avoid convicting the innocent. The political conclusion was equally bad: We wanted Rampart to be over, wanted to survive it without systemic collapse, but we did not want to know what had actually happened.

Even some of the prosecutors didn't want to know. Kathleen discovered a dropped line of critical questioning in transcripts of prosecutors interviewing Rafael Perez. The transcript inexplicably fell silent after Perez claimed he had carried his misconduct to other CRASH units. The avalanche of questions that should have followed this zinger never came. The transcript stopped cold because no one had the stomach to follow evidence on the most important question of the entire mess: Did the corruption go beyond Rampart CRASH to other divisions? No one wanted to know.

By the time we completed our investigation in 2006, we had synthesized an enormous amount of information spanning thirty years of reports and investigation records. We had interviewed more than two hundred experts in LAPD and the criminal justice system, five former LAPD interim and permanent chiefs of police, more than thirty deputy and assistant chiefs, commanders, and captains, the heads of four police unions, hundreds of rank-and-file officers, FBI and other law enforcement agents, current and former police commissioners, select members of the Christopher Commission, and two convicted former Rampart CRASH officers, including Rafael Perez, whose fascinating interview I conducted in a Pennsylvania federal prison. Our non–law enforcement interviews were even more extensive, covering the views of federal and state judges, prosecutors, defense counsel, city attorneys, public defenders, plaintiffs' counsel, authors of prior reports on LAPD, investigators, journalists, law professors, community leaders, and consultants to prior investigations. All tallied, our panel had heard eight thousand years of experience in LAPD and the Los Angeles criminal justice system.

After we'd considered all of that wisdom, there was only one conclusion to draw. Despite the valiant efforts of many, LAPD and its sister institutions had not only failed to protect the Los Angeles criminal justice system against CRASH crimes, they had also failed to competently investigate the scandal. If obscuring the extent of corruption had been the goal, it would have been difficult to imagine a more effective game plan. As one federal prosecutor put it, Rampart was the movie *Chinatown*: a scandal too dangerous to comprehend. We had stumbled into the baffling territory of systemic denial.

Fortunately, we did not have to make this dismal tale of past breakdown the sole focus of our report. We focused instead on the road ahead and Beck's campaign to transform Rampart Division and win community trust. We made the entire first half of the report about the Rampart renaissance even as we warned that as soon as Beck and his innovators left, the division would revert back—not to corruption but to easier search-and-destroy policing. We wove the report around the officers' quotes, backing up the conclusions with a chorus of officer voices making profound and honest remarks about their jobs.*

The most important point of the report was not the failed criminal investigations, the cynical police mindscape, or Captain Beck's Rampart renaissance. It was the section that explained how society's decision to use a "thin blue line" model of policing had helped spawn the cowboy culture, centurion conduct, and insularity that had led to Rampart. It didn't excuse torture by gun roulette or planting evidence any more than it excused gang abuse of Pygmy, but it explained the origins of LAPD's bunker mind-set and exposed our collective role in reinforcing the conditions that fed it.

---

*Please visit www.powerconcedesnothing.com for links to the interviews of *Rampart Reconsidered*.

The thin blue line, the lean model of policing that deploys too few officers for the size of the population, is designed to keep people safe in "good neighborhoods," on the right side of that line, and people in "bad neighborhoods," on the wrong side of it, contained. The thin blue line was at the vortex of the spirals of destruction and despair. For anyone tempted to dismiss this notion as sociological pablum, consider the day I was driving Molly's BMW convertible in Watts, draped in Barbara Bush pearls, power earrings, and a St. John suit. Officers in two squad cars on Century Boulevard spotted me, decided that I must have mistakenly strayed into the wrong neighborhood, and pulled me over for the sole purpose of offering their immediate escort "back to safety." This instance of beneficial color caste and class profiling only confirmed what we all know: Women who look like me are supposed to be on the safe side of the line. Therefore, I don't belong in Watts.

Officers in our interviews had said it over and over again:

"What we do down here is suppression; it's not safety, it's containment to make sure it doesn't spread to good areas."

"We're here to maintain control between civilization and utter chaos."

"We have only enough police officers here to make certain that the wealthier neighborhoods stay safe ... [T]he question that ... Los Angeles has to confront is ... do we want to make the whole city safe?"

As we finalized the draft, I knew that this most critical point would never be engaged because it required us to face the ugly fact that our safety was structurally dependent on Watts's endangerment; that by design, all resources were arranged to ensure safety on the right side of the thin blue line and nowhere else.

For eighteen months, Kathleen, Brent, the blue-ribbon-panel members and I had roller-coastered through the Rampart CRASH cover-up, exposed deep systemic corruption, and revealed massive investigation failure. For what? At the end, I told Kathleen and Brent that far more important than showing lessons not learned or writing the last epitaph for the biggest police scandal in L.A. history, we had verified a compelling community-based crime-fighting model that would win the future; we had opened an astonishing window into the soul of policing; and we had created bonds with cops that would end my fifteen-year war with LAPD and start the partnership I'd envisioned at the Hollywood Reservoir over ten years earlier.

We presented our final report, *Rampart Reconsidered: The Search for Real Reform Seven Years Later*[26] to the Police Commission on July 13, 2006, at a special meeting held in the ornate City Council rotunda. Commission president John Mack, the legendary leader of the Los Angeles Urban League, was as surprised as I was to see three League directors express "qualified support" of the findings. Bratton thanked us and accepted our challenge to cowrite the last chapter, which we'd left blank as an invitation for an ongoing joint venture and a jointly drafted conclusion.

Three months later, as I was beginning to fear that the chief had shelved our report and that my bid to flip it into an ongoing partnership had failed, Bratton called me into his office. On his conference room table was a stack of paper, each page of which had a line splitting it down the middle. On one side, in orange ink that matched the color of our report cover, were "Connie's Recommendations," and on the other, in LAPD blue ink, were Bratton's translations. He had taken the panel's ideas and made them his own. My invitation for an ongoing partnership had received Bill Bratton's RSVP. The Rampart investigation had concluded, but the relationships created during its run had just begun.

Chapter 19

STUCK ON STUPID

Throughout Parker Center, we spotted the orange cover of *Rampart Reconsidered* on desks and tucked under the arms of command officers. I had no delusions that they'd read it. I was just relieved LAPD hadn't pitched it into any bonfires—and that my real goal, Bratton's alliance, had been achieved. The investigation had cemented my role as an outside adviser to the chief and placed me inside the castle. To the horror of some, Bratton renewed my facilities badge, and my Prius took its spot amid the sea of Crown Victoria police sedans in the parking lot. The chief told me to finish the reform work with now Deputy Chief Beck, Assistant Chief Jim McDonnell, and Gerry Chaleff, his politically savvy civilian chief in charge of consent decree compliance.

Few understood the vital role that Gerry's deep knowledge of LAPD played in Bratton's effort to get LAPD to shed its old-guard exoskeleton. The right promotions, rear-flank protection, and political moves would not have happened without him. Like an annoying terrier, I attached myself to Gerry to help counter resistance to the consent decree, collect intelligence, and help command staff properly investigate, respond to, and learn from crises like the heartbreaking police shootings of two-year-old Susie Pena and thirteen-year-old Devin Brown. This catalytic work inside Parker Center was essential because the few LAPD change agents like Beck and Sandy Jo MacArthur who knew how to transform the department needed our challenges, questions, and strategic backup for the hand-to-hand combat that it took to carry out Bratton's vision.

It would take seven years of dueling inside the castle—but fighting alongside Bratton, his brain trust of outside advisers, powerful allies, and John Mack's Police Commission meant that our police clients now had a fair shot at winning the battle for LAPD's soul after all. It did not take nearly that long to see the budding change. Months before our investigation ended, Assistant Chief Earl Paysinger, the talented rhino-hide chief of LAPD operations, had reached out to arm-wrestle with me about LAPD's future. I about fell over in 2005 when Paysinger called me on my first cell phone, demanding to know if Bo was with me. He had just issued a top alert in response to a police radio report that a Bo Taylor had been shot. It was another man, but this unprecedented LAPD concern over a gang intervention worker told me things were changing.

Bratton's invitation to come inside meant that finally I no longer had to expend the tons of energy it took to fight LAPD from the outside. I could now redirect that voltage into gangland. Not a moment too soon. Progress with LAPD did not mean that it or the city had gained any better idea about how to roll back the alarming spread of gang violence. And now it reached people like us. Over the six years since 1997, gangs had shot the daughter of one of our LDF secretaries, murdered the husband of another staffer, and gunned down the brother of our Advancement Project computer tech in front of his church as he left choir practice.

The fight was now personal. And it was clear why we were losing. Cops kept doing revolving-door arrests of the same gang members, and the city kept doing L.A. Bridges, a tiny, underfunded gang prevention and intervention program supervised by city employees who knew next to nothing about gangs. However, by May 2003 that had begun to change. While Kathleen and I were winding down the last months of the Rampart investigation, Martin Ludlow, a charismatic and energetic labor leader, had won election to the Los Angeles City Council's Tenth District, which included a gang hot zone of housing units known as "The Jungle." The prior summer, seventeen shootings had happened in that hot spot. Ludlow felt like he couldn't wait to get sworn in before acting. Summer was a month away, and he feared for kids like Trevon Taylor.

Trevon, an eleven-year-old who loved baseball, and his older brother, Mahlon, had grown up in the Jungle. They had never been in serious trouble until Mahlon got sent to an L.A. County juvenile detention camp for an offense that in the suburbs would have received counseling. In camp, fellow inmates who were gang members from his neighborhood forced Mahlon to join their gang. When Mahlon was discharged, no one from county probation had assessed the damage done during his detention or the risks he would face upon release. No one coordinated his release with Child Services or arranged for a reentry/rehabilitation team. The only reentry team to greet Mahlon was the gang. When Mahlon refused to bang, the gang snatched Trevon and executed him with a bullet to the head in his front yard.

Trevon's murder devastated Ludlow just as the plight of the Jacksons, Zunigas, and Pygmy had galvanized me. They all had fallen prey to gangs in part because of the banality of bureaucratic evil—the indifference of its ineptitude. The day after his election, Ludlow, determined to destroy the lethal complacency that had killed Trevon, called the L.A. Bridges staff to find out how many kids they had rescued from gangs in the Jungle.

They informed him they did not know how many kids had been retrieved from the gangs in the councilman-elect's district. That was not their job. Ludlow asked them what plans they had to stop a repeat of the prior summer's shootings and fatalities in the Jungle. They said none. That also was not their job.

Ludlow decided it was his job and gathered Bo, me, the Community Coalition, and several others at his campaign headquarters. He announced that the Jungle was going to go from the previous year's "Summer of Death" to a "Summer of Success," that we would "wrap around" each child a safety net to keep every kid in that neighborhood safe. He told Bo to line up his gang interventionists to bargain with the local gangs for safe passage and "permission" to operate in their territory. He put his leftover campaign cash on the table, raised another three quarters of a million from the California Endowment, and signed on Guillermo Cespedes to run the round-the-clock programs needed to create the bubble of safety. He delivered the jobs that gang leaders had demanded. He browbeat LAPD into doing foot patrols and cooperating with the gang interventionists they despised. He forced a reluctant Department of Water and Power to keep the local park's lights on at night and a resistant Recreation and Parks Department to keep the gyms open past midnight for basketball and soccer. He had Dominique DiPrima from Stevie Wonder's radio station, KJLH, hosting music jams and talent contests with prizes for rap and hip-hop songs about nonviolence. He and Cespedes got teachers tutoring, coaches running games, churches cooking for the kids, businesses offering jobs, and dozens of volunteers working round-the-clock creating activities. Late at night, Ludlow took home with him the kids from abusive homes so they'd be safe.

At the end of the eleven weeks, the crime stats told the story. Youth gang crime had plummeted—zero shootings, zero batteries, zero rapes, zero deaths. A year prior, during these very same weeks, gangs had shot three kids to death, wounded more than a dozen more, gang-raped several girls, and sprayed the neighborhood with gunfire. By forcing all hands on deck, including those of the gangs, Martin Ludlow, Guillermo Cespedes, and a small army of parents, coaches, pastors, cops, teachers, gang interventionists, government agencies, and civil rights lawyers had kept the kids in his worst gang hot spot safe—in the heat of summer.

This was the army that had not been there for Pygmy, the Jacksons, or the Zunigas. We had gone beyond cease-fire pacts, behavior modification courses, candlelight vigils, and midnight basketball to a neighborhood-wide child safety strategy that kept a large number of kids safe, fed, and learning. Bo and I were ecstatic. An entire community had refused to lose a single kid, and it had worked.

Local news stations covered this triumph, and the *L.A. Times* celebrated the results on its editorial page. But just as we had predicted that Captain Beck's turnaround of MacArthur Park would revert after he left, so did that neighborhood when the Summer of Success ended. The money ran out, and the kids found themselves back in the Jungle.

That summer was only the beginning of Ludlow's fight for child safety. The new councilman was on fire about L.A.'s gang emergency, but when he arrived at city hall, he found zero interest in the problem. The council just didn't get it. Crime was down, headlines were good, and nice areas were safe. So what urgent gang problem was there? Los Angeles, the gang capital of the country, had $9 million a year to subsidize golf courses but no funds for Ludlow's Summer of Success program that saved kids' lives.

It also had no permanent committee on gangs. So Ludlow chaired a temporary ad hoc committee on Gang Reduction and Youth Development (GRYD). He recruited Councilman Tony Cárdenas, who had coauthored the first statewide bill to fund gang intervention; Janice Hahn, the councilwoman for Watts; and Ed Reyes, the councilman for the Rampart area.

They decided that the only way to snatch the city's head out of the sand would be with a new report that documented why the city had failed to reduce gang culture, influence, and growth.

When Ludlow called me with this idea, I was just finishing *Rampart Reconsidered*. Within days of its submission, I dived right into this new investigation of L.A.'s response to gangs. I called a team of experts who had been battling hot-zone violence for years before I even discovered Watts. They all said yes—epidemiologists, gang anthropologists, public health physicians, criminologists, cops, teachers, trauma experts, bureaucracy experts, gang intervention experts, community leaders, and gangsters. To the dismay of many in city hall, we won the contract to tell L.A. why its gang strategy was stuck on stupid.

We already knew how to keep kids in gang zones safe and create healthier, violence-free ecosystems. We had to organize resources so that the Summer of Success became the Year of Success. We had to coordinate ourselves and our agencies to offer safe havens for the kids who ran to gangs to escape pain and abuse; offer alternative activities to banging; strengthen mental health and emotional resilience; offer floundering families the kind of support they needed and wanted; force graveyard schools to educate; and provide jobs, jobs, and more jobs.

If we knew what to do, why do another report? Just as it had with Rampart, the city already had ignored three prior reports on its gang program; without a political plan for its use, a fourth would end up as one more excuse for not acting. But Ludlow, Cárdenas, and Hahn needed to throw a grenade into the City Council rotunda. And they needed our all-star team to assemble it.

For our leadership, I called Bill Martinez, the former head of the County Youth Gang Services; Billie Weiss, an expert in gang prevention at the UCLA Center for the Study of Injury Prevention; and Father Greg Boyle, founder of Homeboy Industries. We signed on seven gang intervention practitioners: Bo Taylor, Melvyn Hayward, Stan Muhammad, Mustafa Fletcher, Khalid Shah, Jeff Harmon, and Shontese Williams. We rounded up experts like Wes McBride, a thirty-four-year veteran gang deputy from LASD; Peter Greenwood, a former Rand criminologist; Patricia Giggans and Cathy Friedman, experts in violence against women, from Peace Over Violence; Howard Uller and Tony Massengale, experts in gang intervention; Jorja Leap, a UCLA gang anthropologist; Maria Casillas, an urban education expert; Cecilia Sandoval, a community engagement leader; Dr. Ali Modares, an expert in demography; the Vera Institute, for funding analysis; and a ream of other experts in government structure, evaluation design, community development, and gang prevention. Most important, we consulted with two public health experts, two epidemiologists, and professors in gang studies Malcolm Klein, Diego Vigil, and Cheryl Maxson. Finally, we convened a large community advisory team of seventeen community leaders and agencies. When we submitted our response to the bid, it included twenty experts. By report's end, we had engaged more than fifty.

For a project this big, I had to find a director to manage the experts, direct my staff, help me navigate the politics, and produce the report.

John Kim, our Advancement Project office manager and director of our Healthy City IT platform that was Google for civic entrepreneurs, suggested Susan Lee, a Yale- and Berkeley-educated lawyer. I liked her instantly. She was smart, blunt, analytical, and outwardly unflappable. Luckily, Susan had been ready for a change. She could no longer stomach the waves of lost kids in Koreatown, where she headed up the Korean Youth and Children Center. She had just mourned the death of a youngster whom she'd hired to get off the streets. Saving one troubled kid at a time would never dent the problem; L.A. had too many. There was, however, a slim chance that if we wrote and wielded it right, this gang report could trigger systemic action. By the end of the lunch, she had agreed to take a leave from KYCC to produce our opus.

It was the smartest move I could have made. Her no-nonsense manner and intense competence calmed the anxious political staffs and bureaucrats who feared what our big team would write. Like any good lawyer, Susan could thwart specious political attacks, but she also could go toe-to-toe with our feuding academic experts and mediate the inevitable friction in a wildly diverse team. We charted our plan and began our colonoscopy on L.A.'s failed approach to gangs.

After a massive amount of research and assessment by our teams, the facts we marshaled on L.A.'s gangland drew a staggering landscape. Within its nearly five thousand square miles of sun-splashed splendor, the County of Los Angeles had a virulent gang epidemic. It had a gang violence epidemic. And it had a youth gang homicide epidemic that had raged for twenty years. Law enforcement estimated we had a thousand gangs and eighty thousand gang members, half of which operated in the 470 square miles of L.A. City. After twenty-five years of spending more than $25 billion on a war on gangs, the L.A. region had six times as many gangs and twice as many gang members. In our mass incarceration strategy, we had arrested more than 450,000 youths under eighteen in a ten-year period. Our experts also determined that

L.A.'s violent gang crime cost California taxpayers more than $2 *billion* every year. For every gang murder Bo and Fred had helped prevent, the taxpayers had saved $1 million in direct costs and $16 million in indirect costs. The cost in human lives, however, had been far greater.

Since 1980, people in L.A.'s hot zones had suffered 7,000 gang murders, 100,000 people shot, more than 50 police officers killed by gangs, and at least 16 gang intervention workers killed. One of our epidemiologists, a former expert for the World Health Organization, concluded that "Los Angeles is to violence what Bangladesh is to diarrhea, which means the crisis is at a dire level requiring a massive response." One prominent criminologist determined that the petri dish of L.A.'s high-crime neighborhoods had spawned "a violent gang culture unlike any other," and that culture had created a regional "long-term epidemic of youth gang homicide and violence."

I found it sobering to hear scientists and sociologists confirm my distorted lens on the violence. My years in the tiny shooting zones patrolled by Fred and Bo were not a scientific basis for understanding the broader impact, if any, of what I was seeing. This study was. Our experts had connected the dots from bad policy to gang expansion and the triple whammy of epidemics from L.A.'s gang culture.

The bottom line was that L.A. had the wrong paradigm. Our epidemiologists, to whom I'd handed the reins of our report, told us that the street gang culture was so entrenched and widespread that it required the same public health strategies used to reverse serious epidemics.

As one expert put it, when you have a malaria epidemic, you don't hand out fly swatters to swat one mosquito at a time. You change the norms of behavior, conditions, and vectors that help spread the disease. You hand out nets, rub kids down with insecticide, avoid going outdoors at dusk or dawn, kill all mosquito eggs, drain all standing water, spray the swamp and anything else in which mosquitoes thrived. L.A. was arresting one gang member at a time—swatting mosquitoes—and doing nothing to stop the spread of the mentality, ideology, or culture of gangs. Indeed, with multiple arrests of the same gang members, L.A. was swatting the same mosquitoes over and over.

Another expert, Jorja Leap, explained it with an equally compelling analogy: If violent gang culture is cancer, the police are the surgeons who cut out the tumor—i.e., lock up the bad guys. But if that's all you do, the cancer will return and spread. To prevent that, you have to follow up with chemo, radiation, nutrition, lifestyle changes, checkups, and support groups. Then you have to heal. Well, L.A. had been repeatedly cutting out the same tumor without doing anything to prevent the disease from metastasizing or growing a more virulent strain. Yes, we absolutely had to arrest the violent and anyone who committed serious crimes, but we could not stop there and expect the problem to recede.

We also showed that more than 850,000 non-gang-affiliated kids lived in the county's gang hot zones and that 90 percent of them reported being exposed to serious violence. Worse, nearly 33 percent exhibited levels of post-traumatic stress disorder and clinical depression that exceeded those of our soldiers returning from Iraq. Not all of this trauma could be laid at the feet of gangs, but gang violence could take a great deal of credit for making the environments extremely unhealthy for kids.

With all of this, the L.A. region failed to fund effective prevention and intervention programs. The city spent on prevention only twenty-four cents a day per hot-zone child, while it lavished $1 million per elephant for the zoo's new elephant preserve. And the malpractice of L.A. County agencies continued. Mahlon was not the only child who had been jumped into gangs while in county custody.

As we synthesized gang studies, Susan and I cringed at the academic dueling (the Ph.D.'s couldn't even agree on the definition of "gang") and at the thin record of research. Only one long-term study of L.A. gang violence had been completed, and it showed that just one factor strongly correlated with significant reductions in gang violence: jobs. How could we know so little about such a big problem?

We didn't need studies to act; we could see enough of what worked to reduce violence, and we could recommend future research to pinpoint what worked to reduce gang joining and influence. Father Greg Boyle was right: For hard-core gang members ready to change, jobs stopped bullets. Patti Giggins of Peace Over Violence was right:

Socializing girls to reject abuse stymied the violence. Martin Ludlow and Geoffrey Canada were right: For non-gang-involved youth, passionate leadership with control over a defined neighborhood whose families were organized for educational achievement also worked. After twenty years of organizing fourteen low-income blocks in Harlem, Geoffrey Canada had produced droves of healthy, college-bound kids. In an L.A. gang zone, he would have had to first win permission from the local gangs. Reliance on private efforts alone would not undo the damage by L.A.'s public institutions. In L.A., public schools and agencies had to be in the mix, if for no other reason than they were a huge part of perpetuating the problem.

I learned an unexpected lesson from the research. Obsessively focusing on the gang was a bad idea. It boomeranged by making the gang stronger, more cohesive, and more attractive. I had been right to help Fred protect the kids of Jordan Downs, but I'd made a big mistake in helping Grape Street do community-friendly stuff. I had made an even bigger mistake with truce enforcement. Instead of validating the gang's status, I should have dealt solely with individuals to help reduce the killing. Finally, experts showed that we had paid too little attention to the girls, who were a key to altering the behavior of the boys and the dynamics of the gang ecoculture. One researcher half-jokingly suggested that we could end gangbanging overnight if we made access to girls conditional on leaving the gang.

We submitted seventy recommendations in support of the main mandate to move from a suppression-driven war on gangs to a public health campaign against the violence and trauma of the hot zones.[27] Our prescription was for L.A. institutions, families, and schools to organize themselves for safety and trauma prevention.

First, establish the political mandate to provide basic safety for every child and commit to sustaining long-term solutions that create safe ecosystems for kids in poor high-crime areas.
Establish a quasi-independent office of Gang Violence Reduction and hire a creative gang czar to run Summer of Success–like

strategies. The vision is for every child to be able to walk to school safely, attend school safely, do after-school activities safely, and return safely to a violence-free home.

Second, move beyond crime suppression to public health and family health models that address the unmet needs of children that drive them to join gangs, and get universal preschool and educare for all poor kids.

In an epidemic, there are too many children affected to avoid systemic responses. Fortifying families and young children pays unimaginable dividends on every front but requires cross-agency multidisciplinary coordination.

Third, get police to do strategic suppression that collaborates with communities.

You can't do Summer of Success in a war zone, so street safety has to be in the first phase of any public health strategy. Police have to cooperate with the community and refrain from Operation Hammer policing that alienates the community and strengthens gangs.

Fourth, find boys healthy male role models and reduce girls' attraction to violence.

Instead of ceding our kids to gangs, we have to help them seed a counterculture that sees power in achievement; attraction to nonviolent, positive manhood; and aggressive socialization of girls to reject violent male behavior.

Fifth, focus on the alternatives, not the gang.

Violent street gangs are just a symptom of a sick ecosystem. Focus on creating enough alternatives, compete for the kids to reduce the gang's appeal, and help families shield kids from gang recruiters.

Sixth, turn local schools into accessible community centers.
Schools, often the only facility available, should serve as centers for mental health, family and juvenile counseling, education, and jobs.

Seventh, adequately fund local service providers.
Invest in local experts, and sustain high levels of funding for effective groups like Community Build, A Place Called Home, Para Los Niños, and Homeboy Industries that do the early-childhood education, reentry, and gang prevention work. All rehabilitation funds should be taken from prisons and agencies and given to effective community groups. The $55 million cost to substantially increase safety in a hot zone is one fifth of the tab for redecorating the Getty Museum and about as much as the city spent on its nine elephants in 2009.

Eighth, transform hot-zone schools from gang recruitment centers and educational graveyards into engines of upward mobility.
L.A. hot-zone schools are a major vector of the gang epidemic because they channel high-risk youth into county prison schools and fail to educate the remainder at a high enough level of achievement.

Ninth, coordinate and redeploy wasted public funds into strategies that can reduce gangs and violence.
Departments in L.A. County operate in rigid silos, spending more than $900 million on youth programs that do not reduce gang growth or the PTSD of kids in the hot zones. The county spends $157 million on programs with "gang" in their title but has no idea what a third of those programs do or why gangs continue to thrive. That money and the rabbit-warren structures that waste it have to be organized to carry out results-based public health solutions with local leaders.

Tenth, dismantle the infrastructure of savage inequalities.
If I'd learned anything from my journeys with Fred and Bo,
it was that we, the body politic, had found a hundred ways
to redline, blueline, greenline, and brownline underclass communities into isolation and convert their neighborhoods into
dumping grounds. We then pretended the deadly conditions
resulted solely from some natural order or their behavior, and
refused to see how our policies not only ended upward mobility but passively resurrected the systemic exclusions of Jim
Crow. From containing violence in their "bad areas," to excus-
ing chronic education malpractice, ignoring catastrophic 50
percent unemployment rates, destroying families with parent
incarceration for addictions that the rich indulge with impunity, to spending ten times as much on the Department of Animal Services than on the Department of Human Services,[28] to
herding two thirds of underclass men into the gang-controlled
crime factories we call prisons, to disqualifying ex-felons from
jobs, Los Angeles built its hot zones as deliberately as the pha-
raohs built the pyramids.

Gang hot zones are the blowback of structured isolation and
planned exclusion. As Molly and I found out during lunches with
several top economists, we actually write the poorest people out
of the equations: Economic forecasting models do not include the
underclass because the assumption is that they will never join the
mainstream economy. The poorest of the poor are not in the economic forecasts or the recovery projections. They are, however, in the
projections for prison beds.

In addition to dozens of specific directives, like create a gang
reduction office and hire a gang czar, these ten steps formed the
skeleton of our report.

By late fall 2006, we had completed our meta-analysis. Susan and
I wrote the final report in the weeks leading up to Christmas, and

Susan, Pilar Mendoza, and Leticia Ramirez powered through the production of the maps and voluminous appendices over the holiday. We titled the report *A Call to Action: A Case for a Comprehensive Solution to LA's Gang Violence Epidemic* for two reasons. First, we wanted to raise an alarm. Second, we wanted to force politicians to face the fact that a complex epidemic required holistic, systemic, and politically difficult solutions. If we'd given them the usual menu of safe à la carte options that partially address the problem, they would have skipped the systemic approach and cherry-picked a bunch of politically safe and totally inadequate programs.

We also made the report really big. With appendices, *A Call to Action* was an intimidating thousand pages long and weighed twelve and a half pounds. We were determined that it not join its predecessors as a dust collector on bureaucrats' bookshelves. After we finished the production, I warned an exhausted Susan that we were going to have to defend our tome as if it were a death row inmate. Far from being thanked, we were about to become *piñatas* for politicians unprepared to accept our verdict: The L.A. region was stuck on stupid when it came to fighting gangs.

With the whole report before us for the first time, its bite and potential for explosive impact suddenly became clear. There was something in it to anger almost everyone. Our report told L.A. that, aside from a few promising pilot programs, it had the wrong politics, wrong policies, wrong personnel, and wrong strategies for reversing gang expansion. And it told L.A. politicians to stop wasting time posing for "tough on crime" photo ops with AK-47s and fix government's fractured, uninformed, and wasteful approach to gangs.

"Fasten your seat belt, Susan," I advised. "This is going to be a bumpy ride."

Chapter 20

A CALL TO ACTION

At first the gods seemed to be with us. *A Call to Action* landed smack in the middle of public panic over a 34 percent spike in gang crime in the West San Fernando Valley, a white middle-class area that was not supposed to have gangs. The press latched on to *A Call for Action* as if it were a life buoy. The *Daily News* trumpeted it as "LA's Marshall Plan for Gangs" and applauded our criticism of city policy, politics, and programs. *La Opinión* and the *Los Angeles Times* wrote several articles, as did independent neighborhood papers. After two weeks of heavy coverage, the report became a phenomenon. It also triggered some odd reactions. I turned down invitations from three mayors of other cities to become their gang czar. A few politicians called to complain that I was unfairly making them look weak on crime, completely missing the point. The knives I'd warned Susan to expect started coming out.

Ad hoc chairman Tony Cárdenas held a hearing on January 17, 2007, to officially receive *A Call to Action*.[29] A thousand people packed city hall's marble and brass rotunda. The line-up of county and city officials to testify in support of our report's message was unprecedented, and amazing panels of mothers of murdered children, religious leaders, public health experts, intervention workers, and all manner of advocates all voiced robust backing of the report.

The strongest support, however, came from law enforcement. Sheriff Baca wrote his own declaration of gang emergency, designed a gang coordination center, and assigned Lieutenant Cheryl Newman to the mission of getting our recommendations enacted. Chief Bratton publicly refused to tamp down his vocal support, and assigned his most capable and recently promoted innovator, Deputy Chief Charlie Beck, to work with us on the gang intervention training academy. Within one week of the headlines from our report, FBI Special Agent in Charge Robert Loosle had asked for a meeting at his office, where his tabbed and highlighted copy of our report took up half of his desk.

For these law enforcers, our call to action was a late no-brainer.

Outside of four major foundations and six politicians who "got it," our most reliable allies with any power would turn out to be the press, the L.A. Chamber of Commerce, L.A. County Sheriff Lee Baca, and LAPD chief Bill Bratton. I was not amused at the irony of getting vigorous support from more conservative bodies while having to force to the table some of my liberal friends in power.

After a month of fire-hot press coverage, in February 2007 the ad hoc committee decided to slow things down and hold several months of hearings because, as one member explained, the city "was not ready" for the big changes that the report urged. I was too stunned to respond.

Not ready? The committee was no doubt right. The report was scary. It required people to change how they did their jobs; its ideas were too big and too complex, even with diagrams of simpler phased-in steps. They were also right that Susan and I were pushing too hard for action and rubbing lots of people in City Hall the wrong way. They had expected us to behave like other contractors—write what the city wanted, get paid, and then go away.

To us, however, it was not a contract. It was a pact for social change. And *A Call to Action* was not a report. It was a vehicle to accomplish a mission. How many more had to die while L.A. leaders got ready?

After three studies, chronic incompetence, and a mounting death toll, Susan and I were not willing to lose the momentum. Chief Bratton and Sheriff Baca were also done with waiting. Ad hoc committee member Janice Hahn, who represented Watts and had helped form the Watts Gang Task Force, immediately began working on a $50 million initiative to pay for wraparound safety programs. Assembly member Karen Bass drafted legislation, and state senators Mark Ridley-Thomas and Gloria Romero called hearings to begin moving the comprehensive public health model into practice. Congresswoman Lucille Roybal-Allard funded a training center. Most other politicians settled for cautiously praising the report without reading it; they would later balk at many of its politically costly demands. Councilman Cárdenas was right on this point—to other city hall offices, *A Call to Action* had been about as welcome as a *60 Minutes* investigation. Newspaper editorials decrying the slow response of the council and Mayor Villaraigosa to *A Call to Action* began a new drumbeat for a faster response.

Even my old friend Antonio Villaraigosa, who had beat James Hahn and Bernard Parks to become mayor of Los Angeles in May 2005, hesitated. For a month and a half, the mayor's office had declined public comment about our report. Behind the scenes, one of Villaraigosa's top staffers abruptly left a briefing on it and declared, "The mayor is not doing this."

I understood their reluctance. Antonio Villaraigosa had run as "the education mayor," not "the gang mayor." He had an ambitious agenda, but gangs were not on it. That's what Bratton was for. Who were we to change a mayor's agenda? Between mayoral torpor, Ad Hoc's exploration, and the emerging gripes about *A Call to Action,* I could see that city hall had no intention of fundamentally changing anything. If we let them, they would turn our report into a big fat doorstop. We had to get the mayor engaged. I told Susan that ringing editorials were nice, but in L.A., nothing for poor people gets done without the mayor. I did not care what he thought his agenda was.

The safety of kids in gang zones had to be on it. If the mayor wanted to say no, he would have to say it to my face.

In early February 2007 I followed him to a cocktail fund-raiser at the City Club. His staff members blanched as I pushed my way through them to his side and asked to meet with him alone. For a nanosecond the mayor looked slightly affronted that anyone would breach his bulwark. But it was gone in a flash, and he slipped cleanly into guarded affability and told his scheduler to fit me in—with no staff.

I met with Susan to strategize. "What do we want from him?" I asked the woman who was fast becoming my right and left brain.

"No one in city hall wants to face the magnitude of change needed," she said. "They're all running for cover. Just get the mayor to consider what we're saying."

That should have been easy to do. I had first met Villaraigosa fourteen years earlier, late one night in my LDF office at Ninth and Olive. I had returned from dinner to work through the night on our bus riders case against the Metropolitan Transit Authority, and I'd been surprised to see a stranger waiting on my couch. He introduced himself as a former alternate member of the MTA. He had dropped by to give me a declaration in support of our case to stop the agency's looting of the bus system. He thought MTA was giving L.A.'s half a million poor bus riders the shaft, and he felt it was the right thing to do. I admired him for ignoring the crap he would get for testifying against his former agency.

In the years since that night, we had fought the same fights, standing up for immigrants, women, police abuse victims, the racially excluded, and later on, after he became speaker of the California Assembly, for children in need of new schools. At each stage of his ascent up the power ladder, I had always been able to reach him, to convince him to do the right thing.

I did not know whether the old Antonio still existed. It had been hard to see him through the fog of celebrity that followed his mayoral victory. I would soon find out.

The morning of March 8, 2007, I arrived at city hall early. I liked the updated artwork in the waiting area. The brazen strokes, bright colors, and ethnic themes echoed the new L.A. After ten minutes, a small woman in a suit and matching pumps came out. She led me through the towering dark wood doors that opened into the long corridor leading down to the mayor's chambers. We headed down the hall, exchanging small talk, but I slowed at the unmistakable bark of yelling.

"Goddammit!" the mayor was shouting. "She's been a friend of mine for twenty years! I can meet with her alone. Now leave!"

Oops. I walked past two crestfallen Homeland Security deputies, one of whom turned to the mayor to suggest that she join the meeting after twenty minutes. Who knew I posed such a threat to Homeland Security? He brushed her aside and greeted me with open arms and a hug.

"Hello, my friend. Come in," he said quietly, ushering me into the large yellow-and-beige-hued office. "Something to drink?"

He looked good. His handsome face had aged for the better—more chiseled, tan, and lived in than I remembered. His energy was older, too, more formidable and focused. A full swagger had replaced the plucky confidence of his younger labor-organizing days. The vulnerability and openness had vanished years ago, always the first casualties of elected office. In their place was a dark under-vibe that I recognized from the street. His eyes no longer sparkled, but they were vibrant, probing, and cool.

All told, he wore power well, like a long heavy coat of veiled control.

Declining refreshment, I thanked him for seeing me and told him how good he looked. I took a seat on the couch to the left of his chair. He strolled around his office for a spell, talking energetically about the dozen things he wanted to get done while in office. He was still savoring his historic victory. His secretary finished whatever she was doing at his desk and left. We were alone.

Amid the banter, he had been sizing me up. At that moment I was no longer a friend. In his mind, I had generated for him bad press and a dangerously impractical mission—reduce not just gang crime but also epidemic gang violence and culture. This meeting would determine in which box he'd put me—ally, foe, or "frenemy."

He made it around to his chair, settled in, and looked directly at me for the first time. He was poised and alert, but his familiar tone grew intense as he turned to his passion, mayoral control over the public schools.

"You know, these frickin' schools, man," he started in with his street vernacular that I loved, "they're killing these kids' futures. I've got to get control. I mean, look at what Daley's done—I just got back from being with Bloomberg, man, he's rockin' that place, turning it upside down and getting real results. Look, I fundamentally believe there's nothing more important. Education is *the* civil rights issue of the twenty-first century."

I thought, *Nicely done—use civil rights against a civil rights lawyer.* It was also what he fervently believed. Fair enough. I absolutely agreed with him. I could have argued that very little education happened in gang zones, and a mayor in charge of schools would have to make them safe enough for learning. Or that the two failures were linked to each other and to hobbling ecocultures that had to be changed.

But I was not there to have a pissing match over which emergency came first. I was there to pull out the cotton that his staff had put in his ears about our report. I had little chance of moving him beyond no to embracing our mission unless I did the one thing I almost never did: show what was in my heart.

Before my half hour was up, Antonio had to see my passion and that I would not be moved from securing fundamental safety for these kids. He had to understand that I was not blaming him for any failure, just myself. He also had to know why I was mounting this battle, come hell or high water.

I dived in.

I took stock of the battles we'd fought together. Noting all of the cases we'd won that gave folks at the bottom the tools to change the odds stacked against them, I said the great lawyers on our teams had reason to be proud. We'd racked up billions in relief and won enough civic awards to fill Dodger Stadium. But I told the mayor that all of that success meant nothing. It meant nothing because we left our clients and their children to survive in danger zones that we'd built. I told him that when I looked at the kids trapped in these gang zones—the same kids we both so desperately wanted to get educated—there was only one honest conclusion: My entire award-winning career was a failure, because at the end of the day, our poorest kids could not walk to school without fear of dodging bullets, could not learn because they had war levels of PTSD, could not play outside or go to a park because the gangs made it too dangerous.

"What do my court wins mean if half a million kids lose in gang zones?" I asked. "What do my awards mean when funeral directors are on television begging L.A. to stop filling their cemeteries with children?"

I explained that *A Call to Action* was not another dry report. It was about our failure to deliver the first of all civil rights: the right to safety. I told him that dead kids can't learn. Chronically stressed kids don't thrive. He needed to understand that this was the hill I was dying on.

I ended it there.

There was no need to bare Pygmy's graphic plight or the agony of the Jacksons and Zunigas. This was enough of what weighed on my heart. The old Antonio would heed this kind of clarion moral call. All justice junkies did.

He was fully facing me, leaning forward and searching my face. His eyes were not moist, like mine, but they were burning. I had reached him.

"No, no, Connie, now, let's get something straight: You are no failure. Hell, you're a hero—one of my heroes. You've done more— Look, I'm clear that we've got to take this on. Of course I'm with you. We've got a chance to turn *all* of this around. We have to, because nobody else is going to frickin' do this heavy lifting. You're saying..."

He was listening. I went on to explain our push to treat violence as a disease and the gang epidemic as a public health threat. And I went over the difference between fighting gang crime and reducing the attraction to gangs.

"Mayor, gang *crime* is not the focus here—gang *culture* and gang *violence* are."

As I suspected, he had never heard any of this from his staff. I made it clear that we were not talking about the 5 percent of gangsters doing the drive-by shootings. They had to be locked up, and it would be nice if we didn't let them run our prisons as their drug distribution headquarters. We were talking about the three hundred thousand kids trapped in the city's gang zones who never joined a gang but lived in terror because of them. Even Chief Bratton and Sheriff Baca agreed that what we'd been doing wouldn't work. We had to step up our response.

I thought, *The police get it—what's up with you people in city hall?*

I knew what was up. Politics. If there was anything our work had shown, it was that most politicians did not focus on poor people unless forced to, and they never did anything politically risky unless given no other choice. Almost none took on the deeply entrenched, structural disadvantages built in to our skewed priorities, tax codes, and criminal justice laws—they'd have risked drive-by labeling as socialists. As Robin Hood lawyers seeking to reset the priorities, we regularly had to create leverage and political pressure to force change. Our school construction case settled after we got the billionaires who funded the governor to call him and say they wanted it settled. Our MTA case on behalf of bus riders settled because we got Washington to withhold MTA's federal rail funding. When politicians refused to engage on something important like gangs, I rallied cops, armed the press, and crossed my fingers that they'd prosecute the case in print. This mayor got poor people but, understandably, did not want to add a dangerous issue to his agenda.

I reminded him that in Summer of Success, Martin Ludlow had already done a wraparound strategy that the press agreed had worked. Martin had raised money, forced city departments to work at midnight, twisted arms to get the police to act right, engaged the civic and religious sectors—and made them all work together like an orchestra. I told the mayor that our report had been based on Martin's Summer of Success with the added mandates to rope in the county agencies, gang-proof the schools, and support a student- and neighborhood-led cultural movement against the violence.

"Mayor," I said, "we have to go from a *summer* of success to a *year* of success. And that means doing what our report says."

I ended with Martin's epiphany over Mahlon and the gang execution of his baby brother, Trevon.

Antonio hit the arm of his chair with his fist and cursed the county for running gangster factories and releasing kids into death traps. Forty minutes had gone by, but he waved off his worried-looking secretary, who had poked her head in to rescue him. For another ten minutes, he quietly reminisced about growing up in a gang neighborhood. How his mother had struggled to keep him out of their local gang's grasp. How he'd had to dodge the traps, fend off street thugs. How guys who could not master books found power in guns. And if not for the efforts of a special teacher and his mother, how close he, too, had come to taking that dead end.

Then the old Antonio was done.

I summed up my pitch by asking the mayor to just think about what we were proposing and offered flexibility—he did not have to skin the moose the way we had, but it did have to be a moose and not a mouse. He nodded. I took satisfaction that it was a thoughtful nod, not a "pretend to be listening" or "she's crazy, get her out of here" nod.

"We'll figure something out, my friend," he said, standing to embrace me.

The mayor's response came a month later, in his State of the City address. He had invited the entire L.A. gang intervention world to hear the speech. Or so Molly told me. Somehow I missed both the invitation and the event. The mayor, clearly expecting me to attend, noted my absence in his remarks and complained afterward to Molly. He'd given his response to our meeting, and I wasn't even there to hear it.

His entire State of the City address was about gangs. He had announced a new Los Angeles gang reduction strategy, a new Office of Gang Reduction and Youth Development, and the hiring of the city's first director of gang reduction and youth development. The gang capital was about to get its first gang czar. More important, the mayor announced the creation of eight Gang Reduction Zones—all in the most dangerous areas of the city, not safe or easy areas, as our report had recommended. My hat was off—it took guts to plunge into the city's worst gang zones and plant a flag, and this mayor was one of very few who would take that enormous risk, even with the support of his police chief. In these zones, the mayor said, suppression would be backed up with comprehensive gang reduction strategies. The big news was that the mayor had adopted our mandate to change games—go beyond Whac-A-Mole suppression to the "healthy neighborhood and prevention" approach. He also adopted a number of other ideas set out in *A Call to Action*—"one-stop resource centers," coordinated services, and "multi-disciplinary intervention teams."

"I guess he heard you," quipped Susan as we went over the text of his address the next day. We marveled again at how much hand-to-hand combat it had taken to get this far. But even with the mayor coming around, the fight was not over. It was just beginning. As press criticism of the City Council's failure to act on our report mounted, the council finally took a bold stand for—another report to review our report. This time by City Controller Laura Chick.

It was amazing how a council that spent a pittance on gang prevention could find millions for studies it never followed. But if the council had wanted our report buried, Laura Chick was the last person to whom they should have turned. Before she became the city's first woman controller, I had never thought of an audit as a weapon—or a controller as a crusader. (On the one occasion I publicly fought by her side, an observer dubbed us "Thelma and Louise.") She had been one of the first elected officials to praise our demand for a new strategy, and she did not intend to waste taxpayer money doing an unproductive second report. She wrested control over the study from the council and set out to force council action. During the eight months that it took for the controller's team to produce this second opinion on L.A.'s gang dysfunction, Susan and I plunged headlong into the tornado of work that had whipped up in the wake of *A Call to Action*.

What a whirlwind it had sown. Things had taken off in a hundred chaotic directions. In response to the headlines demanding the new direction, "tough on gangs" prosecutors and politicians had lined up press conferences to defend their undying determination to lock up anything that so much as walked by a gang. Others defended the "gang obliteration" strategies that we had shown actually increased gangs, and still others decided they needed a gang bill with their name on it. Some responded even more mindlessly, like the councilman's deputy who slapped together a midnight basketball game between rival gangs that ended with a fight and ambulances. (He defended this malpractice by claiming that with all of the headlines, his boss needed "to be seen doing something on gangs"!) Some police departments posted TOP TEN MOST WANTED GANGSTER lists—and gang members called our office to complain that they had not made the cut. I was half expecting the Saddam Hussein–inspired deck of playing cards with their faces on the back—or a gangsta reality show.

Luckily, others in this circus responded more productively, albeit as disjointedly. Within the first eight months following our report, Governor Arnold Schwarzenegger had eight of our expert co-authors fly up to Sacramento and brief his staff. He thereafter appointed his own gang czar, Paul Seave, and I joined his advisory board. In late June 2007 Mayor Villaraigosa made good on his promise and hired L.A.'s first gang czar, Jeff Carr, a reverend who used to run a neighborhood community center in central L.A. While Jeff figured out what he'd gotten himself into and how to do a job with no budget, Councilman Cárdenas's committees of gang intervention workers hammered out a two-prong definition of intervention. State Assembly leader Karen Bass requested our help in drafting legislation with Assembly Speaker Fabian Núñez's office to require recipients of state gang reduction funds to coordinate services in comprehensive strategies. Senator Mark Ridley-Thomas cochaired a California Senate hearing with Senator Gloria Romero and convened his Neighborhood Congress to act on our report. Sheriff Baca convened his clergy council, assigned Lieutenant Cheryl Newman to our shop, and set out his plan for a gang emergency operations center. The Los Angeles Unified School District passed a resolution approving the report and declared that its seven hundred thousand children should attend safe schools.

Back at the Advancement Project, Susan and I shook our heads at this mind-bending jumble of activity following the report. We should have called it *A Call to Chaos*. While waiting for Laura Chick to kick us up to the next gear, we doubled down on pushing the public agencies to collaborate, creating a model for school safety, keeping law enforcement on the right track, and helping street and gang intervention get ready to run a training academy that Sheriff Baca and LAPD chief Bratton asked us to take on. LAPD Deputy Chief Charlie Beck, who by now was a daily partner, assigned Sergeant Curtis Woodle and Sergeant Lloyd Scott to join Lieutenant Cheryl Newman and Detective Ray Bercini as full-time staff to push *A Call to Action* into policy. Advancement Project staff had barely adjusted to the daily stream of former gang members in the office and now had to contend with the presence of police officers and their unnerving guns. Our oddball team began by helping the most advanced gang intervention groups to organize the Community Crisis Violence Intervention Professionals, a union of intervention leaders, to enforce standards and set policy for hard-core street gang intervention experts. Twelve gang intervention organizations signed on, and within a year, despite some factional disintegration, they were moving and seconding motions and writing letters to Congress about gang policy.

With the help of the Jewish Family Foundation, we also jumpstarted the Association of Mothers of Murdered Children (AMOM) in hopes that they would someday do for gang violence what Mothers Against Drunk Driving (MADD) had done for drunk driving—organize everyone from politicians to bartenders into a movement that changed the norms about driving drunk. We needed the parents of murdered children to galvanize everyone from their neighbors to funeral directors to change the norms that accepted youth gang homicide. In addition, with the help of Fred Ali at the Weingart Foundation, we hired a team of gang intervention experts to take the Pat Brown training model to the next level and codify what former gangsters knew about reducing, interrupting, and diverting gang violence; mediating cease-fires; and keeping hospitals, schools, and other public spaces as NVZs—no-violence zones. Perhaps most important, we kept our heavy focus on working with police to change their training, tactics, and mind-set and build on their new willingness to work with gang intervention.

As all of these disparate efforts gurgled along, Susan, Lieutenant Cheryl Newman, Sheriff Baca, and I took a doomed run at cracking the impregnable Los Angeles County government. County Supervisor Burke had passed a motion for the county to enact the comprehensive gang reduction strategies we had recommended, but it was almost meaningless. The county, a $23 *billion* colossus responsible for regional welfare systems and local prisons, was basically immovable—even with the best of tools and intentions. In part, this was because of the mountains of rules, funding constraints, silos, and *Dilbert* mentality that bollix all bureaucracies. But mainly, it was because it was so big, and the five county supervisors who ran it like five separate duchies were unchallengeable micromanagers who squelched innovation. How far could we go when the staff of one office referred to the "G-word" because they were not allowed to say the word "gang"? Despite the best efforts of Bill Fujioka, who was a big supporter of our gang report before he took over the helm of the county as its first CEO, any bid to change county gang policy faced the same odds as a baby seal during clubbing season.

In that first year following the report, we could only wonder at the yawning gap between the frenzied hive of activity and the seamless coordination needed for the "all hands on deck" strategies that our epidemiologists recommended. Out of it all, the mayor's Office of Gang Reduction and Youth Development (GRYD) remained the only power platform dedicated to the community and family side of reducing gang violence. As such, we had to help Laura push through its breech birth, even if it was a barely funded shell.

Eight months after she took on the council's request for a second opinion, Laura Chick delivered her verdict on Valentine's Day 2008 at the California Endowment. At a power-studded press conference, Baca, Bratton, and the rest of L.A.'s top law enforcement officials; the mayor; Governor Schwarzeneggar's gang czar; Janice Hahn; a bevy of prosecutors; and a roomful of journalists awaited her findings. Laura stood before a wall of television cameras and ordered the City Council to not only heed *A Call to Action* but to place the new Office of Gang Reduction and Youth Development in the mayor's office and give it the $19 million wasted on ineffective gang programs. She had affirmed our strategy and ended the city's first gang program, L.A. Bridges.

Bratton and Baca, chuckling over remarks to the press that Laura and I were women "who must be obeyed," hugged me and whispered pledges of even more help. I thought, *This is a milestone.* It had been a year and thirty-three days since *A Call to Action* hit the press. It had taken every waking moment since then to get my friends in office to stop denying the scale of change needed. Yet even after the Taser jolt from Laura, we saw none of the urgency or alacrity that politicians fired up for other emergencies, like a Lakers basketball championship parade.

It was now 2008. Since the insane crack wars of the late '80s and early '90s, safety in the gang zones had improved substantially. The war with LAPD's brass was largely over, the women of Jordan Downs no longer used bathtubs as bulletproof beds, and visible crime continued to decline. It was a beginning that had taken twenty years to forge, but it was only a beginning.

A Call to Action had culled years of expertise from dozens of activists, academics, and agencies, and because of Laura Chick and Antonio Villaraigosa, it had jump-started a change in the city's approach to gang activity. But we had a long way to go before gangs no longer dominated hot zones, and an even longer way before the county's nearly one million kids in them enjoyed minimally adequate safety and the right to a viable education.

Chapter 21

CALIFORNIA INSURGENCY

Ten days before Laura's press conference, Bo Taylor learned the devastating news that he had Stage 2 mouth cancer. It was spreading fast, and I accompanied him to the hospital to help him sort through the terrible options. His only real choice was to undergo radical surgery within six weeks. With the surgery, he had a shot at living five years or more. Without it, Bo probably had seen his last winter. When we left the hospital, I thought he understood what he had to do. But the shock was too much for him to accept. As the window for survival closed and he turned away, my heart broke.

Despite or perhaps because of his illness, Bo, who had left Amer-I-Can to work with USC football coach Pete Carroll a few years earlier, intensified his street peace work. He was going to go out fighting his way and sticking to his dream. I began to reconcile myself to his cruel fate and to the fact that without him, once again there would be no trusted guide to navigate the endless risks of gangland. Through Bo's nationwide network and Bill Martinez, who ran the first gang intervention courses at the Pat Brown Institute, I had met dozens of other dedicated gang intervention workers from whom

I'd learned much. But none could take Bo's place. His absence would end my long journey through the world of black gangs.

It was just as well. The fact that L.A.'s gang landscape had become dominated by Latino sets was an even more pressing reason to exit. I knew close to nothing about Latino gangs, and the chances of finding someone who could teach me were next to none.

Or so I told Susan in February 2008.

After publishing *A Call to Action,* Susan had stayed on to become my permanent Director of Urban Peace. In May 2008, she walked into my office and announced that she had received a strange call from a guy who told her, "You don't know me, but you need me." At first she thought it was another escapee from the jail's mental ward, but after talking to him, she decided that if half of what he said was true, he was worth my time. From Susan, this was a rave review. Nothing impressed her. She was the only person I knew who had found Yale Law School so underwhelming that she transferred to Berkeley for a more interesting legal education. I had learned to heed her advice.

On June 17, 2008, I met with Ron Noblet, a silver-haired, square-jawed former marine who had grown up in East Los Angeles, Latin Kings territory. His ramrod bearing was reinforced by his blunt and deliberate way of speaking, as if his life depended on being absolutely clear. Ron, I would later learn, had almost no filters and no deference. He told me that our report had nailed the city's dysfunction and black gang dynamics but that little of it applied to Latino gangs.

I agreed and told him that because we had no way of learning enough about the Latino, Asian, or prison gangs to avoid making dangerous mistakes, Susan and I were exiting gang intervention.

He leaned forward and said, "That's why I am here." He explained that in the forty years he'd done gang intervention, he had never seen the kind of political opening for gang work that we'd created. "You cannot leave now," he said. "You have to see it through."

Despite Ron's disturbing answers to my vetting questions (why wasn't he dead? and how many times had he come close to dying?), I decided to work with him. He did not have the normal résumé of a gang interventionist. Violence fascinated him in a strange academic way. In college, he had studied the violent blood feuds of Slavic tribes, and for twenty years, he had lectured at USC's Delinquency Control Institute on the cultures, norms, and structures of different kinds of violent organizations: street gangs, prison gangs, drug gangs, cartels, mafias, insurgencies, militant islamists and other religious extremists, militias, revolutionary armies, terrorists, paramilitaries, and nation-state militaries.

On the streets, Ron had worked mostly on his own, sometimes on behalf of churches, schools, or academic researchers. Without betraying anyone, he could more often than not explain the reasons for a gang killing or fight—who had crossed whom, and why, and what the feud affected today. Without divulging names, Ron translated the hidden triggers of violence, the unseen alliances, power plays, blood ties, ambitions, boundaries, betrayals, sanctions, codes, norms, and relationships. I had no delusion of understanding any of it, but for the first time, the closed world of Latino gangs became reachable for the very limited task of keeping families out of the line of fire.

The risk of working with Ron was worth taking. While he could help with gang intervention, his best contribution would be as a veteran marine with friends in DOD, the war colleges, and all branches of military service. Right before meeting him, I had just received an unsettling call from a DOD captain who said he needed our help because L.A.'s gangs were like the insurgents the U.S. military was battling in Iraq. With the *Call to Action* battles behind us, and a team member with military expertise, maybe we could interact intelligently with military players seeking our advice. At least that's what I thought when, right before Barack Obama's election, Lieutenant Cheryl Newman asked me to address a military team coming out for a site visit to assess L.A. gang strategy in February 2009.

Under Sheriff Baca's orders, Cheryl organized this visit and arranged for me to meet the head of the assessment team, Commander Gan,[30] the night of his arrival, February 2, 2009. I knew little about him except that he had been Special Forces in Vietnam at the same time as my dad; he spoke several languages; and he had coauthored manuals on counterinsurgency. Known for having a high IQ, chain-smoking, and rarely smiling, the commander was a decorated counterinsurgency expert who had helped General David Petraeus keep Iraq from swirling down the drain. After reading his résumé, I knew I'd be meeting a Bronze Star/Legion of Merit soldier who had predicted the nature of twenty-first-century warfare and had just helped rescue our dumbest political misadventure since General Custer's Last Stand.

I had no delusion of helping him, but I hoped that he might help us.

The commander's advance team, just returning stateside from Baghdad and en route to Afghanistan, had arrived in L.A. that afternoon and were waiting for him in the noisy bar area of the Omni International Hotel. Lieutenant Newman, Detective Bercini, LAPD sergeant Marie Fellhauer, and Ron were already jawboning and drinking with the young military advisers when I found them. I declined a drink and ignored the banter among the throng of the advance team and our cops. Forty minutes later, Commander Gan swept into our circle. His face held no expression except seriousness. He did not smile as he shook my hand but acknowledged me with a bare upturn of the left side of his mouth as I shouted some banal greeting over the atrocious music. He turned to greet our local police and Ron, paid brief attention to his men, and then sat back down across from me.

He settled into his chair and calmly sized up our group. His face had a gaunt, sunken look, as if he had lost weight recently or spent too much time on planes. I remember thinking that poignant eyes did not belong in that cadaver-like face, right before moving my chair closer to ask how we could help him.

"Ms. Rice," he responded unforgettably, "I am hoping that you can help me figure something out . . . *How do you provide security amidst despair?*"

For an instant I wasn't quite sure he had said what I'd heard. The noise had surged, but I also couldn't quite process that a man steeped in the business of death—and trained to scorch the earth if necessary—

had used the word "despair." That was a compassion word, a word from my world, not his. But then he added, "How do you keep people with no hope safe?"

"Hope." Another word from my world. Either he was practicing effective psy-ops on me, or this man really got it better than almost every civilian I knew. He had not flown to L.A. to review routine police tricks. Just as Army MASH surgeons come to L.A. to train on our abundant gunshot victims, this counterinsurgency commander had come to learn about *security amidst despair*. I thought nothing could get deeper than that. But I was wrong.

Two days later, the commander summoned me for a final dinner meeting at the hotel's patio restaurant. He had listened to our presentation on gang violence on his first day and had just finished two long days in the field with LAPD and LASD operations and gang officers. His assessment of L.A.'s gang terrain was complete.

On the patio, nestled in the concrete canyon between the lighted skyscrapers towering above us, the commander smoked cigarettes and bantered with Ron, Cheryl, and Marie. Halfway through his second shot glass of Jack Daniel's, he moved us to a table inside and instructed me to sit next to him, listen, and take notes. He had a mission for me, one that he could not have imagined before coming out to L.A. After we ordered dinner and more drinks, he leaned toward me and looked me in the eye.

"Connie, you have to raise gangs to a transnational threat," he began. "I want you to come to Washington. You have to raise the alarm in Washington. You said something important yesterday. You said that L.A. may be on the road to Sicily—"

"Road to Palermo," I quietly corrected.

"Yes, even better." That slide had listed the factors leading to Italy's descent into partial Mafia control and had listed parallel conditions of L.A.'s gang hot zones. The commander had noted that Fallouja had the same dynamics, from feudal politics and gang control to chronic joblessness.

"I want you to do a new report, ten pages or so, called 'The Road to Palermo.' Connect it to what you and Ron said about Mexico's cartel vulnerability, the cartel connections to the prison gangs, and the prison gangs' creeping control of the streets."

He paused to sip more of his liquor as I scribbled across the yellow legal pad.

"I like the fact that you don't just talk, you act," he continued. "And I like the alliance you have with your police. That's important and advanced."

At least we'd done something right.

"You know what has to happen. You understand what we call the holistic approach, and you are fighting to force government to do it—just like we are in Iraq and soon in Afghanistan. And you and Ron can counter the mentality of gangs because you understand it for what it is—male and dumb."

Make that four things done right. Dinner arrived. We paused for a moment.

As he ate, he listed a number of people to brief and then pushed aside his plate and pulled the shot glass closer. I dropped the pen to take a quick bite of food before resuming the most important note-taking I'd done since my capital punishment days.

He said that our time spent fighting bureaucracies that do not want to change mirrored his struggle in Washington and overseas: How do you get bureaucracies to cooperate, sublimate rivalries, and sacrifice turf for the larger mission? The agency bickering was, he noted, what had gotten us killed in the first place.

He took another sip. I stole another bite of my lukewarm food.

I had no idea what the rest of the table was doing. I was jotting down names and key phrases as quickly as I could. My head was hurting—I hated going to Washington. Our Bronze Star–winning commander, however, was just getting started. He talked for another fifteen minutes while I scrambled to get his words on paper.

We ordered dessert, and he left the table for a cigarette. Ron asked if I was okay. I said I didn't know. When he returned, the commander allowed the waiter to put one more shot glass in front of him. It had been four hours of drinking, and he could not have been more lucid. When he picked up his train of thought, it had turned dark.

"I can't believe," he began with a heavy sigh, "that I'm over in Iraq fighting insurgent threats, and I come out here to L.A. and find out it's in my own damned backyard." He sipped before delivering the blow. "Let me tell you what you have out here, Connie. You have in Los Angeles what we call a sustained, incipient, parasitic insurgency."

I stopped breathing.

He had more.

"And," he went on in the same calm but serious tone, "you have no ability to counter it. In LAPD and LASD, you have superb local police—they are some of the best I've ever observed. But they are applying elegantly executed tactical responses to an enduring strategic threat, and it cannot work."

I put my pen down. The room blurred as the other conversations gurgled on. He finished the last of his Jack Daniel's, went around the table to shake everyone's hand in genial farewell, and then headed out of the restaurant. In what was left of my mind, I silently wished him luck in our latest quagmire, Afghanistan.

And then, silently, I cursed him.

In shock and aggressive denial, I drove home, blaring Aretha Franklin's rocking version of "Eleanor Rigby" and killing three sticks of gum. Once home, I fed a grumpy Sinbad, the jet-black, green-eyed tomcat who'd taken over my house after Jaws died, took some sleeping pills, and climbed into bed. Seven hours later, I woke up to a whining feline and a full-blown case of the flu.

I thought hard about the commander's words. *It cannot work.* He had banged the gong on our collective amateur hour out here in L.A. Rightly so, even though I'd decided that gangs did not satisfy the political takeover element of a real insurgency (they didn't need to; our policies gave them everything they needed to thrive). The commander was nonetheless right that we were incubating a nascent national security threat while L.A. politicians played musical chairs and our prisons hosted criminal networks that boosted the danger. But his words sparked multiple fears. Talking about gangs as transnational threats could license more dumb political hysteria. It also could unleash more *mano dura* "war on gang" strategies, even though he clearly eschewed futile obliteration in favor of the community fortification of "Three Cups of Tea"[31] and Condi's Clear, Hold, Build. It would take a ton of skill and loads of luck to replace our mindless policies with the strategic patience required to build up vulnerable communities in order to starve down an insurgency.

This, however, was no time for fear. The commander was right. We had underdiagnosed the problem. It wouldn't be enough to switch from suppression to public health and violence reduction. We were sleepwalking down the road to Palermo and needed to wake up and take a U-turn.

The good news was that he had confirmed our approach to countering gang reach. Clear the danger, hold the stability of safety, and build a community too healthy and hopeful for gangs—or any other danger—to take root. Or, as Father Greg Boyle put it, he had never met a kid with hope who joined a gang.

If a decorated military commander and a pacifist Jesuit priest agreed that safety and hope were the answer to providing security amidst despair, what else did we need to know?

After Commander Gan left L.A. for Afghanistan, our military and transnational encounters grew, including meetings with war college staff; travel to Central America with FBI gang experts; briefings with Condi, retired general Stan McChrystal, former secretary of Homeland Security Michael Chertoff, and General Robert Holmes, who flew up to Cambridge in April 2009 to hear Baca, Bratton, and me jointly deliver the Forum Address at the Harvard Kennedy School.* But it was the Gan encounter that reset the default template of this work.

Of all the epiphanies along this roiling journey, nothing rocked

---

*For pictures of the Kennedy School event, please visit www.powerconcedesnothing .com.

my mind more than the commander's challenge. Not just because he'd lifted the curtain to reveal the larger threat. Not just because he'd linked L.A. to the same emasculation and dearth of upward mobility that seeded violent cults overseas. It was because he had given me the one argument for saving the underclass that we could not ignore: Conditions in gang hot zones and prisons were spawning lethal threats to the middle class. Chief Bratton had issued a similar warning when he stated in 2004 that "too many . . . safe neighborhoods close their eyes to the threat . . . mistakenly believing it . . . can be contained to certain [neighborhoods] . . . But residents of . . . areas once considered havens from violence are [increasingly] being attacked . . . as gangs . . . expand their territory . . ."[32] No one heeds lawyers, but who ignores a top counterinsurgency expert *and* America's top police chief?

When he heard my "Road to Palermo" talk, the commander recognized the dangerous waters that L.A. was blindly entering as it celebrated historic drops in gang crime but missed the rising tide of gang power. He had found the following story of my own capitulation to gang power particularly telling. In 2007 two mothers of murdered children had asked me to sue the gangs whose members had ruthlessly gunned down their kids. Instead of the killers' houses and money, these grieving women wanted the gang members' children— to save them from *la vida loca*. Although no court would ever permit it, I thought their vision was brilliant and moving, and I began preparing the case. After checking with top prosecutors and police, I was devastated to have to drop it. As one deputy chief put it, "You file this, and you and your clients will be dead by sundown."

If gangs determine what a powerful lawyer and the mighty arm of the law can and cannot do, who's really in charge?

The commander knew the answer to that question. He noted my other "Road to Palermo" markers of how mainstream Angelenos dance to the rhythm of gang norms: Businesses pay prison gang "taxes" because police cannot protect them. Prosecutors drop cases because we can't protect witnesses. First-graders dive under desks at the sound of gunfire. Meter readers intermittently forgo hot zones to avoid gang cross fire. Students skip school because of gang threats. For safety, Sheriff Block segregated prison phones, showers, and cells by gang and by race. My staff changed Urban Peace Academy courses after gang objections. The city's gang czar seeks gang cooperation to avoid endangering children. Gang interventionists have to seek a "license to operate." Prisons routinely lock down for gang kill orders. And when a principal says that his campus is "okay because we're a Blood school," the adults have not only noted gang norms but surrendered to them.

We accommodate gang norms because in our gang-saturated situation, it is unsafe to do otherwise. Gangs are too entrenched in the neighborhoods, families, and culture to do otherwise. Until we carefully deflate their influence with positive alternatives that indirectly wall off their reach into families and drain their underground clout, their norms will increasingly dictate our options. The commander had revived an old warning with new urgency: The failure to end the spiral of despair will lead us to the same creeping and ultimately crippling corruption of mainstream institutions by street gangs and crime cartels seen in Sicily, Italy, and Guerrero, Mexico.

Los Angeles leaders still fail to see what the commander instantly recognized: Improved policing, temporary summers of success, and even steep drops in gang crime are "elegant tactical responses" that, by themselves, will not stop the rising tide of gang power. We scour the globe for a handful of violent extremists and spend billions to protect vulnerable villages overseas but slash protections for vulnerable Americans and leave them to a violent network that expands every year. L.A. is not alone; the rest of the country is also stuck on stupid.

Chapter 22

THE GHOSTS AND THE GLORY

In time, the web of transnational issues sparked by the commander's warning and several subsequent encounters with other military experts would eventually replace the street-level work that had kept me up at night for twenty years. But not before a transition broke my heart and new milestones sent all of us down a road both more perilous and promising.

When the commander left for Afghanistan in February 2009, Bratton had been riding the bucking bronco of LAPD for over six years. He had not only stayed in the saddle but presided over historic crime drops every year and transformed LAPD's leadership. He had survived the inevitable setbacks, including the stunning 2007 MacArthur Park May Day police riot in which LAPD officers had been filmed running down grandmothers with strollers, chasing fleeing priests, and battering journalists with cameras. Bratton's swift responses to crises like these, five years of record-low crime, and consent decree compliance were enough for him to seek and win reappointment as chief of police in 2008, the first chief in fifteen years to do so.

Since the Rampart investigation, my relationship with Chief Bratton had grown. He called me in on the MacArthur Park May Day fiasco and had begun to listen to my ideas about changing LAPD's mind-set and incentives. We had cinched our bond, strangely enough, in a slave artifact store. A few weeks after the "Mac Park Melee," I found at Sable Images—a slavery artifacts shop on Crenshaw Boulevard—an old antebellum poster that blared: BEWARE ESCAPED SLAVES OF BOSTON POLICE. THEY ARE SLAVE CATCHERS & WILL RETURN YOU TO SLAVERY!! I bought it for Bratton. Not because he had started his policing career in Boston but because the poster struck me with just how long we'd all been trying to overcome the headwinds of that stormy history. In some ways, we were still fighting the Civil War. I framed it in a heavy black frame and attached a plaque that read, *To Chief Bratton. This poster reminds me of the 300 hundred years of crippling headwinds we are trying to reverse. Thank you for having the courage to change the wind. Your Colleague in Civil Rights, Connie Rice.*

I had no idea how he'd take being given a poster about police being slave catchers, but I gave it to him anyway. He graciously acted like he was delighted. He cleared a space for it on his cluttered wall and took it around to show his appalled command staff, who looked at it and blanched. He then said he wanted to visit Sable Images. At the small shop, he looked at the Sambo toys, pickaninny corkscrews, posters of slave auctions, photos of lynchings, maps of plantations, slave bills of sale. As we viewed these painful items, we talked quietly about how astounding it was that the things in the shop had been part of a system for owning fellow human beings. And then he found the collection of plantation police badges. They looked just like modern police badges, except "Greenacres Plantation" was where "City of Los Angeles" was on today's badges. He bought one of them; posed for pictures with Gail, the owner, and me; and then, forty minutes later than he'd planned, returned to Parker Center.

The progress under Bratton notwithstanding, there still was so much yet to do—everything from establishing effective supervision and competent investigations to securing basic safety in the hot zones. Less than a month after the city celebrated six years of city-wide declines in crime, a hot spot in Newton Division had exploded in a three-day spate of twenty-two shootings that resulted in three deaths and required massive redeployment of officers and use of Jerald Cavitt, one of the region's best gang interventionists, to shut down a deadly gang war. This calamity was followed by an outbreak of midday shootings by the Avenues gang that locked down an entire neighborhood and endangered school kids.

My long list of things left to do in police reform, however, would have to be for the chiefs who followed Bill Bratton. He had done enough. No matter how anyone looked at it, his had been an extraordinary run. Yes, he owed former mayor James Hahn the greatest debt for sacrificing his political career to make him chief, and in part, he owed his success to Gerry Chaleff, Rikki Klieman (Bratton's wife), the chief's talented team of brass, Judge Gary Feess's firm enforcement of the consent decree, John Mack's unusually skilled Police Commission, Andre Birrotte's deft mastery as inspector general, and Mayor Villaraigosa, who had backed Bratton to the hilt.

But the main reason LAPD was on the right road was because of Bratton. Public trust in LAPD had risen with every racial group, and LAPD had finally, after a century of refusing to do so, accepted civilian control. No chief serving two terms could transform LAPD down to the squad room or finish my checklist. The reform finish line was way down the road, and it would be up to us to choose the chief of police to take Bratton's baton across it. While it wasn't perfect, to those of us who never could have imagined such progress, the LAPD transformation under Bratton seemed pretty close to miraculous.

Sadly, there would be no miracles for Bo Taylor. At the end of July 2008, Coach Pete Carroll called me and said I needed to come to a USC rally that Bo would be attending. It was time to say goodbye. I took one look at his swollen, abscessed face and knew his battle would be over soon. He hesitated to face me, but this was no time for vanity or who had been right or wrong. I held him and told him I loved him and to go with God.

Three weeks later, my car phone rang as I headed east across the Santa Monica Freeway. LAPD sergeant Curtis Woodle, the gang officer with whom I'd worked ever since the Rampart investigation, told me to pull the car over. Bo had died an hour earlier. He had been in a car just outside of San Diego, driving down to Mexico in search of another phantom "cure." Woodle asked if I was okay. I asked if I needed to drive down and bring Bo back to L.A., but Woodle was already on his way. His friends on San Diego's police force were standing guard over his body until Woodle arrived. I bit my lip at the thought that an LAPD sergeant would bring Bo home. I thanked him, pressed the hang-up button on my steering wheel, and wept.

At Bo's huge funeral, dignitaries filled the stage. Mayor Antonio Villaraigosa, actor Danny Glover, Sheriff Lee Baca, Coach Carroll, Minister Tony Mohammad, LAPD assistant chief Earl Paysinger, Ms. Shabazz, and dozens more. Bo would have cared far more that in the audience, from black and brown communities all over California, stood a hundred or more of the men he had turned from violence, the men with whom he had shielded thousands of children from the mayhem of gang hot zones. Their standing salute would have meant more than all of the politicians and celebrities combined. At two in the morning the night before the service, I had written a poem, "Farewell to the Son of Thunder," so that, if asked to speak, I would have something that forced me to keep my composure. When I took the podium, determined not to look at his body laid out in a coffin not fifteen feet away, I thanked Bo's family for letting us steal so much of their time with him, and then I wept through a reading of my tribute to the Son of Thunder:

> The passion of fury ran in your veins,
> Honed and driven by unrelenting pain.
> Born of anguish in a sea of wasted blood,

Your mission of mercy, you seared in love,
A Sentinel of the Streets bending the wind,
You ran on empty to save every kid.
A whirlwind of rescue, a roving shield,
Abrasively determined, with indomitable will.
You screamed out loud: NOT ANOTHER KID;
NI UN NIÑO MÁS!
For the Son of Thunder, the time to end the killing had
    Long ago passed.
Well, Bo Taylor, you have been heard.
Because of you, there is an army on the move.
Foes who are now friends, will take it from here.
And we promise, my friend, to end the river of tears.
Our Sentinel of the Streets will watch no more,
He's lain down his sword, but his fight rumbles on.
The Son of Thunder has indeed gone home,
But his mission unfinished is now ours to be borne.
And when Bo's kids are finally safe, we will celebrate his love
And listen for his applause in the thunderclap above.

James Ingram later turned these words into lyrics for a searing song that he wrote in Bo's honor: "Not Another Kid."* He sang it for me over the phone, and we both wept. James couldn't have given a better gift to Bo's memory.

It was at the end of Bo's long memorial ceremony, however, that his greatest triumph came. As I stood outside the church, watching his devastated family pile into the limousines that would take him to the cemetery, my heart leaped as LAPD officers halted his hearse. They were making way for the uniformed motorcycles lining up at the church gates. They switched on their lights to flashing and doubled up to flank the hearse on all sides. As they pulled out in front of the procession, they turned on their sirens to lead Bo in honor

*To hear the song, please visit www.powerconcedesnothing.com.

formation to his final resting place. He had to be happy watching an LAPD honor guard pay tribute to a gang member turned hero.

My sentinel of the streets was gone, and no one would replace him, but the work had to go on.

Almost a year later, on July 17, 2009, Judge Gary Feess, whose firm enforcement and repeated extensions of the consent decree had held LAPD's feet to the fire, had finally seen enough sustained progress to release the department from the federal control that my old partner Bill Lann Lee had imposed in response to Rampart corruption. Judge Feess ended the consent decree, returning full control of the department to its leaders for the first time in seven years.

A month later, Bill Bratton caught me on my car phone early in the morning. "Hi, kid," he said, "afraid I've got bad news, and I didn't want you to hear it from the press: I'm leaving very soon." I had half expected this news when his house went on the market the month before. I responded half jokingly that he was breaking my heart. He laughed and said he wouldn't have it any other way.

I drove on and thought back over my work as an inside agitator or, as an African-American friend described it, my "Mandela after apartheid" role. It wasn't a bad tally: getting inside LAPD to figure out what was going on; winning their trust while reinvestigating the Rampart scandal; documenting Charlie Beck's transformation of Rampart Division; learning the lowdown of policing from hundreds of officers; addressing their fears; forging ties between police and gang intervention; pushing the city and county to step up gang violence reduction efforts; boosting officer and gang intervention training; helping Baca and Bratton join forces; and helping Bratton reframe policing and racial reconciliation. Each experience had created relationships that exceeded any expectations going in, and many had become significant for the work. A few had become significant personally.

That afternoon Bratton publicly announced that he would be

leaving by September 2009. We both knew there was only one LAPD leader who had transformed himself enough to take up Bratton's baton. The campaign for the next LAPD chief had just swung into full gear. I first called Gerry Chaleff. Whoever took the helm from Bratton would still need Gerry's unique skills. And there were only two candidates for whom Gerry would stay.

I called Charlie Beck and told him he had to go for it. He knew why. Bratton had transformed the top of LAPD, but Beck understood like no one else how hard it would be to push those changes down to the streets, into the back of LAPD's squad rooms, and into the hearts of street cops. He had done it at Rampart Division, and he was the only command officer with a track record of winning, not forcing, 180-degree changes in warrior cop thinking and behavior. He was also the only command officer besides Commander Pat Gannon who defended gang intervention and the need to change LAPD's approach to gangs. But this was a big decision that would entail a maddening selection process. He needed to think about it.

Running for chief was a little like running for pope—or vice president. You can't be seen seeking the post, but if you don't kiss the right rings and pay homage to the right power brokers, you can get knocked out of contention. Depending on the occupant of Getty House, the mayor's mansion, it could mean getting lost in a guessing game figuring out the real advisers, most of whom didn't know LAPD from LTD. When Beck said he would run, I flew into full campaign mode to inject facts and knowledge into the selection process. I laid down my markers in a Sunday *L.A. Times* op-ed that outlined the remaining reforms the next chief of police would have to tackle.* It audaciously told the mayor to choose Bratton's successor solely on his or her ability to finish that agenda.

The next chief was solely Mayor Antonio Villaraigosa's choice. It was not my place to tell him which candidate to pick. My job was to make sure he asked the right questions, understood what had truly

*Please visit www.powerconcedesnothing.com to read the editorial.

been accomplished in LAPD, what was left to do, and what kind of leadership could successfully drive the nascent changes permanently into LAPD's DNA. Police Commission President John Mack began the national search, and the mayor enlisted Warren Christopher, the former secretary of state and the namesake of the Christopher Commission, to head a small group of prominent lawyers who would help him think through the selection. The mayor tapped Ron Olson, Stewart Kwoh, Judge Lourdes Baird, and me. The mayor knew I had a parking space at Parker Center, had worked with all of Bratton's top command, and had encouraged most of them to apply for the chief's job; he still ordered me to join the Christopher group. I got word to Beck that our contact had to end for the duration of the search. I wished him luck and turned to helping Mr. Christopher respond to Hizzoner.

In the meantime, Bill Bratton ended his whirlwind of farewell tributes to him and his wife, Rikki Klieman. Who could begrudge them a few dozen victory laps? Amid all of the glittering million-aires' galas, I wondered if they'd still make time for our Advancement Project tenth anniversary garden party at Steve and Molly's beauti-ful Mediterranean Spanish home in Pasadena. We were honoring Genethia Hudley-Hayes for being our field general in storming the Bastille of LAUSD to get the schools built; former mayor Richard Riordan for bankrolling our takeover; and Sheriff Baca and Chief Bratton for their joint transformation of law enforcement. We hadn't planned on it also being our farewell to Bratton, but it would be. The late-October 2009 event unfolded in 90 degrees of heat and Mol-ly's rose-ringed garden. It was packed with more than four hundred well-wishers, sipping cool drinks and sampling the food stations.

I presented our award to Sheriff Baca, going back to the days when, before anyone else in law enforcement, he'd had the vision of helping the community rather than suppressing it. I recalled his quip: "Connie sues you to let you know that she wants a relationship." And I shared his response during the Pitchess race riot, when he had snapped that people were dying and he didn't give a damn about getting reelected. I lauded his vision and dedication and thanked him for his friendship. He accepted the award with warm grace.

I said the next award was going to "Rikki Klieman's husband" and that anyone who understood Bratton's success understood the tremendous work she had done in her own right raising huge sums for battered women. As for Rikki's husband, he had contributed a little something to L.A., too. I thanked Bill Bratton for showing LAPD how to police without destroying trust; how to see people with compassion instead of contempt; and for pushing his vision of policing as a spark for racial healing instead of the flashpoint of racial violence. Then I cracked everyone up with the image of our Scottish-American chief sorting through slave artifacts and plantation police badges with two black women. At the podium, the chief said a few kind words about my help and a few pointed ones about my incessant prodding, and then, while unwrapping a package, said, "Since Connie thinks she is the chief of police anyhow, I brought a little something that reflects her rank in our department." He held up a big 3-D replica of his four-star LAPD chief of police badge with my name on it. He handed it to me amid prolonged audience applause. I was speechless, but thinking that starting as arch-antagonist and ending as honorary chief was not a bad journey. As I looked back to our awkward beginning, Bratton's affectionate acknowledgment that day was a sweet moment.

The party behind us, I turned full-time to Mayor Villaraigosa's search for Bratton's successor. After extensive interviews, the Police Commission had picked as finalists Assistant Chiefs Jim McDonnell and Mike Moore and Deputy Chief Charlie Beck. The horse race had tightened, and they were turning into the final stretch. On Tuesday, November 3, 2009, my home phone began ringing at six A.M. It was an A.M. news radio station wanting to know the mayor's choice. I told them nothing and hung up. The media frenzy had begun. Two hours later, the mayor's staff called and asked if I could be at Getty House in an hour for a press conference. Now the phone was ringing off the hook. I threw on a dark navy 1940s-style dress, matching pumps, and lots of sunblock. I flew down the mountain in my Prius, listening to radio speculation about the tightly guarded choice all the way down. I reached the mayor's leafy Hancock Park neighborhood in record time and parked my car one street over. Halfway to the corner, I paused to strike the right posture before passing by the sixty cameras and satellite trucks spilling from the Getty House driveway and into the street. Anxious officers swept me inside. In the living room, among the waiting, I smiled back at Jeff Carr, the mayor's new chief of staff, who was grinning from ear to ear. Everyone turned as the vestibule doors opened from the patio.

The mayor and Chief Designate Charlie Beck entered into the simmering excitement and began shaking hands. I exchanged a knowing smile with Beck but nodded him away to pay attention to the commissioners and everyone else. We had not talked in weeks, but our reunion would have to wait. The mayor looked relaxed and in control. Beck looked elated, even a little giddy, but completely at ease. I thought to myself, *Well done, Antonio, well done.*

At the outdoor press conference in the middle of the sun-drenched driveway of Getty House, the mayor strode to the podium and introduced his new chief of police as a man of integrity, loyalty, and humility. He noted LAPD's fabled but troubled legacy, praised Beck's vision of constitutional and effective crime fighting, but lauded above all Beck's fealty to continuing the changes Bratton had begun.

As he spoke, standing in the broiling sun, it hit me like champagne bubbles shooting through my veins just how much it had taken all of us to get to that driveway. The reins of LAPD, so ignominiously lost after Rampart, were being handed back, but not to Daryl Gates's LAPD. Charlie Beck, a new kind of leader, took the podium. He looked lovingly at his family beaming to his left, and nodded respectfully to the police commissioners and the three Christopher advisers arrayed on his right. Beck gripped the podium with both hands, looked out at the wall of cameras, and without notes or teleprompter, introduced himself as an LAPD veteran who understood the "ghosts and the glory" of the LAPD. He pledged to stay the path of constitutional, compassionate policing and promised that on his watch, LAPD would never return to the pain of the past. He pledged to continue earning the trust of all of L.A.'s people; it was the right thing for the city but also what he, a father of two young LAPD officers, had to do for his kids. The speech was humble, authentic, and eloquent. It was quintessential Charlie Beck.

The mayor swept his new chief of police off to town hall greetings across the city. At the first stop, in an auditorium near the African American Museum, more than a thousand people awaited them. When they entered, the place exploded into thunderous ovation. Handlers tried to usher the mayor's procession onto the stage, but Charlie spotted a big gathering of gang intervention workers waiting down front, and he broke from the entourage to race over to the guys. Taco, Gerald, Skip, Kenny, Melvyn, Johnnie, Vickey, and a dozen other interventionists engulfed him in an ecstatic huddle, jumping up and down, pumping their fists, and cheering. Onlookers gaped at LAPD's new chief hugging gang interventionists. Charlie Beck was their chief. And LAPD was on the way to becoming the community's department.

War with LAPD's leaders had ended. The good guys had won, for now.

I could only think of Bo and how he would have cherished the meaning of that moment. He was there. Fred was there. As were Pygmy, Trevon, the Jacksons, the Zunigas, and the thousands of men, women, and other children who had perished. They floated behind the cheering throngs along with the ghosts of cops who had died and mothers who had tried. Their slain expectations haunted the jubilation and mocked its promise. Almost twenty years after I first parked my car outside Jordan Downs, the folks fighting every day for dignity and opportunity still had only a shadow of the safety and viable schools that my neighborhood took for granted.

If only for a moment, though, I held on to that remarkable scene for what it was. The snapshot of Charlie and the guys for me was as sweet as the moment Barack Obama stepped through the Capitol Balcony door: one chapter of history closing as another, more hopeful chapter opened.

How it ended would be up to us.

Chapter 23

BENDING THE WIND

I am the great-granddaughter of slaves and slave owners. As an Ivy League–educated lawyer, I have collected fully on America's promise—cresting atop my family's meteoric rise from legal chattel to legal counsel in three generations. I detract nothing from my hard work, but without the sacrifice of prior pioneers, my family's talent, and the advantages of being light-skinned, I would not have reached the mountaintop that Martin Luther King Jr. glimpsed right before his death. It took only striving for me to walk through the doors rammed open by unheralded abolitionists, resistant slaves, conductors of underground railroads, suffragists, Pullman porters, Tuskegee Airmen, and thousands of courageous freedom riders from every race. It took even less to run on the gains won by luminaries of the civil rights revolution: from Jackie Robinson's determination on the diamond to King's sermons on the Mount, from Marian Anderson's triumph on the Washington Mall to Thurgood Marshall's victories in the halls of justice. We all stand on their shoulders and are eternally in their debt.

I am free. But because far too many are not, I declined the playgrounds of profit to take up the battleground for access. With teams of clients, lawyers, experts, and allies, I have waged exhilarating campaigns storming today's Bastilles—battling police brutality, fighting discrimination, attacking the incompetence of public education, championing women's rights, empowering bus riders—and crusading for freedom from violence. Through courts, legislatures, and elections, we have forced the systems that are supposed to extend opportunity to do so. My colleagues and clients should take great pride in the fights we've led and won. We have changed the odds for millions of children and families. We have helped transform important institutions. The value of our work exceeds $20 billion but in many ways is worth much more. We are respected for being smart, fearless, and effective advocates who, *Los Angeles Magazine* remarked, "ha[ve] picked up where Clarence Darrow left off."[33] That's high praise, and while I wouldn't go that far, we've racked up a record that any civic entrepreneur would be proud to own.

In personal praise I cannot accept, the same magazine designated mine as "the voice for LA's oppressed." Pretending for an absurd moment that this could ever be true, that voice has yet to cut through our denial that erasing the poor sows the seeds of our own demise. That voice has failed to pierce the din of distraction to warn that we ignore King's vision of full inclusion at the risk of destroying ourselves. Only universal opportunity—safety, health, and viable education—can repel the danger nesting in our kill zones. Just ask the military.

Until we extend the ladder of self-determination to the children trapped in our barrios, ghettos, reservations, suburban Sowetos, rural rust belts, and hidden hollers of Appalachia, we cannot indulge the rich getting richer ever faster. Not until we deliver the "wholesale, drastic and immediate social reform" that King demanded can we rest.

King never gave up that vision, not even when depressed and sensing his doom. A week before he met his assassin's bullet in Memphis, a troubled Martin Luther King Jr. found his way to Harry Belafonte's Manhattan refuge. King had just returned from a dispiriting confrontation with Amiri Baraka, the poet and self-styled revolutionary, who was calling for black liberation through violent upheaval. King had argued for nonviolent resistance but knew he had failed to persuade the angry young leaders who were tired of turning the other cheek. Belafonte could see King's turmoil and asked his friend what was wrong. King turned to him and, of America, said, "I fear that we are integrating into a burning house."

Startled, Belafonte asked the man who had a Dream, "Then what is it that we must do?"

King replied, "We must become firemen."

Ever since Harry told me that story, it became clear to me that I've been a smoke jumper fighting the flames of endemic inequality that fueled the rage King faced that night. This is the story of my journey into some of those firefights, and their lessons about why, in the midst of extraordinary advancement for our nation, becoming firemen was not enough. Why our landmark cases and winning campaigns are not enough. Why our remarkable progress in L.A. is great, but not enough.

Yes, compared to the madness of the crack wars twenty years ago, even our hot zones are markedly less violent. In 2005 our kids stopped killing one another enough to end L.A.'s twenty-year youth gang homicide epidemic. Together, we have even made a few astounding leaps: In 2010 Mayor Villaraigosa's Summer of Success–like program, called Summer Night Lights, produced a jaw-dropping 57 percent plunge in gang homicides near the parks that stay open past midnight. That is a transformative level of impact—one that should have prompted the county to immediately reengineer all agencies to duplicate the magic of that public-private partnership. All the program did was extend the wraparound stability and resources that freed the residents of the hot zones to save lives. Their efforts averted $100 million in homicide costs and showed that when hot zones receive a thousand jobs and coordinated round-the-clock attention from talented agency workers, police, parents, and neighborhood organizations, the people will change the norms so that the killing plummets. As Guillermo Cespedes, the brilliant "gang czar" who runs SNL, puts it, if you make it possible for the community to choose vitality over body bags, they will choose life every time.

However, no one should mistake going from crack-war chaos to the stability of entrenched gang dominance—or a summer of park success—as the Dream for which Martin Luther King Jr. died. Fifty percent dropout rates and 40 percent unemployment rates are just improved levels of failure, and reducing violence is just the tourniquet that stops the hemorrhaging. King refused to confuse our adjustment to poverty amidst "overflowing material abundance" with justice, noting that "our moral values . . . sink . . . as our material wealth ascends."[34] The main difference today is that the rich are much richer, and we now admire greed, not King's sacrifice for an integrated destiny of shared prosperity.

The unacceptable bottom line is that our progress over the past twenty years has not even begun to turn kill zones into Harlem Children's Zones. It has not brought the jobs needed to survive without crime. It has not slowed the spread of gang ideology, which is now global, with Grape Street Crips cliques in London and Perth, Australia. It hasn't put a plug in expanding gang control—which grows as the cartels terrorizing Mexico move into L.A.'s gang hot zones. On July 19, 2010, the leading Los Angeles newspaper, *La Opinión,* took the baton from endangered Mexican journalists and ran the headline: LOS ZETAS YA ESTÁN EN LOS ANGELES. Translation: "The Zeta Cartel Is Already in Los Angeles."[35] The article explained how the Mexican drug cartel the Zetas had merged with California prison gangs and taken over two L.A. street gangs. This is the beginning of the transnational threat that Commander Gan saw.

Mission accomplished?

Not even close. Palermo is still what's in our MapQuest destination box.

We need to wake up and smell the cordite. Despite tremendous strides, when it comes to our poorest children, we have dropped the baton. In 2011 what could I honestly say to the women of Jordan Downs who sent me to help their men with a truce? That their children no longer have to sleep in bathtubs to deflect bullets but their grandkids could still die at any moment for wearing the wrong color? What could I tell the Zunigas? That Latino families in Jordan Downs no longer get torched to death but are regularly terrorized with home invasion robberies? And to the black families bombed out of Ramona Gardens, that they would still struggle to live there safely? What could I say to Mahlon? That in 2011 he would still be jumped into a gang during county custody, and the gang would still "pop" his baby brother, Trevon? And to Trevon, would the only good news be that the city now has a gang czar, but that L.A. County would still do too little to shield him from his executioners? And what would I tell Fred? That Markham Middle School, behind which he operated his Cross Colours Foundation, has reduced its dropout rate from 75 percent to 50 percent, but is still so violent that it cannot retain permanent teachers, and in November 2009 it inspired yet another *L.A. Times* editorial entitled "Markham's Not Working"?

This is not good enough. We have work to do.

I have learned many lessons on the quest for social justice in our poorest hot spots. I have learned to reject the inevitability of kill zones; we build them, and we can dismantle them. I've learned to reject the invisibility of poor areas; we erase them at our peril. I've learned to pay the price of going against my tribes and to stand alone when it counts. I've learned to leave the order of courtrooms to take instruction from the streets. I've learned to win in the gladiator rings of politics and confront the staggering dysfunction of bureaucracy. I've learned to quarantine the strategic incontinence of elected officials by blocking them off from the money, like we did with the school construction bonds. I've learned to sideline torpid incompetence by co-creating nimble entrepreneurial alternatives like the school construction unit run by our Navy Seabees and the Gang and Youth Development Office. I've learned to push people beyond pilots to do the systemic change that complex problems require. I've learned to lock in long-term solutions, put the professionals in charge, and block politicians from diverting progress for their short-term political needs. I've learned that suing cops earns their respect but helping them to change earns their trust. I've learned to make adversaries into allies and, when necessary, to sue my friends and even my own board members, because it doesn't matter who holds it—power concedes nothing without a demand.

Above all else, I've learned to reject false choices. There is no choice among fixing individuals, institutions, or ecosystems; we have to fix them all. There is no choice between the work of charities or harnessing the public sector; the whole spectrum is required, because a thousand points of light can reduce the dark but cannot replace the sun. There is no choice between instilling righteous values and individual responsibility, on the one hand, and the systemic solutions we seek, on the other; the former are the bedrock for success in the latter. There is no choice between reforming a police culture of war and reversing a community cult of death; both are essential. There is no choice between abandoning the poor and saving the middle class; they are inextricably linked. There is no choice between engineering real opportunity and ending the anti-achievement ethos that shuns scholars; both must happen. And there is no choice but to heed King's warning that only radical restructuring can deliver America's promise of a just and prosperous multiracial democracy.

King predicted that we would duck the heavy lifting needed to achieve universal opportunity because it would require the "radical restructuring of society itself," a "revolution in values," and "the drastic reforms that will save us from social catastrophe."[36] As King put it, "[America] must recognize that justice ... cannot be achieved without radical changes in the structure of our society."[37] A nation that enriches more defense contractors than it invests in viable educations for its poorest children requires the radical restructuring King prescribed. A nation that sends more of its people into poverty than into the middle class requires the radical restructuring King prescribed. A nation that incubates dangerously violent subcults in its prisons and poverty zones requires King's restructuring.

King got this one right, but he underestimated how much America would change. Barack Obama's election as president of the United States is a stunning milestone, and no one would have rejoiced more than King when the president-elect stepped through that Capitol

Balcony door, the son of a free African, to finally close slavery's Door
of No Return. Despite those who keep marching to the dark drumbeat of division and heeding the harbingers of hate, nothing could
dim the joy of the black voter who cradled an urn of his mother's
ashes as he marked his ballot for Obama and began the "momentous
dawn of 'our new day begun. . . .'" Not even the eruption of ignorant
vitriol from "birthers," immigrant bashers, homophobes, and Islamo-
phobes that followed the election of our first black president could
darken that day. Many of our clients, the poorest of the poor, cheered
despite knowing that the "reach of prosperity" and "span of opportunity" invoked in the Inaugural Address have never extended to them,
even in the most prosperous of times. They listened to Obama's
sobering call to strive through the looming "winter of our hardship,"
knowing that folks at the bottom had clung perilously to the brink
of survival for an entire ice age. As President Obama girded America
to brace for the deepest economic plunge since the Great Depression, my clients and I scoffed at economists on television quaking
over "horrifying" prospects of 10 percent unemployment. Had they
bothered to count them, they'd have found an underclass that, for
more than twenty years, has been engulfed by 50 percent unemployment, 60 percent male incarceration, and epidemic violence. Our
experts fret over a Great Recession but ignore the permanent Great
Depression beneath their penthouses.

The "fierce urgency of now" burns anew, as does King's warning
and the Dream he commemorated before a different throng gathered
on that same Mall forty-five years earlier. That Dream—for an integrated, fair, safe, and prosperous democracy—barely survives forty
years of Southern Strategy race baiting, wrecking-ball destruction
of safety nets, failure of public institutions, unhinged greed from our
banking and financial sectors, and the vitriol of drive-by politics. But
multiracial democracy will not survive de facto segregation and a
permanent underclass, a caste of American untouchables abandoned
to prisons, and an underground economy increasingly dominated by
gangs that grow in power and reach. We need a little less hope and a
whole lot more audacity to meet this emergency.

The "fierce urgency of now" is not just to save the middle class from the ravages of casino capitalism and jobless recoveries. It must also be to douse the flames in our basement and reach back for the forgotten. We must rekindle the hope of the hopeless—dismantle the new Jim Crow and remove the threat posed to us all by the deadly conditions festering in the hot zones. We must invest the cost of achieving our greatest credo, *E Pluribus Unum,* or pay the price of losing the greatest democracy ever created.

I believe that as we race to counter global economic and climate collapse, we are finally being forced to confront our folly and become transformative. And this presents a chance—perhaps our last—to end entrenched deprivation and extend real opportunity into every barrio, holler, reservation, ghetto, and glen. Until every child from Harlem, East L.A., or Looxahoma, Mississippi, no longer faces the likelihood of living unhealthy, ignorant, and poor, or dying violently and way too early, we need to pick up King's baton and run like the wind. Until we make good on the first duty we owe all children—the safety sufficient for them to learn and thrive—we need to heed King's warning to douse the fire in our own basement. If we don't, the flames will spread to engulf us all. If we do, we will go beyond closing the Door of No Return to opening the door of universal opportunity—and with that, realize America's promise and King's Dream.

My quest for safety in the kill zones as the first step to realizing King's vision began the moment I understood that children died every day for simply wandering into the wrong neighborhood. It is a mission that has tested everything I've become to repay those who advanced "freedom from fear" and "freedom from want" on a much riskier vigil than mine. In my mind, our ancestors are watching. When the time comes to join them, I do not plan on explaining how indifference kept us from delivering the basic safety upon which freedom rests.

Not on my watch.

Epilogue

The demands of getting the right police chief selected, fighting off opponents trying to derail the Urban Peace Academy, warding off the increasing political meddling with the school building program, helping the gang czar, and keeping the Advancement Project funded during a recession—all while struggling to write this book late at night—kept me from spending as much time with my family as I would have liked. But not even the Great Recession of 2009 prevented my annual trek home for Thanksgiving. Even dispersed across five states, the Band of Five still sets my compass. My parents, in the winter of their years, continue to thrive and fuss at each other under the watchful eye of Phillip, who in 2011 was still affiliated with Harvard Medical School and practicing at North Shore Hospital in Massachusetts. At age seventy-eight, my mom was still working, and we couldn't get her to stop teaching—or sending her two unmarried kids articles on the merits of arranged marriages. In between events with her network of friends, she spends her time tending to her siblings, giving her kids instructions, and keeping my dad on the straight and narrow. Dad wrote and self-published his memoir, *Mixed Bag,* an exploration of his life and quest for meaning. When he's not friending his grandkids on Facebook, he spends his days reading, playing golf, and walking his Connecticut Reservoir and his Lettuce Lake Park in Florida. Norman and Rosalind have been busy raising Ashley and Ryan and building a formidable anesthesiology medical practice, a real estate business, and a mansion in Dallas. At least Norman and Roz know how to make money. Phil, ever like his sister, works way too much for way too little, but I am relieved that he lives within driving distance of our parents. Phil and I tussle over his daughter (my niece), Kristen Nicole Rice-Jones, whom I rechristened with my middle name to Kristen LaMay. In 2012 she got accepted to every graduate school to which she applied, and Phil accused me of being a corrupting influence and the reason she wasn't going to medical school. As for my former and only ex-husband, Dick Berk, he thrives as a brilliant stat and sociology professor and remains my best expert and great friend.

By 2007, visiting once a year and calling twice a month wasn't enough, so I also began winging it east to spend my birthday with my parents at my dad's Tampa, Florida, condo in April, before the tropical heat sets in. On my fifty-third birthday, Mom, Dad, and I watched a young alligator bask in the sun at Lettuce Lake for an hour. For a moment I began contemplating the unthinkable, my world without them, but quickly reentered denial and willed them to live another fifteen years. After all, ninety-five is the new eighty! Besides, they need to write a book on good parenting, a priceless skill they know in their bones.

May they live forever.

Afterword

When the story of *Power Concedes Nothing* comes to an end, Los Angeles police chief Charlie Beck has just taken the baton from Bill Bratton, the transformative chief who turned LAPD around and got it through the agony of federal consent decree control to end its brutal policing. Since *Power Concedes Nothing* was published and Bratton's departure in 2010, I regularly have had to pinch myself to certify that I'm not dreaming. L.A. has seen an astounding (57%) drop in gang murders, and even the violent Nickerson Gardens housing project murder rates have dropped, with only one homicide reported since August 2011. The city's other gang crime has plummeted for five years in a row, and, with my help, L.A.'s brilliant "gang czar," Guillermo Cespedes, has guided gang neighbors to reduce gang violence steadily. Guillermo also has pioneered efforts to keep the youngest members of gang families from joining the family business, an effort I affectionately call the "Michael Corleone project." There has never been violence reduction like this. None of this is accidental—all the changes are the result of work by Chief Bratton, Chief Beck, "Gang Czar" Cespedes, neighborhood leaders, LAPD change agents, and my team.

Best of all, Chief Beck and I have created a specialized unit of cops dedicated to community policing in the relentlessly violent public housing projects. I named it the Community Safety Partnership (CSP) and demanded that it reverse policing's typical incentive for arrests. At my insistence, this is the sole LAPD unit in which cops get promoted for showing how they *avoided* arresting a kid; where cops get awards for how they have bonded *with* people in the ghetto—not hunted and harassed them. And while Guillermo, Beck, and I keep the political leadership on board with all kinds of risky gang reduction strategies, the CSP unit weaves its magic by solving the problems of poor blacks and Latinos of Jordan Downs, Nickerson Gardens, Imperial Courts, and Ramona Gardens. The cops call it "relationship-based policing." And while at first the residents screamed at me for creating a "police state" in their housing projects, they now agree CSP is a blessing. To have cops who want to help them solve problems and counter the gangs' presence with the 24/7 presence of safety is more than a blessing—it has changed their world.

There is, of course, always a huge price to be paid anytime you color outside the lines or leave your tribe to forge peace with enemies. After my years of suing LAPD, I now have such a close relationship to LAPD that my liberal friends blog that I've gone to the "dark side." Indeed I have. But it has been worth it.

Charlie Beck and I have always known that the gangs dominate poor LA communities because they never leave. The cops never stayed long enough to make things safe. And I was worse—packing up my briefcase and exiting for the tree-lined safety of my quiet neighborhood every evening, leaving the families of Watts to the gun-toting gangsters lurking in the shadows. Like every other privileged Angeleno, we had accepted the danger of gang neighborhoods like we accept gravity. And no one ever demands a change in that formula.

Well, we did—we demanded and orchestrated a big change. Here's how.

Shortly after Beck became chief in 2005, my partner, Susan Lee, the stoic, super-capable lawyer who runs my programs, came into my office to report on a horrific home invasion of a Korean family by the Grape Street Crips. The gangsters had taken the family's belongings and then marched the women upstairs for gang raping.

I went nuts. I got in my car, drove down to the new LAPD headquarters building, burst into Beck's office, and demanded to see him. This wasn't about Beck; it was about my abject failure. Twenty years earlier, Barry Litt, Mercedes Márquez, and I had sued the Los Angeles Housing Authority over the relentless violence of the housing projects. The dominant gangs of each development terrorized racially isolated families. Back then the Hazards gang firebombed black families in Ramona Gardens, and Grape Street Crips terrorized Latino families in black-dominated Jordan Downs. Barry, Mercy, and I "won" the housing violence case, but nothing changed.

Now, twenty years later, I was hearing about yet another racially isolated family targeted for home invasion and rapes by Grape Street? I couldn't bear it. Our case had not only failed to fix the problem, but twenty years later things seemed worse for new families. How could I have abandoned these poor people without fixing the problem? It was unforgivable. I had to find a way to prevent home invasions and ensure every kid in Jordan and Ramona could walk to school safely.

But who was I kidding? It was going to take ingenuity and humongous will to end-run the gang dominance and bureaucratic inertia. The truth is that we accept violence in housing projects like we accept gravity. I knew how to change this, but needed the power to make it happen. I was going to need LAPD. Luckily, unlike the twenty years I chronicle in *Power Concedes Nothing*, I no longer faced Chief Daryl Gates's LAPD with its casual racism and hatred of civil rights lawyers. I had Chief Charlie Beck, with whom I'd grown up.

In his office, an apprehensive Beck sat me down and asked what had happened. He closed his eyes in pain as I related the Korean family's Jordan Downs/Grape Street nightmare. I was close to tears by the time I finished, approaching the female emotionalism that cops hate. Charlie told me to calm down because we—he and I— were going to fix this.

"What do you want?" Chief Beck began the negotiation, looking into my eyes to increase the chance of reading me right.

"I want fifty cops—for real community policing."

"Okay, done," he agreed.

"And ten supervisors—so no breaks in coverage happen."

"Okay."

"And I want the positions to be pay grade advanced."

As I continued making demands, Beck paused, mulling how radically I was planning on changing policing. But he agreed with my vision. And so the Community Safety Partnership policing project was born. My final demand was that these cops commit to staying in the projects for five years so that they really learned the community and who was who. He reluctantly agreed, and the Community Safety Policing Unit was born.

I couldn't believe it. Susan and I had hit the jackpot: a policing unit that we would help shape ourselves! We finally had a shot of getting cops who would focus on solutions to community problems, not cops looking for some "action." These CSP cops would get rewarded for getting to know the community and solving folks' problems instead of arresting them. This was more than huge. For twenty years we'd been suing just to get constitutional policing; I had never dared dream of getting anything beyond that.

Beck put Deputy Chief Pat Gannon, a longtime ally of ours, in charge of the program. The other issue was convincing the community. Was it ready for this experiment? I crossed my fingers and hoped to fly. I knew some folks in the housing projects would throw a hissy fit upon hearing about this venture—and they did. I was just relieved they were blaming me and not the new CSP officers.

The hating didn't last long, however. The CSP cops gathered community members on the first day and asked what they wanted done. The grandmothers said they wanted the alley behind Grape Street cleaned up. It was a disgusting throughway, full of human waste as well as used mattresses, where people shot up drugs and conducted open air sex. Public Works personnel had refused to clean it up because the gangs were too dangerous. The next day LAPD had the alley filled with trucks and power hoses to remove the mattresses, syringes, and filth. By the time CSP and the grandmothers were done, you could have done surgery in that alley. The grandmothers were elated.

Next, after hearing from concerned doctors that several elderly residents had undiagnosed diabetes, CSP cops arranged for a trailer with doctors and medical equipment to visit the project and test everyone in Jordan, Nick, and Imperial for diabetes, hypertension, and other diseases. When the cops learned that almost all of the grandparents lacked bifocals, they delivered more than three hundred pairs. They set about raising money from wealthy Westsiders after hearing from a school principal that kids couldn't afford the computers the teachers wanted them to have. CSP officers sponsored back-to-school giveaways with backpacks full of school supplies, clothes, athletic equipment, and sports uniforms. At Thanksgiving, LAPD threw a dinner at USC for the residents and awarded all their "public housing partners." On and on it went. The best part came every month with the crime stats: crime plummeted to levels never seen before. Gang activity completely receded. Beyond providing services, the most important change, however, was in the unit's arrest policy. CSP cops only made arrests of the violent, dangerous, or seriously disruptive. They did no arrests for pot, jaywalking, or lacking a visa, and absolutely no arrests to fill an arrest quota.

While I guessed that the CSP cops were winning a few hearts and minds in the community, it took a crisis to show me that I had underestimated how deeply some CSP cops had bonded with folks in the projects. It was in February 2013, during the Christopher Dorner catastrophe. For folks living on a glacier, Dorner was the LAPD cop who set out in February 2013 to kill LAPD officers in vengeance for his firing for lying about his supervisor's actions. He had posted online a list of his targets. At the top of his kill list was Charlie Beck, followed by Phil Tingirides, the captain over the CSP unit, and a whole host of officers with whom we worked daily. My blood went cold.

Dorner, who had specialized training in mobile inshore undersea warfare, actually had the skills to carry out his threatened rampage.

LAPD had no choice but to take him seriously. When the rogue cop launched his killing spree, his website screamed about racism, racial abuse, and discrimination, and he implored the black community to support him. The former SEAL was on a racial bender to avenge his firing from LAPD by killing as many LAPD cops as he could. There was no way this was going to end well.

When Bratton had fired Dorner in September 2008 for lying about a supervisor's misconduct, it must have been a crushing blow. It didn't just end his dream, but his whole sense of self. I had met Dorner a few years earlier, and he struck me as prickly, overly proud, and fragile in that way that big, puffed-up men can sometimes be. After LAPD, Dorner at least still had had his SEAL identity to hold on to, even if he was working in a Navy supply office. But when in late 2012 the Navy dismissed him too, he must have felt he'd lost everything. My guess was that if he had no job that let him be a hero, he decided it was time for him—and a whole lot of his LAPD enemies—to die.

Pop psychology aside, the point is that LAPD cops were being hunted. And there is nothing on the planet more dangerous than a cornered or hunted cop. And in this case Dorner *and* the LAPD force were cornered and hunted. LAPD went to DEFCON 10—ready for nuclear warfare. I'd never seen them like that, bristling for war. Then again, they had never needed protective details for themselves and their families. Every LAPD cop was determined to stay alive and kill Dorner. The intensity was indescribable—on and cracking—and I felt like we were all holding our breath.

On the first day of the crisis, Chief Beck called. "Connie, can you do your thing with the press?" he asked. I told him it had been years since I'd done my preemption number where I blanket the press with my presence and message. Back in those days there were 10 channels; now there were 500, not to mention the Internet, of which I knew nothing. Beck wanted someone like me—knowledgeable and not hostile to the LAPD—to dominate the coverage. I promised to try. Immediately, I penned a good *Los Angeles Times* op-ed on the fast breaking story that put me at the top of the web feeds on the hunt for Dorner. The next day I had seventeen television interview requests, from the BBC and Al Jazeera to CNN. I had forgotten what media saturation felt like and remembered the old days when I taped three TV shows a week and regularly had television trucks parked outside my home. I always had given good interviews.

Beck called to thank me for a "terrific piece" in the *Los Angeles Times.* He warned me that the crisis was going down fast and to prepare for the worst. He would call to let me know he was safe when it was over. We knew what lay ahead—the possibility, if Dorner were successful, of dead LAPD officers, many of whom I would know, and the certainty of one very dead Dorner. Anyone who sets out to hunt LAPD must expect to die.

On the second day of the crisis, I found myself on several radio shows, debating morons who defended Dorner as some kind of black Robin Hood avenging the black community against the racist LAPD. Under their theory, the neighbor they had a fight with last year had the right to kill their kids as revenge. Who justifies the murder of cops' innocent kids? I asked on the air. But I understood. This was the sting of community memory. Dorner had triggered the hundred years of LAPD's racial humiliation, excessive force, unjustified killings, and other abuses of the black community. That past may have begun to recede, but it would take generations to erase. Every time we hit a speed bump like Dorner, the pain of history would jostle to the foreground again. For now, Dorner had ripped the scab off of the community's racial wounds.

By the fifth day of the crisis, Dorner had murdered the daughter of an LAPD captain; murdered her fiancé; killed two cops from the inland valleys; kidnapped, shot, and hospitalized others; and, according to the helicopter film on TV, was now setting fire to the San Bernardino mountain cabin in which he appeared to be cornered. It was midday and I was sitting in the lunchroom of our office, watching the takedown on CNN. An hour later, the TV proclaimed him dead.

My phone rang. It was Deputy Chief Bobby Green, who ran South Bureau and was the top official at CSP. "Connie, it's over." I could hear his Bluetooth; he was driving.

I thought back to a time twenty years ago when Bobby Green would rather have been waterboarded than talk to me. Back then, I'd had him in mind with every LAPD lawsuit I'd ever filed: an intense blue-blooded, shock-and-awe cop who seemed to be full of contempt and without compassion or empathy. But twenty years later, Green was second only to Emada and Phil Tingirides in enthusiasm for the Community Safety Partnership policing unit. He was still scarily intense, but now he was an empathetic convert—which is probably how he thought of me too. Not that either of us had changed our spots—I was still a Prius-driving, MSNBC-devoted, Whole Foods–shopping liberal, and he was still a Crown Vic–driving Fox News conservative. Yet I enjoyed being his partner in the most important experiment to change American policing in the country.

"Hi, Chief—I saw it on TV. Are you okay?" I asked.

"I'm good. Everyone's okay, tired but okay," he said. For a long spell we commiserated over the trauma and shock of the last few days as Dorner plowed through his death binge.

"When's the last time you slept?" I asked.

"Five days ago," he answered.

"That's too long. I am going to talk you up to Simi Valley while you drive—to make sure you don't veer off the road."

He laughed his assent, but I wasn't giving him a choice. I began by lamenting the radio shows I'd had to do that week, challenging the defenders of Dorner and explaining where the LAPD was today. I said to Green that he and I should teach a course called "Why They Hate Us" to explain to young cops the troubled racial history of LAPD and why the community would revert and identify with a cop like Dorner. And then I lit into a long screed about how this catastrophe was going to damage a decade of racial progress. About two minutes into my tirade, Deputy Chief Green interrupted.

"I disagree, Connie."

"What?"

"I don't think the damage is as bad as you fear."

"Chief, people made 'Run Dorner Run' T-shirts—they called him the black Robin Hood. . . ." I protested.

"But," he interrupted again, "didn't you hear what happened with Phil?" he said, referring to Captain Tingerides, the leader of CSP for Jordan, Imperial, and Nickerson. I hadn't.

Green then told me that when the Blood Bounty Hunters of Nickerson went online and saw that Dorner intended to kill Phil, they got their guns and called to tell him they were coming to his house to protect his family and weren't leaving until Dorner was dead.

My spine went cold. I was speechless. Green couldn't possibly have said that Bloods volunteered to risk their lives for an LAPD captain.

"That can't have happened," I declared.

"It did. And when we told Beck, he joked, 'Well, hell, if I'd known that, I could have saved all this overtime and relied on the gangsters!'"

I laughed, but for the rest of the conversation I was in shock. No wonder Green wasn't as alarmed over the fallout. He had seen something that should have been impossible: poor blacks defending LAPD in a racially charged crisis. When I later confirmed that it had actually happened, I could only guess that the Bloods had watched the Tingerideses help their grandmothers, coach their kids, and buy their kids everything from computers to shoes—and they were not going to let them die.

It is hard to fathom the meaning of this incident. I am still adjusting to the reality of it. But I now knew just how deeply bonded to the project residents that at least a few CSP officers had become. And we were only two years into the CSP program. How far would we be able to go?

I take nothing away from our astounding progress with the Community Safety Police unit, but *Power Concedes Nothing* is not just a police reform story. It's a story of the dangers of leaving the children of our ghettos and barrios to molder in poverty. We send our cops into the kill zones, where our poorest kids try to survive, but we don't think to remove the poverty or the dangers the kids and the cops face. And we never question the deadly assumptions that the rest of us hold about children of color and the poor that fuel mindless policy that keeps the kill zones intact.

Trayvon Martin is exhibit A of how deadly unfamiliarity, fear, prejudice, and the failure to integrate can be. Martin Luther King Jr. implored us to integrate because racially isolated people never learn to trust one another, get comfortable with one another, or share each other's fate. I go home to my safe neighborhood while the kids of Watts see so many threats they have permanent PTSD. But people like me feel no urgency to make the kill zones or the kids suffering in them safe. At King's insistence, we may have ended apartheid—desegregated—but we never did what he said was absolutely necessary: integrate. Without integration, there can be no end to "to fears, prejudice, pride, and irrationality, the barriers to a truly integrated society." The same holds for police reform; you can force cops to comply with a court order or consent decree, but that will not change their hearts and minds. They have to do that with transformative police leaders and help from people who understand them. CSP was definitely an example of cops' hearts and minds changing, but it wasn't the first. That was during the Occupy L.A. demonstration.

The protest movement, which seized on the pain of the economic 99 percent, reached the West Coast late in fall 2011. Other cities' cops had been on TV, shown beating and brutalizing Occupy denizens and bungling the takedown of their encampments. Hundreds of protesters announced the arrival of the Occupy revolution in Los Angeles by blanketing the grounds of L.A.'s City Hall with scores of pup tents in September 2011. The tent city covering the grounds of City Hall was also directly in front of the new LAPD headquarters building. I held my breath to see if Beck was ready to try my suggestion that he treat them as protected protesters and not as vermin to be removed. I needn't have worried. Each day, Beck walked through the Occupy camp, joshing and chitchatting, asking if everyone was all right and letting them know that, as long as the mayor was okay with them, Beck was there to make sure they could protest safely and fully. His only request was that they remain peaceful and not light up their blunts in front of him.

After a few months of communing with the marijuana-infatuated Occupy folks, Beck was a rock star with some of them and a respected presence with most others. When I walked through the pot-soaked camp, I could see that Beck's cops were under strict restraints. It was a marked contrast with the militarized approach of NYPD. As months of the Occupy L.A. dance went on, I knew the politicians would eventually call for an end to it, and I only hoped it wouldn't be while I was home with my parents in Connecticut for Thanksgiving. While sitting in my mom's kitchen over the Thanksgiving holiday of 2011, my mother called me to the phone with "It's LAPD." I raced to the phone in fear. I needn't have worried. The Occupy camp was still intact. The deputy chief on my mom's phone had called to tell me that they, LAPD, had served Thanksgiving dinners to the "Occupy people."

"We thought you'd be proud of us, Ms. Rice," he explained. I was too stunned to say anything, except, of course, that it had been a nice gesture. When I asked him if LAPD understood that most of the Occupy folks were vegan, the officer asked what that was. I just congratulated him for a humane gesture and hung up. Serve Thanksgiving Dinner to protesters? What had I done to LAPD?

On the day I returned to L.A. I got two calls telling me to get down to City Hall. Mayor Villaraigosa had ordered LAPD to end the Occupy encampment. The previous day Beck had gone into the camp to advise the Occupy leaders to evacuate everyone before his cops had to dismantle the camp. He said he didn't want to hurt or arrest anyone, but if they resisted or obstructed officers, that would happen. He explained that the cops coming through to take the camp down would not talk with them or answer questions or be like him, friendly and helpful. He then advised them on what to do if they got arrested and said he regretted having to end it this way. That night a thousand officers swarmed out of City Hall and into the camp. When the grounds were cleared, not one person had suffered a serious injury. No cracked heads, broken bones, or gunshot wounds. In New York, Seattle, and a number of other cities, police forces had looked more like Bull Connor all over again, clashing with and brutalizing Occupy protesters in order to end the camps. But not in L.A. Beck had pulled off something close to a miracle. The one objection was over LAPD's lack of detention strategy that left arrestees absurdly stranded on buses in handcuffs for more than six hours. On the whole, however, I was amazed.

Just as the country will soon be, LAPD is now like Los Angeles itself, majority of color. For that reason alone, there is no way we are ever going back to the days of casual racism, condoned brutality, and open contempt for the colored public. Also gone were the days when twenty-seven cops would stand around while LAPD beat Rodney King's teeth out of his mouth. But whether the entire force will reach the levels of community fluency we are seeing with the CSP unit is another question and in my mind doubtful. Many folks on the street in Watts and East L.A. would disagree that LAPD has changed at all. And I know why—most cops haven't; they think the same way they did when Gates was chief. There is a long way to go. Stay tuned. It is an amazing experiment in real time.

LAPD, though, is only one barometer of progress. Martin Luther King Jr. would tell us that it is equally if not far more crucial to engineer upward mobility, integrated power sharing, and opportunity than to get humane police, although one can't exist without the other. And right now we Americans are engineering *downward* mobility and less equality of opportunity as capital, automation, and outsourcing truncate jobs and earnings of everyone who wasn't born with a trust fund. As King noted, "An edifice that produces beggars needs restructuring." And he meant radical restructuring—not marginal tidying up. To undo the centuries of concentration of wealth, we have to do what King called "radical reconstruction of society itself." It's time to return to the economic dynamics of the 40s, 50s, 60s, and 70s, where the middle class shared in the prosperity of the nation and the top 1 percent did not expect robber baron returns while the rest of America sank into poverty. King was clear: a revolution of values, a radical redressing of inequities for the 99 percent and quality education for poor kids are the minimum of what we need to do. Whether we have the will to even raise these issues is unclear. What is clear is the price our kids will pay if we blindly and blithely continue down our current path.

In Los Angeles, we have traveled a distance that no one had thought possible twenty-five years ago. When I talk to other police departments around the country they are mesmerized by stories of LAPD's transformation. The top of LAPD has changed its DNA; the rest of the force has yet to follow but is poised to try. If they succeed, I will be able to write the coda to *Power Concedes Nothing,* an ending that tells the story of unprecedented police partnership and fluency with the poor community. Without equally big transformations in policy for upward mobility and equality of opportunity, there will be no similar ending for our democracy. That is the frontier to which *Power Concedes Nothing* speaks. It is the frontier that we all must conquer if just democracy and the "promised land" King glimpsed right before his death are to become our reality.

—Connie Rice
September 2013

Acknowledgments

I f I thanked everyone who should be thanked for making my journey and this book possible, the list would run forever. The folks on its pages are just a few of many to whom I am indebted. So many people and their important stories or contributions got dropped after my eight-hundred-page first draft got whittled down into a readable book. Here is where their significance receives a nod.

Power Concedes Nothing exists because key people supported my effort to write it. Snatching time to write, often late at night, was hard to do. So was unlocking the compartments into which I'd stored the memories. But this book would never have happened without the following people. I need to thank my agent, Mary Evans, for calling after seeing me on Bill Moyers's *NOW* and demanding, "Where is your book?" Thanks also go to Scribner editor in chief Nan Graham, who took a chance on a first-time author, and to Paul Whitlatch, her associate editor, who had the patience of Job throughout. I could not have cut down the *War and Peace*–sized first draft without the skilled assistance of Maryanne Vollers. Kathleen Salvaty, Adrienne Byers, Justine Lewis, and Richard Larson, great friends that they are, read multiple drafts and kept me on track. My law partner, Molly Munger, excavated the research on my slave-owning relatives and then dragged me to meet their stunned descendants. To Susan Lee, thank you for taking the leap off the cliff with me and expertly shouldering the tremendous load of our work; this book would not have been completed without you.

Mom, thanks for charting out your family tree, and Dad, thanks for writing your memoir, *Mixed Bag,* and helping me sort out the Rices.

I am deeply grateful to the financial supporters of our work. None of today's progress would have been possible without the long-standing support and guidance of the Weingart Foundation, the California Endowment, the California Wellness Foundation, Open Society Institute, the Broad Foundation, the Ralph M. Parsons Foundation, the Riordan Foundation, the James Irvine Foundation, the Jewish Community Foundation of Los Angeles, the Crawford Family Foundation, the Rose Hills Foundation, Edie and Lew Wasserman, Carol and Frank Biondi, and the Annenberg Foundation.

This book is dedicated to my parents, so it goes without saying that they; my brothers, Phil and Norman; and my Aunt Betty, who is my second Mom, have my deepest gratitude. I am also steeply indebted to Dick Berk, my statistics guru, former husband, and eternal friend. Outside of my family, my first thanks go to our clients who risked losing their careers, sanity, and even their safety to forge fairness for everyone else. To Terry Tipton and Myrna Lewis, who led the charge in *Tipton v. LAPD,* thank you for sacrificing your careers so that the women in today's LAPD have a fighting chance. You carried a crushing load with uncommon grace for so long, and led the other brave women and men of that case who helped break the Blue Grip: Janine Bouie, Neadie Moore, Kathy Age, Kathy Daviller, Joe Peyton, Kathy Spillar, Abby Liebman, and Chief Penny Harrington. To Kevin Williams, thank you for never surrendering your integrity or high standards. To Rene Rodriguez, thank you for risking all as a rookie cop to stand up for Tyisha Miller. My gratitude also goes to Detective John Hunter, the Latin American Law Enforcement Association, and the Law Enforcement Association of Asian Pacifics for demanding the fair promotions in the LAPD that resulted in today's majority minority and growing female force.

Reginald Denny, thank you for your spirit of forgiveness during the '92 riots and for understanding why we, as part of Johnnie Cochran's legal team, could not vindicate your civil rights in court. To Reverend Cecil "Chip" Murray, thank you for being L.A.'s leading light of faith and justice for so many decades. To Reverend

James Lawson and Reverend William Epps, thank you for shielding the victims of unwarranted police-dog attacks with your stature and great congregations. Reverend Lawson, words fail to describe the debt our nation owes to you for being the architect of the nonviolent civil disobedience that felled the evil of Jim Crow.

To Geronimo Pratt, it was a privilege to help Johnnie finally win your freedom. Billy Moore, thank you for showing me the meaning of rebirth through Christ. Ms. Sarah Farmer, you have my eternal gratitude for the chance to witness true grace as it led you to seek freedom for one of the men who murdered your brother. To David Baldus, Charles Pulaski, and George Woodworth, thank you for documenting the bias in capital sentencing. Warren McCleskey, thank you for carrying the case that will one day help end the death penalty.

To the many unsung heroes of Watts, all of us owe a great debt. Thanks, however inadequate, are due to leaders like Arturo Ybarra of the Watts Century Latino Organization, Gregory Thomas of Kush Reaching Out, Inc., Tim Watkins of the Watts Labor Community Action Committee, the Watts/Willowbrook Boys & Girls Club, the Watts Gang Task Force. And special thanks to Mother Alice Harris and Mother Lillian Mobley. To Kikanza Ramsey, Ted Robertson, Eric Mann, and all of the other intrepid leaders of the Bus Riders Union, thank you for forcing L.A. to get a new fleet of clean, gas-burning buses and for giving L.A.'s half-million bus riders a voice that cannot be ignored. To Tom Rubin, thank you for your selfless courage in being our whistle-blowing transit expert; we'd have never won billions of dollars for the bus system without you.

My gratitude also goes to the Honorable Damon J. Keith. Judge, thank you for the privilege of serving in your chambers, for demonstrating the just rule of law, and for putting up with a feminist law clerk. And to the Honorable Terry J. Hatter, thank you for always having the courage to extend America's promises to the excluded. And to Judge Gary Feess, thank you for your staunch determination to make the LAPD consent decree produce the accountability mandated by the Christopher Commission. To Warren Christopher, thank you for leading Los Angeles's elite to finally rein in the LAPD.

And to Judge James Hahn, thank you for demanding a transformative chief of police even though it cost you your political career.

I am indebted to many great lawyers, starting with my mentors at LDF. To Jack Boger, thank you for teaching me to do the impossible. To Lani Guinier, you have been my model and have shown me the priceless skill of envisioning what no one else can see. Julius Chambers, thank you for showing me the power of patience and for hiring me against your better judgment. To Elaine Jones, you will never know the immense admiration you inspire or how you taught me to embrace my opponents when you warmly greeted Senator Jesse Helms. For thirty years, Tony Amsterdam has been my muse; my gratitude for his wisdom and encouragement is unending. To Bill Coleman, thank you for believing in LDF's Los Angeles office. My thanks also go to Tim Ford, Ted Shaw, Patrick Patterson, Judith Reed, Jim Liebman, Clyde Murphy, James Nabrit III, Jack Greenberg, Steve Winter, Steve Ralston, Norman Chachkin, and Gail Collins. To Julia Boaz, thank you for the adventure and friendship of a lifetime. And my special thanks go to Velma, Oscar, and Earl for watching over Julia and me, and for serving LDF for so long.

My heartfelt thanks go to my closest colleagues in the L.A. office of LDF, at the Advancement Project, and a few other places. To Bill Lann Lee, I can never thank you enough for being my linebacker and friend, and for putting LAPD under the consent decree. To Kevin Reed, thank you for your daunting skill and tight camaraderie. To Robert Garcia, thank you for making it possible for me to play the good cop. To Chandra Ellington and Shedralyn Pulliam, thank you for your unflagging support. Patrick Patterson and Ted Shaw, thank you for bringing me back to LDF. To Penda Hair, Gerald Torres, and Judy Browne, thank you for jumping out of the plane with us, landing without parachutes, and co-creating a great organization. As for you, Molly Munger, there isn't a bin big enough to capture all that I owe you. And to my law partner Steve English, thank you for spearheading *Godinez*, being my friend, and sharing Molly. To Genethia Hudley-Hayes, thank you for being implacable and for singing in the key of my soul. And to Alton Hayes, thank you for loving and protecting both of us. To Roy Romer, Captain Jim McConnell, Captain Guy Mehula, and the other Seabees, this book does not tell our story, but thank you for giving Los Angeles's children the school buildings that they deserve. And to Roxanna Godinez and the Community Coalition, thank you for having the courage to lead the lawsuit that began it all.

To Barry Litt, thank you for adopting me, teaching me the right way to settle a case, and showing me the meaning of unconditional support. To Carol Sobel, thank you for teaching me to represent female cops, for sharing your golden gift of laughter, and enabling my shoe-shopping addiction. To Johnnie Cochran, thank you for teaching me how to quadruple the value of a case and to never stop fighting for the freedom of an innocent client. Mercedes Marquez, thank you for daring to confront black-brown violence and for showing me what a human stealth bomber can achieve. To Sam Paz, thank you for being a one-man juggernaut against police abuse when so few knew how.

To Ramona Ripston, Paul Hoffman, Mark Rosenbaum and the many other talented lawyers of the ACLU of Southern California, and to our law school allies, Erwin Chemerinsky, Laurie Levenson, Gary Williams, Merrick Bobb, and Gary Blasi, thank you for being our partners in the virtual firm of Fairness, Equity & Justice. To Antonia Hernandez, Teresa Bustillos, Tom Saenz, Hector Villagra, and the dozens of other legal eagles at MALDEF, thank you for joining forces with us and leading the charge to the new Los Angeles. To Stuart Kwoh, Julie Su, and the great legal team at the Asian Pacific American Legal Center, thank you for attacking today's slavery and always pushing for consensus. To Hugh Manes, Carol Watson, Don Cook, Robert Mann, and the other legal warriors who pioneered Police Watch, without your fearless vanguard, there would have been no path to constitutional policing in Los Angeles County.

The Advancement Project's gang work is done by our amazing Urban Peace staff, under Susan Lee's masterful direction. Susan, thank you for being my partner and for your amazing leadership of the staff, the city, law enforcement, and me through uncharted riptides. To Pilar Mendoza, thank you for your superb analysis and even better teamwork. To Fernando Rejon, thank you for managing the Urban Peace

Academy for gang intervention with sublime skill and humility. Antonio Crisostomo-Romo, thank you for copiloting so ably. Maribel Meza and Jamecca Marshall, thank you for your dedication and assessments that change the city. To John Kim, thank you for your partnership, your extraordinarily skilled copiloting of AP, and for making my vision of computer-generated maps of neighborhood profiles a reality.

To Howard Uller, thank you for your ardent generosity with your formidable knowledge. To Anthony Thigpenn, if your genius had found the political response it deserves, King's dream would be a reality. To Father Greg Boyle, you are a guiding light and inspiration to us all. Bill Martinez, thank you for leading the way to professional gang intervention. Tony Massengale, your deep understanding of communities with gangs has been invaluable. To Jaime Regalado, thank you for creating the first gang intervention academy. To Brenda Shockley and Community Build, thank you for your unparalleled excellence. To Carol Biondi, thank you for a driven passion to save incarcerated kids that carries us all. Very special thanks go to James and Debbie Ingram, who have supported this work with their hearts and talent. To Gina Belafonte, thank you for getting us through the Urban Peace Awards and sharing your dad. To Danny Glover, thank you for riding shotgun and helping us stay on the bronco. And to Paul Alan Smith, a.k.a. "Too Tall Paul," thank you for adopting the guys and our mission.

I owe an especially steep debt to the many gang workers and interventionists who have taught me over the years. To Fred Williams, thank you for trusting me to join your journey of atonement and for explaining the realm of black gangs. My deepest gratitude goes to Darren "Bo" Taylor for his friendship, his relentless spirit, and his leadership of so many through the passage from "predator" to "peacemaker." To Daniel "Nane" Alejandrez and O.T., thank you for teaching me to think with my heart and to tap the spirit of the eagle. To Calvin Hodges, "thank you" does not begin to match the nobility you showed in throwing yourself onto a child to take the bullet of a drive-by shooting; your sacrifice inspires all. To Black, thank you for putting everything on the line to keep the peace, and for letting me tag along during the shuttle diplomacy. Melvyn Hayward, your dedication, immense ability, and integrity remain unrivaled. To Mike Garcia, thank you for taking the leap to work with us and for pioneering how to keep hospital emergency rooms safe from retaliation shootings. To Ben Owens, your diplomacy and dedication to community intervention have played a key role in our progress. To Jerald Cavitt, your fierce dedication inspires; the city does not know what it owes for the wars you have averted and the lives you have saved. To David Kuaea, thank you for your peerless wisdom and support. Ron Noblet, thank you for so generously illuminating the complex world of *la vida loca* and for your blind devotion to violence reduction. To Skipp Townsend, thank you for your gifted translation and for making the teaching of intervention to law enforcement so successful. To Johnnie Godinez, thank you for your years of leadership on the streets and your spirit of cooperative inclusion that has helped overcome the factions. To Coach Carroll and Aquil Basheer, thank you for carrying Bo during his illness.

To Jim Brown and the men of Amer-I-Can, thank you for a life-saving curriculum and a fierce vision of community reclamation. To the many other intervention leaders who have built the Urban Peace Academy and run the city's LAVITA gang intervention academy, you have my deep gratitude for the professionalism and dedication you have shown: Mike Areyan, Russell Martinez, Mike Cummings, Michael Godoy, Stan Muhammad, Kenny Green, and Paul Carrillo. And to Luis Rodriguez, thank you for combatting violence with the healing powers of culture, art, and love.

My thanks also go to Vicky Lindsey, Pam Carolina, Sister Soulja, Kelli Dillon, Cecilia Muniz, Adela Barajas, Susan Cruz, Kim McGill, and the other women of gang intervention who have taught all of us their indispensable perspective on this work. To the mothers of murdered children, your voice is our conscience and the soul of this work. To Billie Weiss, thank you for teaching me so much, lending your formidable network, and starting us all with the Violence Prevention Network. And to Patti Giggans and Belinda Walker, thank you for creating for girls the exit ramps out of gangs and the lifelines out of abuse. To Jorja Leap, we have all learned from your longevity in this field. To Jeff Carr, thank you for taking nothing and making the Office of Gang Reduction and Youth Development a viable reality. To Guillermo Cespedes, thank you for so ably taking the baton from Jeff, for bridging our tribes, and for teaching me to think like a jazz musician. And to Blinky Rodriguez, Bobby Arias, and Big D, your mission has rescued many, many from *la vida loca*.

Many politicians made critical contributions along the way. Special mentions go to Martin Ludlow for the Summer of Success and making us respond to Trevon's death; to Laura Chick for forcing the city to respond coherently to *A Call to Action*; to Tony Cardenas for leading the charge in making gang intervention touchable; to Antonio Villaraigosa for having the guts to dive into gang hot spots, launch the gang intervention training academy, and insist that unsafe areas get extra resources first; to Janice Hahn for her fearless embrace of the Watts Gang Task Force and the moxy to almost win $30 million a year for this work; to Karen Bass for spearheading the charge to save all exploited children; to Mark Ridley-Thomas for championing this work and King's vision; to Bill Fujioka for aggressively pushing the comprehensive public health approach to violence reduction; and to Yvonne Burke for quickly pushing the county to back our report. And to Mayor Dick Riordan, a special thanks for showing why bad education is a crime that demands redress and why democracy requires the rich to invest in the well-being of the many.

To John Mack, Andrea Ordin, Rick Drooyan, Rick Caruso, Ann Reiss Lane, Stanley Sheinbaum, David Cunningham, and all of the other determined police commissioners over the decades, thank you for insisting that LAPD finally accept civilian control. And to Andre Birotte, Kathryn Mader, and Jeff Eglash, thank you for pushing the inspector general position past the Blue Grip to viability and effectiveness. And to Jan Handzlik, Andrea Ordin, Maurice Suh, Laurie Levenson, Erwin Chemerinsky, Carol Sobel, Stephen Mansfield, and my dear, late friend Edgar Twine, thank you for carrying the Rampart Blue Ribbon Panel investigation to a successful end. To Bill Rosendahl, thank you for leading the best public affairs programming in the nation and for putting me on television. To Joel Fox, thank you for your friendship and for being a political opponent who solves problems. To Bobbi Fiedler, thank you for caring about me and making our political and other boxes irrelevant. To Arnie Steinberg, thank you for telling me the truth and being an unlikely ally.

Last but definitely not least, I am grateful to the police with whom I've traveled this journey. Brent Braun, your generosity and loyalty mean more than you know. To Jesse Brewer and David Dotson, thank you for breaking the code of silence to aid the Christopher Commission. To Lee Baca, thank you for your steadfast friendship and your vision of healing the world. To Bill Bratton, thank you for righting the LAPD, seeking racial reconciliation, and voicing outrage over broken communities. To Charlie Beck, thank you for our partnership, our friendship, and the honor of calling me your "moral boss." To Gerry Chaleff, the whole city owes you thanks for steering LAPD reform onto the road of success and forcing the cruiser to roll. To Cheryl Newman, thank you for your tireless support and your irrepressible spirit; we could not have moved the post-report agenda as far without you. To Sandy Jo MacArthur, thank you for your indispensable wisdom. And to Pat Gannon, thank you for your steadfast backing and belief that things can change.

Fred Booker, thank you for being an ally for more than two decades. Earl Paysinger, thank you for the insight, the arm wrestling, and the laughter. To "Captain Hannity," thank you for breaking rank to help us. Bernard Parks, thank you for firing many of the abusive officers. Curtis Woodle, thank you for bending LAPD to your prescient vision and will. And Cecil Rhambo, thank you for opening a new road for advancing community policing. To all of the blue angels, thank you for finding a way to cross over the hostility and safely help us. To all of our police clients, thank you for risking everything to advance everyone else. To our military counterinsurgency experts, thank you for sounding the alarm in a way that cannot be dismissed.

And to Harry Belafonte, thank you for the ride of a lifetime.

For a full set of acknowledgments and key photographs, please go to www.powerconcedesnothing.com.

Endnotes

1. Mendel, and several other names in this book, are pseudonyms meant to protect the identities of real people.
2. *The Descent of Henry Head in America*, Hathi Trust Digital Library, 17–18, Idress Head Alvord, 1949.
3. *Mendez* is the landmark school desegregation case that ended California's separate and inferior "Mexican schools" in 1946, eight years before the U.S. Supreme Court ended de jure segregation for the nation in the landmark *Brown v. Board of Ed*.
4. *A Testament of Hope*, 246, edited by James M. Washington, 1986.
5. Ibid.
6. *New York Review of Books*, December 23, 2010.
7. See *Connick v. Thompson*.
8. Billy Neal Moore's death sentence was commuted to life in prison in 1991, based in large part on support from the victim's family first presented in the clemency petition. He was eventually paroled. He became a Pentecostal minister, an author, and a speaker opposing the death penalty.
9. Joe Domanick, *To Protect and Serve*, 12 and 111.
10. Ibid., 115.
11. Ibid., 86.
12. Ibid., 163.
13. Not her real name.
14. *Death at an Early Age*, by Jonathan Kozol.
15. *A Testament of Hope*, 325.
16. Ibid., 557.
17. In *Busriders Union v. MTA*, we sued former LDF and MTA board member Yvonne Braithwaite Burke and MTA executive director Franklin White, a former LDF attorney.
18. Derived from the Declaration of Independence, "When … it becomes necessary for one people … to assume … the separate and equal station to which *the laws of nature … entitle them*, … they should declare the causes which impel them to the separation. We hold these truths to be self-evident, that all men are created equal, that they are endowed … with certain *unalienable rights*, that among these are life, liberty and the pursuit of happiness. That to secure these rights … it is the right

of the people . . . to institute new government, laying its foundation on such principles and organizing its powers in such form, as to them, shall seem *most likely to effect their safety* and happiness." The Constitution of the United States, published by the California Senate, 1991–92, page 20. Italics added.

19. Taken from Magna Carta, 1215, The Great Charter of English Liberty, first-page phrases "liberties unfringed upon"; "freedom . . . considered most important and most necessary."

20. *A Testament of Hope*, 629–30.

21. President Clinton installed Bill through a recess appointment after absurd objections from conservative senators blocked a vote on his nomination.

22. Mayor Hahn lost his bid for reelection in 2005 as a direct result of his dismissal of Parks, who won election to the Los Angeles City Council in 2003 and challenged Hahn in the 2005 mayor's race.

23. "Broken windows" is shorthand for a law enforcement strategy of focusing on fixing the little transgressions, such as broken windows, to prevent lawlessness and more serious crime from finding a receptive environment. New York mayor Guiliani backed Bratton's use of broken windows but got jealous when crime fell and credit fell to Bratton.

24. Bratton said, "We are at the fork in the road where we can now take the high road and improve our relationships with the people we serve rather than continue the practices that lead to tension and mistrust . . . [W]e must . . . through compassionate and constitutional policing . . . improve the relationship between the police and the public we serve. This is particularly true in our poorest . . . neighborhoods . . . I believe the role of the police will evolve . . . to a true partner and catalyst for meaningful social change." *The Beat*, vol. LII, no.1, p. 6.

25. Carl Rowan, *Dream Makers: The World of Justice Thurgood Marshall*, 1993, jacket cover quote.

26. Available at www.AdvancementProjectca.org and www.powerconcedesnothing.com.

27. The full report is viewable at www.AdvancementProjectca.org.

28. The budget for the City of Los Angeles Department of Animal Services is $20,147,443. The budget for human services is $3.6 million.

29. Martin Ludlow had left the City Council to head the County Federation of Labor in 2006, and Councilman Cárdenas took his place as chair of the committee.

30. Not his real name.

31. Refers to the three respectful meetings with local leaders over tea that, if done with enough cultural fluency, will take soldiers from "stranger to friend to family." These are the opening steps that American soldiers learned in order to secure the community into resisting violent extremist infiltration. See *Three Cups of Tea*, Mortenson & Relin, January 2007; *Counterinsurgency, Warfare Theory and Practice*, D. Killcullen, August 2006.

32. *LAPD Plan of Action*, Book II at 5, October 2004.

33. *Los Angeles Magazine*, December 2006, p.160.

34. *A Testament of Hope*, 315.

35. Mexico is engulfed in a war with crime cartels that have infiltrated most police, local economies, and the Mexican political system to a point that threatens Mexico's viability as a sovereign state.

36. *A Testament of Hope*, 315.

37. Ibid., 314–15.

Index